D1426955

The Economist

POCKET WORLD IN FIGURES

The
Economist

POCKET

WORLD IN
FIGURES

THE ECONOMIST IN ASSOCIATION WITH
PROFILE BOOKS LTD

Published by Profile Books Ltd,
58A Hatton Garden, London EC1N 8LX

This edition published by Profile Books in association with
The Economist, 2002

Material researched and compiled by
Andrea Burgess, Marianne Comparet, Mark Doyle, Lisa Foote,
Conrad Heine, Carol Howard, Stella Jones, David McKelvey,
Simon Wright

The greatest care has been taken in compiling this book. However,
no responsibility can be accepted by the publishers or compilers
for the accuracy of the information presented.

Typeset in Univers by MacGuru
info@macguru.org.uk

Printed in Italy by
LEGO S.p.a. – Vicenza – Italy

A CIP catalogue record for this book is available
from the British Library

ISBN 1 86197 424 8

Contents

CONTENTS

Notes

This 2003 edition of the annual *Economist Pocket World in Figures* includes new rankings on refugees, business costs and corruption, immunisation and the environment. The country profiles cover 63 major countries. The world rankings consider 174: all those with a population of at least 1m or a GDP of at least $1bn; they are listed on page 232. The extent and quality of the statistics available varies from country to country. Every care has been taken to specify the broad definitions on which the data are based and to indicate cases where data quality or technical difficulties are such that interpretation of the figures is likely to be seriously affected. Nevertheless, figures from individual countries will often differ from standard international statistical definitions.

Macedonia is officially known as the Former Yugoslav Republic of Macedonia. Data for Cyprus normally refer to Greek Cyprus only. Data for China do not include Hong Kong or Macau. For other countries such as Morocco they exclude disputed areas. Congo refers to the Democratic Republic of Congo, formerly known as Zaire. Congo-Brazzaville refers to the other Congo. Data for the EU refer to its 15 members following the enlargement of the Union on January 1 1995. The euro area of 11 EU members came into being on January 1 1999. Greece joined on January 1 2001 so is not included in our figures, unless otherwise stated.

Statistical basis

The all-important factor in a book of this kind is to be able to make reliable comparisons between countries. Although this is never quite possible for the reasons stated above, the best route, which this book takes, is to compare data for the same year or period and to use actual, not estimated, figures wherever possible. Where a country's data is excessively out of date, it is excluded, which is the reason there is no country profile of Iraq in this edition. The research for this edition of *The Economist Pocket World in Figures* was carried out in 2002 using the latest available sources that present data on an internationally comparable basis. Data, therefore, unless otherwise indicated, refer to the year ending December 31 2000.

In the country profiles, life expectancy, crude birth, death and fertility rates are based on 2000–05 averages; human development indices and health data are for 1999; energy and education data refer to 1998, or latest available; marriage and divorce data refer to the latest year with available figures. In a number of cases, data are shown for the latest year within a range.

Other definitions
Data shown on country profiles may not always be consistent with those shown on the world rankings because the definitions or years covered can differ. Data may also differ between two different rankings.

Most countries' national accounts are now compiled on a GDP basis so, for simplicity, the term GDP has been used interchangeably with GNP or GNI.

Statistics for principal exports and principal imports are normally based on customs statistics. These are generally compiled on different definitions to the visible exports and imports figures shown in the balance of payments section.

Definitions of the statistics shown are given on the relevant page or in the glossary at the end of the book. Figures may not add exactly to totals, or percentages to 100, because of rounding or, in the case of GDP, statistical adjustment. Sums of money have generally been converted to US dollars at the official exchange rate ruling at the time to which the figures refer.

Energy consumption data are not always reliable, particularly for the major oil producing countries. Consumption per head data may therefore be higher than in reality. Energy exports can exceed production and imports can exceed consumption if transit operations distort trade data or oil is imported for refining and re-exported.

Abbreviations

bn	billion (one thousand million)	GNI	Gross national income
CIS	Commonwealth of Independent	GNP	Gross national product
	States	GRT	Gross tonnage
EU	European Union	m	million
kg	kilogram	PPP	Purchasing power parity
km	kilometre	trn	trillion (one thousand billion)
GDP	Gross domestic product	...	not available

World rankings

Countries: *natural facts*

Countries: *the largest[a]*

'000 sq km

1	Russia	17,075	31	Nigeria	924
2	Canada	9,971	32	Venezuela	912
3	China	9,561	33	Namibia	824
4	United States	9,373	34	Pakistan	804
5	Brazil	8,512	35	Mozambique	799
6	Australia	7,682	36	Turkey	779
7	India	3,287	37	Chile	757
8	Argentina	2,767	38	Zambia	753
9	Kazakhstan	2,717	39	Myanmar	677
10	Sudan	2,506	40	Afghanistan	652
11	Algeria	2,382	41	Somalia	638
12	Congo	2,345	42	Central African Rep	622
13	Saudi Arabia	2,200	43	Ukraine	604
14	Mexico	1,973	44	Madagascar	587
15	Indonesia[b]	1,904	45	Kenya	583
16	Libya	1,760	46	Botswana	581
17	Iran	1,648	47	France	544
18	Mongolia	1,565	48	Yemen	528
19	Peru	1,285	49	Thailand	513
20	Chad	1,284	50	Spain	505
21	Niger	1,267	51	Turkmenistan	488
22	Angola	1,247	52	Cameroon	475
23	Mali	1,240	53	Papua New Guinea	463
24	South Africa	1,226	54	Sweden	450
25	Colombia	1,142	55	Morocco	447
26	Ethiopia	1,134		Uzbekistan	447
27	Bolivia	1,099	57	Iraq	438
28	Mauritania	1,031	58	Paraguay	407
29	Egypt	1,000	59	Zimbabwe	391
30	Tanzania	945	60	Japan	378

Mountains: *the highest[c]*

	Name	Location	Height (m)
1	Everest	Nepal-China	8,848
2	K2 (Godwin Austen)	Pakistan	8,611
3	Kangchenjunga	Nepal-Sikkim	8,586
4	Lhotse	Nepal-China	8,516
5	Makalu	Nepal-China	8,463
6	Cho Oyu	Nepal-China	8,201
7	Dhaulagiri	Nepal	8,167
8	Manaslu	Nepal	8,163
9	Nanga Parbat	Pakistan	8,125
10	Annapurna I	Nepal	8,091
11	Gasherbrum I	Pakistan-China	8,068
12	Broad Peak	Pakistan-China	8,047
13	Xixabangma (Gosainthan)	China	8,046
14	Gasherbrum II	Pakistan-China	8,035

a Includes freshwater.
b Excludes East Timor, 14,874 sq km.
c Includes separate peaks which are part of the same massif.

Rivers: *the longest*

	Name	Location	Length (km)
1	Nile	Africa	6,695
2	Amazon	South America	6,516
3	Yangtze	Asia	6,380
4	Mississippi-Missouri	North America	6,019
5	Ob'-Irtysh	Asia	5,570
6	Yenisey-Angara	Asia	5,550
7	Hwang He (Yellow)	Asia	5,464
8	Congo	Africa	4,667
9	Parana	South America	4,500
10	Mekong	Asia	4,425
11	Amur	Asia	4,416
12	Lena	Asia	4,400
13	Mackenzie	North America	4,250
14	Niger	Africa	4,030
15	Missouri	North America	3,969
16	Mississippi	North America	3,779
17	Murray-Darling	Australia	3,750

Deserts: *the largest*

	Name	Location	Area ('000 sq km)
1	Sahara	Northern Africa	8,600
2	Arabia	SW Asia	2,300
3	Gobi	Mongolia/China	1,166
4	Patagonian	Argentina	673
5	Great Victoria	W and S Australia	647
6	Great Basin	SW United States	492
7	Chihuahuan	N Mexico	450
8	Great Sandy	W Australia	400
9	Sonoran	Mexico/US	310
10	Kyzylkum	Central Asia	300

Lakes: *the largest*

	Name	Location	Area ('000 sq km)
1	Caspian Sea	Central Asia	371
2	Superior	Canada/US	82
3	Victoria	E Africa	69
4	Huron	Canada/US	60
5	Michigan	US	58
6	Aral Sea	Central Asia	34
7	Tanganyika	E Africa	33
8	Great Bear	Canada	31
9	Baikal	Russia	30
	Malawi	SE Africa	30

Notes: Estimates of the lengths of different rivers vary widely according to the rules adopted concerning the selection of tributaries to be followed, the path to take through a delta, where different hydrological systems begin and end etc. The Nile is normally taken as the world's longest river but some estimates put the Amazon as longer if a southerly path through its delta leading to the River Para is followed. The level of aridity commonly used to delimit desert areas is a mean annual precipitation value equal to 250ml or less.

Population: *explosions revealed*

Largest populations, 2000
Millions

1	China	1,275.10		32	Tanzania	35.1
2	India	1,008.90		33	Sudan	31.1
3	United States	283.2		34	Canada	30.8
4	Indonesia	212.1		35	Kenya	30.7
5	Brazil	170.4		36	Algeria	30.3
6	Russia	145.5		37	Morocco	29.9
7	Pakistan	141.3		38	Peru	25.7
8	Bangladesh	137.4		39	Uzbekistan	24.9
9	Japan	127.1		40	Venezuela	24.2
10	Nigeria	113.9		41	Uganda	23.3
11	Mexico	98.9		42	Nepal	23.0
12	Germany	82.0		43	Iraq	22.9
13	Vietnam	78.1		44	Taiwan	22.6
14	Philippines	75.7		45	Romania	22.4
15	Iran	70.3		46	North Korea	22.3
16	Egypt	67.9		47	Malaysia	22.2
17	Turkey	66.7		48	Afghanistan	21.8
18	Ethiopia	62.9		49	Saudi Arabia	20.3
19	Thailand	62.8		50	Ghana	19.3
20	United Kingdom	59.4		51	Australia	19.1
21	France	59.2		52	Sri Lanka	18.9
22	Italy	57.5		53	Mozambique	18.3
23	Congo	50.9			Yemen	18.3
24	Ukraine	49.6		55	Kazakhstan	16.2
25	Myanmar	47.7			Syria	16.2
26	South Korea	46.7		57	Côte d'Ivoire	16.0
27	South Africa	43.3			Madagascar	16.0
28	Colombia	42.1		59	Netherlands	15.9
29	Spain	39.9		60	Chile	15.2
30	Poland	38.6		61	Cameroon	14.9
31	Argentina	37.0				

Largest populations, 2020
Millions

1	China	1,446.1		16	Iran	93.5
2	India	1,291.3		17	Egypt	89.7
3	United States	334.2		18	Turkey	82.9
4	Indonesia	261.9		19	Germany	79.9
5	Pakistan	227.8		20	Thailand	75.1
6	Brazil	210.6		21	France	62.4
7	Bangladesh	197.6		22	Britain	60.9
8	Nigeria	184.2		23	Myanmar	57.8
9	Russia	129.7		24	Colombia	56.0
10	Japan	126.0		25	Tanzania	54.9
11	Mexico	125.0		26	Italy	53.9
12	Philippines	101.4		27	South Korea	51.4
13	Ethiopia	100.9		28	Sudan	46.1
14	Vietnam	100.2		29	Uganda	45.8
15	Congo	98.6		30	Argentina	45.3

Largest refugee nationalities, 2000
'000

1	Afghanistan	3,567.2		11	Congo	365.0
2	Burundi	567.0		12	Croatia	323.8
3	Iraq	497.4		13	Azerbaijan	282.6
4	Sudan	485.5		14	Liberia	273.2
5	Bosnia	454.7		15	Western Sahara	165.8
6	Somalia	441.6		16	Myanmar	135.6
7	Angola	421.2		17	East Timor	122.2
8	Sierra Leone	401.8		18	Rwanda	114.1
9	Eritrea	377.1		19	Palestinians	109.8
10	Vietnam	369.1		20	Bhutan	108.9

Countries with largest refugee population, 2000
'000

1	Pakistan	2,001.5		11	Armenia	280.6
2	Iran	1,868.0		12	Zambia	250.9
3	Germany	906.0		13	Uganda	236.6
4	Tanzania	680.9		14	Kenya	206.1
5	United States	507.3		15	Ethiopia	198.0
6	Serbia & Montenegro	484.4		16	India	170.9
7	Guinea	433.1		17	Algeria	169.7
8	Sudan	401.0		18	Sweden	157.2
9	Congo	332.5		19	United Kingdom	149.8
10	China	294.1		20	Netherlands	146.0

Asylum applications by nationality in industrialised countries[a], 2000
'000

1	Serbia & Montenegro	40.6		9	India	10.7
2	Iraq	36.7		10	Sri Lanka	10.3
3	Afghanistan	26.2		11	Pakistan	9.4
4	Turkey	24.9		12	Somalia	8.9
5	Iran	24.5		13	Armenia	8.6
6	China	19.0		14	Congo	8.1
7	Russia	14.8		15	Sierra Leone	7.5
8	Bosnia	11.3		16	Romania	7.4

Industrialised countries[b] with most asylum applications, 2000
'000

1	United Kingdom	98.9		11	Italy	15.6
2	Germany	78.8		12	Australia	12.9
3	United States	63.7		13	Denmark	12.2
4	Netherlands	43.9		14	Ireland	10.9
5	Belgium	42.7		15	Norway	10.8
6	France	38.6		16	Slovenia	9.2
7	Canada	37.9		17	Czech Republic	8.8
8	Austria	18.3		18	Hungary	7.8
9	Switzerland	17.7		19	Spain	7.0
10	Sweden	16.3		20	Poland	4.4

a In 26 industrialised countries.   b In 29 industrialised countries.

Population density

Highest population density
Population per sq km, 2000

1	Macau	24,684	21	El Salvador		298
2	Hong Kong	6,564	22	Haiti		293
3	Singapore	6,502	23	Rwanda		289
4	Malta	1,234	24	Sri Lanka		288
5	Bermuda	1,034	25	Réunion		287
6	Bangladesh	954	26	Israel		273
7	Bahrain	944	27	Netherlands Antilles		269
8	Barbados	622	28	Philippines		252
9	Taiwan	617		Trinidad & Tobago		252
10	Mauritius	569	30	Guadeloupe		251
11	West Bank and Gaza	514	31	United Kingdom		243
12	South Korea	472	32	Vietnam		236
13	Puerto Rico	440	33	Jamaica		234
14	Netherlands	388	34	Germany		230
15	Aruba	362	35	Burundi		228
16	Martinique	348	36	Italy		191
17	Belgium	336	37	North Korea		185
	Japan	336	38	Pakistan		177
	Lebanon	336	39	Switzerland		174
20	India	307	40	Dominican Republic		172

Lowest population density
Population per sq km, 2000

1	Australia	2	22	Angola	11
	Mongolia	2	23	New Caledonia	12
	Namibia	2		Oman	12
4	Botswana	3		Sudan	12
	Canada	3	26	Algeria	13
	Iceland	3		Argentina	13
	Libya	3	28	New Zealand	14
	Mauritania	3		Norway	14
	Suriname	3		Paraguay	14
10	Gabon	5		Somalia	14
11	Central African Rep	6		Zambia	14
	Chad	6	33	Finland	15
	Kazakhstan	6	34	Uruguay	19
14	Bolivia	8	35	Brazil	20
15	Congo-Brazzaville	9		Chile	20
	Mali	9		Peru	20
	Niger	9		Sweden	20
	Russia	9	39	Bahamas	22
	Saudi Arabia	9		Congo	22
20	Papua New Guinea	10		Laos	22
	Turkmenistan	10			

Note: Estimates of population density refer to the total land area of a country. In countries such as Japan and Canada, where much of the land area is virtually uninhabitable, the effective population densities of the habitable areas are much greater than the figures suggest.

Regional variations

Population by region
2000

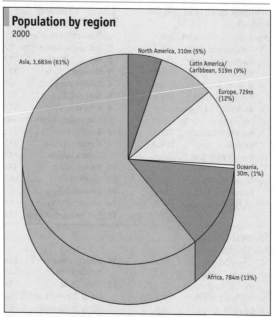

Asia, 3,683m (61%)

North America, 310m (5%)

Latin America/Caribbean, 519m (9%)

Europe, 729m (12%)

Oceania, 30m, (1%)

Africa, 784m (13%)

Land area by region
Sq km, '000

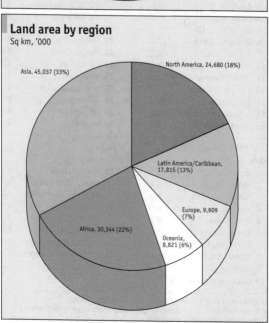

Asia, 45,037 (33%)

North America, 24,680 (18%)

Latin America/Caribbean, 17,815 (13%)

Europe, 9,909 (7%)

Oceania, 8,821 (6%)

Africa, 30,344 (22%)

City living

Highest quality of life index[a]

New York=100, November 2001

1	Zurich, Switzerland	106.5
2	Vancouver, Canada	106.0
	Vienna, Austria	106.0
4	Geneva, Switzerland	105.5
	Sydney, Australia	105.5
6	Auckland, New Zealand	105.0
	Copenhagen, Denmark	105.0
	Frankfurt, Germany	105.0
	Helsinki, Finland	105.0
10	Bern, Switzerland	104.5
	Munich, Germany	104.5
12	Amsterdam, Neth.	104.0
	Melbourne, Australia	104.0
	Stockholm, Sweden	104.0

Lowest quality of life index[a]

New York=100, November 2001

1	Brazzaville, Congo-Braz.	27.5
2	Bangui, Cent. African Rep.	29.0
3	Khartoum, Sudan	31.5
4	Pointe Noire, Congo-Braz.	32.5
5	Baghdad, Iraq	33.0
6	Ndjamena, Chad	37.5
7	Ouagadougou, Burkina Faso	38.0
8	Bamako, Mali	38.5
	Kinshasa, Congo	38.5
	Luanda, Angola	38.5
11	Niamey, Niger	39.5
12	Sanaa, Yemen	40.0
13	Conakry, Guinea	41.0
14	Nouakchott, Mauritania	41.5
15	Port Harcourt, Nigeria	42.0

Biggest cities[b]

Population m, 2000

1	Tokyo, Japan	26.4
2	Mumbai, India	18.1
	Mexico city, Mexico	18.1
4	Sao Paulo, Brazil	17.8
5	New York, US	16.6
6	Lagos, Nigeria	13.4
7	Los Angeles, US	13.1
8	Shanghai, China	12.9
	Kolkata, India	12.9
10	Buenos Aires, Argentina	12.6
11	Dhaka, Bangladesh	12.3
12	Karachi, Pakistan	11.8
13	Delhi, India	11.7
14	Jakarta, Indonesia	11.0
	Osaka, Japan	11.0
16	Beijing, China	10.8
	Manila, Philippines	10.8
18	Cairo, Egypt	10.6
	Rio de Janeiro, Brazil	10.6
20	Seoul, South Korea	9.9
21	Paris, France	9.6
22	Istanbul, Turkey	9.5
23	Moscow, Russia	9.3
24	Tianjin, China	9.2
25	London, UK	7.6
26	Lima, Peru	7.4
27	Bangkok, Thailand	7.3
28	Tehran, Iran	7.2
29	Chicago, US	7.0
30	Hong Kong	6.9

Fastest growing cities

Annual growth rate, 1995–2005

1	Wenzhou, China	9.0
2	Yantai, China	8.4
	Tabora, Tanzania	8.4
4	Mwanza, Tanzania	6.8
5	Jinxi, China	6.7
6	Sanaa, Yemen	6.5
	Toluca, Mexico	6.5
8	Xuzhou, China	6.4
9	Nanchong, China	6.2
10	Ouagadougou, Burkina Faso	6.1
11	Asansol, India	5.4
	Kabul, Afghanistan	5.4
	Rajshahi, Bangladesh	5.4
14	Thane, India	5.3
	Ulsan, Korea	5.3
16	Arbil, Iraq	5.2
	Maputo, Mozambique	5.2
18	Antananarivo, Madagascar	5.0
	Chongqing, China	5.0

a Based on 39 factors ranging from recreation to political stability.
b Urban agglomerations. Estimates of cities' populations vary according to where geographical boundaries are defined.

Highest urban population
% population living in urban areas

1	Bermuda	100	16	Malta	90.5
	Hong Kong	100	17	Argentina	89.9
	Singapore	100	18	Lebanon	89.7
4	Guadeloupe	99.7	19	United Kingdom	89.5
5	Macau	98.8	20	Netherlands	89.4
6	Kuwait	97.6	21	Bahamas	88.5
7	Belgium	97.3	22	Libya	87.6
8	Martinique	94.9	23	Germany	87.5
9	Gaza Strip	94.6	24	Venezuela	86.9
10	Iceland	92.5	25	United Arab Emirates	85.9
	Qatar	92.5	26	New Zealand	85.8
12	Bahrain	92.2	27	Chile	85.7
13	Luxembourg	91.5		Saudi Arabia	85.7
14	Uruguay	91.3	29	Denmark	85.3
15	Israel	91.2	30	Australia	84.7

Lowest urban population
% population living in urban areas

1	Rwanda	6.2	16	Yemen	24.7
2	Bhutan	7.1	17	Malawi	24.9
3	Burundi	9.0	18	Tajikistan	27.5
4	Nepal	11.9	19	Myanmar	27.7
5	Uganda	14.2	20	Lesotho	28.0
6	Cambodia	15.9	21	Madagascar	29.6
7	Papua New Guinea	17.4	22	Mali	30.0
8	Ethiopia	17.6	23	Congo	30.3
9	Burkina Faso	18.5	24	Namibia	30.9
10	Eritrea	18.7	25	China	32.1
11	Vietnam	19.7	26	Gambia, The	32.5
12	Niger	20.6	27	Tanzania	32.9
13	Thailand	21.6	28	Kenya	33.1
14	Afghanistan	21.9	29	Kirgizstan	33.3
15	Guinea-Bissau	23.7		Togo	33.3

Highest city density
Population per sq km

1	Hong Kong	28,405	14	Kolkata, India	11,671
2	Seoul, South Korea	23,908	15	Karachi, Pakistan	10,824
3	Cairo, Egypt	23,148	16	Guangzhou, China	10,417
4	Tianjin, China	21,519	17	Singapore	8,697
5	Manila, Philippines	19,783	18	Brussels, Belgium	7,438
6	Bombay, India	18,247	19	Tokyo, Japan	7,099
7	Surabaya, Indonesia	17,668	20	Istanbul, Turkey	7,007
8	Delhi, India	17,661	21	Vienna, Austria	6,829
9	Jakarta, Indonesia	17,056	22	Sao Paulo, Brazil	6,823
10	Shanghai, China	16,378	23	Kuala Lumpur, Malaysia	5,693
11	Bangkok, Thailand	14,955	24	Amsterdam, Neth.	5,546
12	Beijing, China	14,468	25	Munich, Germany	5,359
13	Mexico city, Mexico	11,676			

Population: *age and sex*

Highest median age[a]

Years, 2000

1	Japan	41.2
2	Italy	40.2
	Switzerland	40.2
4	Germany	40.1
5	Sweden	39.7
6	Finland	39.4
7	Belgium	39.1
	Bulgaria	39.1
	Greece	39.1
10	Denmark	38.7
11	Austria	38.4
12	Hungary	38.1
	Slovenia	38.1
14	Croatia	37.9
15	Latvia	37.8
16	Luxembourg	37.7
	Netherlands	37.7
	Spain	37.7
	United Kingdom	37.7
20	Czech Republic	37.6
	France	37.6
22	Estonia	37.3
	Ukraine	37.3
24	Norway	37.2
25	Portugal	37.0

Highest median age[a]

Years, 2020

1	Switzerland	48.9
2	Italy	48.7
3	Japan	48.0
4	Germany	47.9
5	Austria	47.7
6	Spain	46.8
7	Greece	46.6
8	Slovenia	46.3
	Sweden	46.3
10	Belgium	45.4
11	Czech Republic	44.9
12	Denmark	44.8
	Finland	44.8
	Netherlands	44.8
15	Singapore	44.6
16	Bulgaria	44.3
	Hong Kong	44.3
18	Portugal	44.0
	United Kingdom	44.0
20	Hungary	43.7
21	Latvia	43.6
22	Bosnia	43.5
23	Macau	43.3
24	Norway	43.2
25	Lithuania	43.0

Lowest median age[a]

Years, 2000

1	Yemen	15.0
2	Niger	15.1
3	Uganda	15.4
4	Burkina Faso	15.6
	Congo	15.6
6	Angola	15.9
7	Burundi	16.0
	Somalia	16.0
9	Zambia	16.5
10	Benin	16.6
11	Chad	16.7
	Malawi	16.7
13	Congo-Brazzaville	16.8
	Mali	16.8
	West Bank and Gaza	16.8
16	Zimbabwe	17.0
17	Nigeria	17.2
	Tanzania	17.2
19	Ethiopia	17.3
	Rwanda	17.3

Lowest median age[a]

Years, 2020

1	Niger	15.7
2	Uganda	15.9
3	Yemen	16.0
4	Angola	16.1
5	Liberia	16.2
6	Somalia	16.3
7	Congo	16.4
8	Burkina Faso	16.5
9	Chad	17.2
	Mali	17.2
11	Burundi	17.3
	Congo-Brazzaville	17.3
13	Sierra Leone	17.8
14	Malawi	17.9
15	Ethiopia	18.0
16	Zambia	18.1
17	Guinea-Bissau	18.5
18	Mauritania	18.6

a Age at which there are an equal number of people above and below.

Highest child dependency %[a]

2000			2020		
1	Yemen	105	1	Niger	98
2	Niger	104	2	Uganda	96
3	Uganda	102	3	Angola	95
4	Burkina Faso	101		Yemen	95
	Congo	101	5	Congo	93
6	Angola	98		Somalia	93
7	Somalia	97	7	Liberia	92
8	Burundi	96	8	Burkina Faso	91
9	West Bank and Gaza	93	9	Mali	89
10	Chad	92	10	Chad	87
	Congo-Brazzaville	92	11	Burundi	86
	Mali	92		Congo-Brazzaville	86
	Zambia	92	13	Malawi	82
14	Benin	91		Sierra Leone	82
	Malawi	91	15	Ethiopia	81
16	Zimbabwe	88	16	Zambia	79
17	Ethiopia	87	17	Guinea-Bissau	78
	Nigeria	87	18	Mauritania	77
19	Madagascar	86	19	Benin	75
20	Tanzania	86	20	Oman	74
21	Mauritania	84		Rwanda	74
22	Sierra Leone	84	22	West Bank and Gaza	73
23	Togo	84	23	Gabon	72
24	Eritrea	83		Madagascar	72
25	Guinea	83		Mozambique	72

Highest elderly dependency %[b]

2000			2020		
1	Italy	27	1	Japan	47
	Sweden	27	2	Sweden	38
3	Belgium	26		Switzerland	38
	Greece	26	4	Finland	37
5	Japan	25		Italy	37
	Spain	25	6	Greece	35
7	Bulgaria	24	7	Germany	34
	France	24	8	Belgium	33
	Germany	24		Denmark	33
	Norway	24		France	33
	Switzerland	24	11	Austria	32
	United Kingdom	24		Czech Republic	32
13	Austria	23		Malta	32
	Portugal	23		Slovenia	32
15	Denmark	22		Spain	32
	Finland	22	16	Norway	31
	Latvia	22		United Kingdom	31
	Luxembourg	22	18	Hungary	30
				Netherlands	30
			20	Portugal	29

a Populaton aged 0–14 as % of that aged 15–59.
b Population aged 60 or over as % of that aged 15–59.

Population: *matters of breeding*

Highest crude birth rates

No. of live births per 1,000 population, 2000–05

1	Liberia	55.5	21	Mozambique	41.7
2	Niger	55.2	22	Madagascar	41.5
3	Somalia	51.8		Zambia	41.5
4	Angola	51.3	24	Benin	41.1
5	Uganda	50.6	25	Nigeria	39.5
6	Mali	49.6	26	West Bank and Gaza	39.0
7	Sierra Leone	49.1	27	Togo	38.7
8	Yemen	48.8	28	Eritrea	38.5
9	Chad	48.5	29	Tanzania	37.9
10	Afghanistan	47.3	30	Gabon	37.6
11	Congo	47.2		Senegal	37.6
12	Burkina Faso	46.8	32	Central African Rep	37.5
13	Malawi	44.9	33	Gambia, The	37.2
14	Guinea-Bissau	44.6	34	Cameroon	36.3
15	Congo-Brazzaville	44.2		Pakistan	36.3
16	Ethiopia	43.8	36	Oman	36.0
17	Mauritania	43.7	37	Laos	35.7
18	Burundi	43.5	38	Côte d'Ivoire	35.3
19	Guinea	43.4	39	Zimbabwe	35.1
20	Rwanda	42.1	40	Cambodia	34.9

Lowest crude birth rates

Number of live births per 1,000 population, 2000–05

1	Latvia	7.8	21	Hong Kong	9.5
2	Bulgaria	7.9		Poland	9.5
3	Ukraine	8.1	23	Belgium	9.7
4	Germany	8.2		Bosnia	9.7
	Slovenia	8.2		Finland	9.7
	Sweden	8.2	26	Slovakia	10.2
7	Austria	8.3	27	Georgia	10.3
8	Italy	8.6	28	Romania	10.4
	Russia	8.6	29	Netherlands	10.6
	Switzerland	8.6		United Kingdom	10.6
11	Estonia	8.7	31	Singapore	10.8
12	Czech Republic	8.8	32	Canada	10.9
	Hungary	8.8	33	Denmark	11.0
	Lithuania	8.8		Portugal	11.0
	Macau	8.8	35	Serbia & Montenegro	11.1
16	Greece	8.9	36	Macedonia	11.4
	Spain	8.9		Norway	11.4
18	Belarus	9.1	38	Croatia	11.5
19	Japan	9.2		Moldova	11.5
20	Armenia	9.4	40	Cuba	11.7

Notes: The crude birth rate is the number of live births in one year per 1,000 population. In addition to the fertility rate (see below) it depends on the population's age structure and will tend to be higher if there is a large proportion of women of childbearing age.

The fertility rate is the average number of children born to a woman who completes her childbearing years.

Highest fertility rates
Average number of children per woman, 2000–05

1	Niger	8.00
2	Yemen	7.60
3	Somalia	7.25
4	Angola	7.20
5	Uganda	7.10
6	Mali	7.00
7	Afghanistan	6.80
	Burkina Faso	6.80
	Burundi	6.80
	Liberia	6.80
11	Ethiopia	6.75
12	Congo	6.70
13	Chad	6.65
14	Sierra Leone	6.50
15	Malawi	6.34
16	Congo-Brazzaville	6.29
17	Mauritania	6.00
18	Guinea-Bissau	5.99
19	Mozambique	5.86
20	Guinea	5.83

Lowest fertility rates
Average number of children per woman, 2000–05

1	Armenia	1.10
	Bulgaria	1.10
	Latvia	1.10
	Macau	1.10
	Ukraine	1.10
6	Spain	1.13
7	Russia	1.14
	Slovenia	1.14
9	Czech Republic	1.16
10	Hong Kong	1.17
11	Belarus	1.20
	Estonia	1.20
	Hungary	1.20
	Italy	1.20
	Lithuania	1.20
16	Austria	1.24
	Greece	1.24
18	Poland	1.26
19	Slovakia	1.28
20	Germany	1.29
	Sweden	1.29

Highest teenage birth rates
No. of births per 1,000 women aged 15–19, 2000–05

1	Niger	233
2	Congo	230
	Liberia	230
4	Angola	229
5	Somalia	213
6	Sierra Leone	212
7	Uganda	211
8	Chad	195
	Guinea-Bissau	195
	Mali	195
11	Guinea	168
12	Gabon	161
13	Malawi	152
14	Burkina Faso	151
15	Mauritania	147
16	Congo-Brazzaville	146
	Zambia	146
18	Central African Rep	141
19	Gambia, The	139
20	Nicaragua	138
21	Madagascar	136
22	Mozambique	129
23	Cameroon	127

Lowest teenage birth rates
No. of births per 1,000 women aged 15–19, 2000–05

1	North Korea	2
2	South Korea	3
3	Japan	4
	Netherlands	4
5	China	5
	Sweden	5
	Switzerland	5
8	Italy	6
	Spain	6
10	Denmark	7
	Finland	7
	Singapore	7
13	Belgium	8
	Slovenia	8
15	France	9
	Luxembourg	9
17	Cyprus	10
	Greece	10
	Norway	10
20	Germany	11
21	Austria	12
	Malta	12

The world economy

Biggest economies
GDP, $bn

1	United States	9,837.4	26	Denmark	162.3
2	Japan	4,841.6	27	Norway	161.8
3	Germany	1,873.0	28	Poland	157.7
4	United Kingdom	1,414.6	29	Indonesia	153.3
5	France[a]	1,294.2	30	South Africa	125.9
6	China	1,079.9	31	Thailand	122.2
7	Italy	1,074.0	32	Finland	121.5
8	Canada	687.9	33	Venezuela	120.5
9	Brazil	595.5	34	Greece	112.6
10	Mexico	574.5	35	Israel	110.4
11	Spain	558.6	36	Portugal	105.1
12	South Korea	457.2	37	Iran	104.9
13	India	457.0	38	Egypt	98.7
14	Australia	390.1	39	Ireland	93.9
15	Netherlands	364.8	40	Singapore	92.3
16	Taiwan	310.0	41	Malaysia	89.7
17	Argentina	285.0	42	Colombia	81.3
18	Russia	251.1	43	Philippines	74.7
19	Switzerland	239.8	44	Chile	70.5
20	Sweden	227.3	45	United Arab Emirates	65.9
21	Belgium	226.6	46	Pakistan	61.6
22	Turkey	199.9	47	Peru	53.3
23	Austria	189.0	48	Algeria	53.3
24	Saudi Arabia	173.3	49	Czech Republic	50.8
25	Hong Kong	162.6	50	New Zealand	49.9

Biggest economies by purchasing power
GDP PPP, $bn

1	United States	9,601	21	South Africa	392
2	China	4,951	22	Thailand	384
3	Japan	3,436	23	Iran	376
4	India	2,375	24	Poland	348
5	Germany	2,047	25	Philippines	319
6	France	1,438	26	Belgium	282
7	United Kingdom	1,407	27	Pakistan	257
8	Italy	1,354	28	Colombia	256
9	Brazil	1,243	29	Saudi Arabia	236
10	Russia	1,165	30	Egypt	235
11	Mexico	861	31	Switzerland	219
12	Canada	836	32	Austria	214
13	South Korea	818	33	Sweden	213
14	Spain	760	34	Bangladesh	209
15	Indonesia	596	35	Malaysia	194
16	Taiwan	505	36	Ukraine	183
17	Australia	479	37	Greece	178
18	Turkey	459	38	Hong Kong	174
19	Argentina	446	39	Portugal	170
20	Netherlands	412	40	Vietnam	157

a Includes overseas departments.
For list of all countries with their GDP see pages 234–237.

Regional GDP

$bn, 2000		*% annual growth 1990–2000*	
World	31,500	World	3.3
Advanced economies	25,190	Advanced economies	2.7
G7	21,020	G7	2.4
EU15	7,840	EU15	2.1
Asia[a]	2,220	Asia[a]	7.6
Latin America	2,020	Latin America	3.3
Eastern Europe[b]	760	Eastern Europe[b]	-3.0
Middle East[c]	850	Middle East[c]	3.9
Africa	460	Africa	2.5

Regional purchasing power

GDP in PPP, % of total		*$ per head*	
World	100.0	World	7,560
Advanced economies	57.1	Advanced economies	27,070
G7	45.4	G7	28,800
EU15	20.0	EU15	23,670
Asia[a]	21.6	Asia[a]	3,200
Latin America	8.4	Latin America	7,340
Eastern Europe[b]	5.9	Eastern Europe[b]	6,930
Middle East[c]	3.9	Middle East[c]	5,740
Africa	3.2	Africa	2,040

Regional population

% of total (6.1bn)		*No. of countries[d]*	
Advanced economies	15.4	Advanced economies	29
G7	11.5	G7	7
EU15	6.2	EU15	15
Asia[a]	52.0	Asia[a]	25
Latin America	8.5	Latin America	33
Eastern Europe[b]	6.7	Eastern Europe[b]	28
Middle East[c]	5.1	Middle East[c]	16
Africa	12.2	Africa	51

Regional international trade

Exports of goods and services, % of tot.		*Current account balances, $bn*	
Advanced economies	75.7	Advanced economies	-248.4
G7	47.7	G7	-335.5
EU15	36.0	EU15	-22.5
Asia[a]	9.2	Asia[a]	45.8
Latin America	4.5	Latin America	-48.6
Eastern Europe[b]	4.3	Eastern Europe[b]	27.5
Middle East[c]	4.2	Middle East[c]	60.9
Africa	2.1	Africa	2.1

a Excludes Hong Kong, Japan, Singapore, South Korea and Taiwan.
b Includes Russia and other CIS.
c Includes Malta and Turkey.
d IMF definition.

Living standards

Highest GDP per head

$

1	Luxembourg	43,090	36	Guadeloupe[b]	13,340
2	Bermuda[a]	42,830	37	New Zealand	13,030
3	Japan	38,160	38	Bahrain	11,530
4	Norway	36,020	39	Cyprus	11,490
5	United States	34,940	40	Réunion[b]	11,410
6	Switzerland	33,390	41	Netherlands Antilles[a]	11,160
7	Denmark	30,420	42	Greece	10,670
8	Iceland	30,340	43	Puerto Rico	10,550
9	Sweden	25,630	44	Portugal	10,500
10	Ireland	24,740	45	Barbados	9,740
	Qatar	24,740	46	South Korea	9,670
12	Hong Kong	23,930	47	Malta	9,140
13	United Kingdom	23,680	48	Slovenia	9,120
14	Finland	23,460	49	Saudi Arabia	8,360
15	Austria	23,310	50	Oman	8,330
16	Singapore	22,960	51	Argentina	7,690
17	Netherlands	22,910	52	Libya[a]	7,640
18	Germany	22,800	53	Uruguay	5,910
19	United Arab Emirates[a]	22,670	54	Mexico	5,860
20	Canada	22,370	55	Trinidad & Tobago	5,620
21	Belgium	22,110	56	Venezuela	4,980
22	France	21,980	57	Czech Republic	4,940
23	Australia	20,340	58	Chile	4,640
24	Aruba	19,500	59	Hungary	4,550
25	Kuwait	19,040	60	Croatia	4,340
26	Italy	18,620	61	Costa Rica	4,160
27	Israel	17,710	62	Poland	4,080
28	French Polynesia	16,720	63	Gabon	4,010
29	Bahamas	15,900	64	Malaysia	3,850
30	Martinique[b]	15,600	65	Lebanon	3,810
31	New Caledonia	14,370	66	Mauritius	3,690
32	Brunei[a]	14,280	67	Estonia	3,630
33	Macau	14,170	68	Slovakia	3,540
34	Spain	14,150	69	Brazil	3,490
35	Taiwan	13,950	70	Panama	3,460

Lowest GDP per head

$

1	Burundi	100		Guinea-Bissau	180
	Ethiopia	100	12	Burkina Faso	190
3	Sierra Leone	130	13	Mali	210
4	Myanmar[a]	140		Mozambique	210
5	Eritrea	150		Rwanda	210
6	Malawi	160	16	Bhutan	230
	Tajikistan	160	17	Nepal	240
8	Liberia[a]	170	18	Madagascar	250
	Niger	170	19	Cambodia	260
10	Chad	180		Central African Rep	260

a Estimate.   b 1999

Highest purchasing power
GDP per head in PPP (USA = 100)

1	Luxembourg	133.3	36	Greece	49.4
2	United States	100.0	37	Malta	48.5
3	Switzerland	89.3	38	Bahamas	48.1
4	Norway	86.9	39	Barbados	44.0
5	Iceland	84.2	40	Bahrain[b]	42.3
6	Belgium	80.6	41	Czech Republic	40.4
7	Denmark	79.9	42	Argentina	35.3
8	Canada	79.7	43	Hungary	35.2
9	Japan	79.4	44	Saudi Arabia	33.4
10	Austria	77.2	45	Slovakia	32.4
11	Netherlands	75.8	46	Mauritius	29.1
12	Hong Kong	75.0	47	Estonia	27.4
13	Ireland	74.8	48	South Africa	26.9
14	Australia	73.2	49	Chile	26.7
15	Germany	73.1	50	Poland	26.4
16	Brunei[a]	73.0	51	Uruguay	26.0
	Singapore	73.0	52	Mexico	25.8
18	Finland	72.1	53	Malaysia	24.4
19	France	71.6	54	Trinidad & Tobago	24.1
20	Sweden	70.3	55	Russia	23.5
21	United Kingdom	69.1	56	Costa Rica	23.4
22	Italy	68.8	57	Croatia	23.3
23	French Polynesia	68.4	58	Belarus	22.1
24	Taiwan[a]	66.7	59	Brazil	21.4
25	New Caledonia	64.0	60	Botswana	21.0
26	Cyprus	60.9	61	Latvia	20.7
27	United Arab Emirates[a]	56.9	62	Turkey	20.6
28	Israel	56.7	63	Lithuania	20.5
29	Spain	56.5	64	Namibia	18.8
30	Kuwait	54.8	65	Romania	18.7
31	New Zealand	54.3	66	Thailand	18.5
32	Macau	53.3		Colombia	17.8
33	Slovenia	50.8	68	Tunisia	17.8
34	South Korea	50.7	69	Iran	17.3
35	Portugal	49.8	70	Venezuela	16.8

Lowest purchasing power
GDP per head in PPP (USA = 100)

1	Sierra Leone	1.4	11	Mali	2.3
2	Tanzania	1.5		Mozambique	2.3
3	Burundi	1.7		Nigeria	2.3
	Congo-Brazzaville	1.7		Yemen	2.3
5	Malawi	1.8	15	Madagascar	2.4
6	Ethiopia	1.9	16	Chad	2.6
7	Congo[a]	2.0	17	Rwanda	2.7
8	Guinea-Bissau	2.1	18	Burkina Faso	2.8
9	Niger	2.2		Eritrea	2.8
	Zambia	2.2	20	Benin	2.9

Note: for definition of purchasing power parity see page 231.

The quality of life

Human development index[a]

1	Norway	93.9	44	Estonia	81.2
2	Australia	93.6	45	United Arab Emirates	80.9
	Canada	93.6	46	Croatia	80.3
	Sweden	93.6		Lithuania	80.3
5	Belgium	93.5	48	Qatar	80.1
6	United States	93.4	49	Trinidad & Tobago	79.8
7	Iceland	93.2	50	Latvia	79.1
8	Netherlands	93.1	51	Mexico	79.0
9	Japan	92.8	52	Panama	78.4
10	Finland	92.5	53	Belarus	78.2
11	France	92.4	54	Russia	77.5
	Luxembourg	92.4	55	Malaysia	77.4
	Switzerland	92.4	56	Bulgaria	77.2
14	United Kingdom	92.3		Romania	77.2
15	Austria	92.1	58	Libya	77.0
	Denmark	92.1	59	Macedonia	76.6
	Germany	92.1	60	Colombia	76.5
18	Ireland	91.6		Mauritius	76.5
19	New Zealand	91.3		Venezuela	76.5
20	Italy	90.9	63	Lebanon	75.8
21	Spain	90.8		Suriname	75.8
22	Israel	89.3	65	Fiji	75.7
23	Greece	88.1		Thailand	75.7
24	Hong Kong	88.0	67	Saudi Arabia	75.4
25	Cyprus	87.7	68	Brazil	75.0
26	Singapore	87.6	69	Philippines	74.9
27	South Korea	87.5	70	Oman	74.7
28	Portugal	87.4	71	Armenia	74.5
	Slovenia	87.4	72	Peru	74.3
30	Malta	86.6	73	Georgia	74.2
31	Barbados	86.4		Kazakhstan	74.2
32	Brunei	85.7		Ukraine	74.2
33	Czech Republic	84.4	76	Azerbaijan	73.8
34	Argentina	84.2		Jamaica	73.8
35	Slovakia	83.1		Paraguay	73.8
36	Hungary	82.9	79	Sri Lanka	73.5
37	Poland	82.8		Turkey	73.5
	Uruguay	82.8	81	Turkmenistan	73.0
39	Chile	82.5	82	Ecuador	72.6
40	Bahrain	82.4	83	Albania	72.5
41	Costa Rica	82.1	84	Dominican Republic	72.2
42	Bahamas	82.0	85	China	71.8
43	Kuwait	81.8			

a GDP or GDP per head is often taken as a measure of how developed a country is, but its usefulness is limited as it refers only to economic welfare. In 1990 the UN Development Programme published its first estimate of a Human Development Index, which combined statistics on two other indicators – adult literacy and life expectancy – with income levels to give a better, though still far from perfect, indicator of human development. In 1991 average years of schooling was combined with adult literacy to give a knowledge variable. The HDI is shown here scaled from 0 to 100; countries scoring over 80 are considered to have high human development, those scoring from 50 to 79 medium and those under 50 low.

Economic freedom index[a]

1	Hong Kong	1.35		Belgium	2.10
2	Singapore	1.55		Germany	2.10
3	New Zealand	1.70	23	Cyprus	2.15
4	Estonia	1.80		Iceland	2.15
	Ireland	1.80		United Arab Emirates	2.15
	Luxembourg	1.80	26	Barbados	2.30
	Netherlands	1.80		Portugal	2.30
	United States	1.80		Spain	2.30
9	Australia	1.85	29	Italy	2.35
	Chile	1.85		Lithuania	2.35
	United Kingdom	1.85		Taiwan	2.35
12	Denmark	1.90	32	Czech Republic	2.40
	Switzerland	1.90		Hungary	2.40
14	Finland	1.95		Thailand	2.40
15	Bahrain	2.00	35	Japan	2.45
	Canada	2.00		Norway	2.45
17	Bahamas	2.05		Trinidad & Tobago	2.45
	El Salvador	2.05	38	Argentina	2.50
	Sweden	2.05		South Korea	2.50
20	Austria	2.10		Latvia	2.50

Gender-related development index[b]

1	Norway	93.7	21	Spain	90.1
2	Australia	93.5	22	Israel	88.8
3	Canada	93.4	23	Greece	87.4
4	Sweden	93.1	24	Hong Kong	87.7
5	Belgium	92.8	25	Cyprus	87.2
6	United States	93.2	26	Singapore	87.1
7	Iceland	93.0	27	South Korea	86.8
8	Netherlands	92.6	28	Portugal	87.0
9	Japan	92.1	29	Slovenia	87.1
10	Finland	92.3	30	Malta	85.0
11	Switzerland	91.9	31	Brunei	85.3
12	Luxembourg	90.7	32	Czech Republic	84.2
13	France	92.2	33	Argentina	83.3
14	Denmark	92.0	34	Slovakia	82.9
	United Kingdom	92.0	35	Hungary	82.6
16	Austria	91.5	36	Uruguay	82.5
17	Germany	91.6	37	Poland	82.6
18	Ireland	90.8	38	Chile	81.7
19	New Zealand	91.0	39	Bahrain	81.4
20	Italy	90.3	40	Costa Rica	81.3

a Ranks countries on the basis of ten indicators of how government intervention can restrict the economic relations between individuals. The economic indicators, published by the Heritage Foundation, are trade policy, taxation, monetary policy, the banking system, foreign-investment rules, property rights, the amount of economic output consumed by the government, regulation policy, the size of the black market and the extent of wage and price controls. A country can score between 1 and 5 in each category, 1 being the most free and 5 being the least free.
b Combines similar data to the HDI (and also published by the UNDP) to give an indicator of the disparities in human development between men and women in individual countries. The lower the index, the greater the disparity.

Economic growth

Highest economic growth, 1990–2000
Average annual % increase in real GDP

1	Bosnia[a]	25.6	27	Bangladesh	5.0
2	China	9.6		Botswana	5.0
3	Lebanon	8.8		Malta	5.0
4	Cyprus[a]	8.2		Nepal	5.0
5	Singapore	7.8		Thailand	5.0
6	Ireland	7.2		Tunisia	5.0
	Malaysia	7.2	33	Dominican Republic	4.8
	Vietnam	7.2		Panama	4.8
9	Sudan	6.9	35	Iran	4.7
10	Uganda	6.5		Jordan	4.7
11	Bhutan	6.4	37	Benin	4.6
	South Korea	6.4		Cambodia	4.6
13	Chile	6.3		El Salvador	4.6
	Laos	6.3		Indonesia	4.6
15	Oman[b]	6.2	41	Egypt	4.5
16	Myanmar[c]	6.1	42	Burkina Faso	4.4
	Taiwan	6.1	43	Hong Kong	4.3
18	Syria	5.9	44	Ghana	4.2
19	India	5.5		Namibia	4.2
	Luxembourg	5.5	46	Lesotho	4.1
	Mauritius	5.5	47	Guatemala	4.0
	Yemen[d]	5.5		Pakistan	4.0
23	Israel	5.3		Turkey	4.0
	Sri Lanka	5.3	50	Argentina	3.9
25	Costa Rica	5.1		Bolivia	3.9
	Mozambique	5.1		Guinea	3.9

Lowest economic growth, 1990–2000
Average annual % change in real GDP

1	Georgia	-13.9	20	Macedonia[d]	-0.9
2	Moldova	-9.2	21	Haiti	-0.6
3	Tajikistan	-8.5	22	Mongolia	-0.3
4	Ukraine	-7.9		Uzbekistan	-0.3
5	Azerbaijan	-6.1	24	Rwanda	-0.1
6	Congo[e]	-5.2	25	Albania	0.0
7	Latvia	-4.3		Czech Republic[d]	0.0
8	Russia	-4.0	27	Slovakia	0.2
9	Kazakhstan	-3.7	28	Congo-Brazzaville	0.4
10	Sierra Leone	-3.4		Hungary	0.4
11	Kirgizstan	-3.2	30	Zambia	0.5
12	Bulgaria	-2.6	31	Angola	0.6
	Lithuania	-2.6	32	Cameroon	0.7
14	Turkmenistan	-2.4	33	Barbados	1.0
15	Romania	-2.2	34	Switzerland	1.1
16	Estonia	-2.0		Togo	1.1
17	Croatia	-1.3	36	Kuwait	1.2
18	Belarus	-1.2	37	Central African Rep	1.3
19	Burundi	-1.1		Fiji	1.3

a 1995–2000 b 1990–95 c 1990–99 d 1991–2000 e 1990–98 f 1996–2000

Highest economic growth, 1980–90
Average annual % increase in real GDP

1	Botswana	10.3		Indonesia	6.1
2	China	10.1	13	India	5.8
3	South Korea	9.4	14	Egypt	5.4
4	Oman	8.4		Mongolia	5.4
5	Taiwan	7.9		Turkey	5.4
6	Thailand	7.6	17	Malaysia	5.3
7	Hong Kong	6.9	18	Nepal	4.6
8	Singapore	6.7		Vietnam	4.6
9	Pakistan	6.3	20	Burundi	4.4
10	Mauritius	6.2		Lesotho	4.4
11	Chad	6.1	22	Bangladesh	4.3

Lowest economic growth, 1980–90
Average annual % increase in real GDP

1	Iraq	-6.8	12	Mauritania	0.0
2	Libya	-5.7		Saudi Arabia	0.0
3	United Arab Emirates	-2.1	14	El Salvador	0.2
4	Nicaragua	-1.9	15	Sierra Leone	0.3
5	Trinidad & Tobago	-0.8	16	Georgia	0.4
6	Argentina	-0.7		Sudan	0.4
7	Peru	-0.3		Uruguay	0.4
8	Bolivia	-0.2	19	Panama	0.5
	Haiti	-0.2		Romania	0.5
10	Mozambique	-0.1	21	Myanmar	0.6
	Niger	-0.1	22	Côte d'Ivoire	0.7

Fastest services growth, 1990–2000
Average annual % increase in real terms

1	Bosnia[a]	35.9	8	Malaysia	7.5
2	Georgia[a]	19.0		Uganda	7.5
3	Hong Kong	9.3	10	Armenia[b]	7.4
4	Iran	8.5		Vietnam	7.4
5	China	8.4	12	India	7.3
6	Singapore	7.8	13	Bhutan	7.1
7	Botswana	7.6	14	Cambodia	6.8

Highest services growth, 1990–2000
Average annual % increase in real terms

1	Bosnia[a]	17.2	7	Nepal	10.4
2	Mozambique[a]	16.6	8	Bhutan	10.3
3	Laos	12.4	9	Syria[b]	9.7
4	China	12.2	10	South Korea	8.3
5	Uganda	11.7	11	Sri Lanka	8.1
6	Malaysia	10.8	12	Poland	7.7

a 1995–2000
b 1991–2000
Note: Rankings of highest industrial growth 1990–2000 can be found on page 42 and highest agricultural growth on page 45.

Trading places

Biggest traders
% of total world exports (visible & invisible)

1	United States	15.44	23	Ireland	1.13
2	Euro area	15.33	24	Australia	0.99
3	Japan	8.01	25	Thailand	0.94
4	Germany	7.95	26	Saudi Arabia	0.93
5	United Kingdom	6.62	27	Denmark	0.90
6	France	4.88	28	Norway	0.89
7	Canada	3.81	29	Indonesia	0.80
8	Italy	3.63	30	Luxembourg	0.79
9	Netherlands	3.29	31	Brazil	0.74
10	China	3.18	32	India	0.69
11	Belgium	3.12	33	Finland	0.64
12	South Korea	2.31	34	Turkey	0.59
13	Mexico	2.03	35	Israel	0.54
14	Spain	2.00		Philippines	0.54
15	Switzerland	1.99	37	Poland	0.53
16	Taiwan	1.93	38	United Arab Emirates	0.43
17	Hong Kong	1.39	39	Argentina	0.42
	Sweden	1.39		Puerto Rico	0.42
19	Singapore	1.32		South Africa	0.42
20	Russia	1.31	42	Czech Republic	0.41
21	Malaysia	1.24		Portugal	0.41
22	Austria	1.16	44	Venezuela	0.40

Most trade dependent
Trade as % of GDP[a]

1	Liberia	582.6
2	Netherlands Antilles	206.0
3	Aruba	131.9
4	Malaysia	98.2
5	Singapore	83.7
6	Puerto Rico	79.2
7	Malta	78.2
8	Estonia	74.2
9	Tajikistan	73.6
10	Belgium	73.1
11	Iraq	69.5
12	Panama	65.0
13	Ireland	64.7
14	Slovakia	64.5
15	Bahrain	63.2
16	Czech Republic	60.2
17	Mauritania	59.6
18	Swaziland	58.6
19	Congo-Brazzaville	58.1
20	Hungary	57.9

Least trade dependent
Trade as % of GDP[a]

1	Congo	3.1
2	Somalia	5.3
3	Rwanda	8.1
4	Japan	8.3
5	Argentina	8.8
6	Brazil	9.3
7	United States	10.2
8	India	10.8
9	Tanzania	11.1
10	Burundi	11.4
	Egypt	11.4
12	Cuba	11.5
13	Ethiopia	12.7
	Sierra Leone	12.7
15	Peru	13.4
16	Sudan	13.8
17	Bermuda	14.3
18	Uruguay	14.4
19	Haiti	14.8
20	Euro area	15.1
	Pakistan	15.1

Notes: The figures are drawn from balance of payment statistics and, therefore, have differing technical definitions from trade statistics taken from customs or similar sources. The invisible trade figures do not show some countries due to unavailable data. For Hong Kong and Singapore, domestic exports and retained imports only are used.

Biggest visible traders
% of world visible exports

1	United States	16.24		24	Ireland	0.99
2	Euro area	14.49		25	Brazil	0.90
3	Germany	8.46		26	Indonesia	0.86
4	Japan	6.52		27	Saudi Arabia	0.86
5	United Kingdom	4.99		28	India	0.80
6	France	4.79		29	Denmark	0.77
7	Canada	4.30			Norway	0.77
8	Italy	3.79		31	Turkey	0.70
9	China	3.77		32	Poland	0.68
10	Netherlands	3.21		33	Finland	0.63
11	Mexico	2.77		34	United Arab Emirates	0.58
12	South Korea	2.72		35	Philippines	0.55
13	Belgium	2.69		36	Israel	0.53
14	Taiwan	2.28			Puerto Rico	0.53
15	Spain	2.14		38	Portugal	0.52
16	Switzerland	1.51		39	Czech Republic	0.50
17	Malaysia	1.43		40	Hong Kong	0.48
18	Sweden	1.30			South Africa	0.48
19	Singapore	1.25		42	Hungary	0.43
20	Russia	1.22		43	Argentina	0.41
21	Australia	1.08		44	Venezuela	0.39
22	Austria	1.07		45	Iran	0.35
23	Thailand	1.01		46	Greece	0.33

Biggest invisible traders
% of world invisible exports

1	United States	21.22		24	Turkey	0.74
2	Euro area	16.48		25	Greece	0.73
3	United Kingdom	10.67		26	Norway	0.71
4	Japan	9.10		27	India	0.68
5	Germany	5.97		28	Mexico	0.65
6	France	5.05		29	Israel	0.61
7	Belgium	3.95		30	Thailand	0.60
8	Hong Kong	3.42		31	Malaysia	0.52
9	Italy	3.12		32	Russia	0.47
10	Netherlands	3.10		33	Brazil	0.43
11	Switzerland	2.94			Finland	0.43
12	Spain	2.25			Portugal	0.43
13	Canada	2.17		36	Poland	0.42
14	Luxembourg	2.11		37	Philippines	0.39
15	China	1.42		38	Argentina	0.39
16	Austria	1.39		39	Egypt	0.38
	Singapore	1.39		40	Kuwait	0.32
18	Sweden	1.33		41	Czech Republic	0.28
19	South Korea	1.19		42	Saudi Arabia	0.27
20	Denmark	1.06		43	Indonesia	0.25
21	Ireland	1.00		44	Hungary	0.24
22	Taiwan	0.97			South Africa	0.24
23	Australia	0.89		46	El Salvador	0.23

a Average of imports and exports of goods as % of GDP.

Current account

Largest surpluses

$m

1	Japan	116,880		25	Sweden	6,617
2	Russia	46,317		26	Qatar	5,417
3	Switzerland	32,542		27	Oman	3,347
4	Norway	22,986		28	Denmark	2,507
5	Singapore	21,797		29	Yemen	2,063
6	China	20,518		30	Libya[a]	1,984
7	France	20,430		31	Ukraine	1,481
8	Canada	18,014		32	Syria	1,062
9	Kuwait	14,865		33	Luxembourg	1,011
10	Saudi Arabia	14,336		34	Vietnam	960
11	Venezuela	13,111		35	Ecuador	928
12	Iran	12,645		36	Kazakhstan	744
13	Netherlands	12,355		37	Botswana[a]	517
14	Belgium	11,844		38	Turkmenistan	412
15	South Korea	11,405		39	Jordan	405
16	Thailand	9,369		40	Gabon	390
17	Taiwan	9,316		41	Namibia	358
18	Philippines	9,081		42	Colombia	306
19	Algeria	8,900		43	Aruba	282
20	Finland	8,854		44	Bermuda	197
21	Hong Kong	8,842		45	Uzbekistan	184
22	Malaysia	8,409		46	Bahrain	113
23	Indonesia	7,986		47	Mauritania	90
24	Nigeria	6,983		48	Trinidad & Tobago[a]	57

Largest deficits

$m

1	United States	-444,690		21	Israel	-1,416
2	United Kingdom	-25,590		22	Romania	-1,359
3	Brazil	-24,632		23	Guatemala	-1,050
4	Germany	-18,710		24	Sri Lanka	-1,042
5	Mexico	-18,157		25	Dominican Republic	-1,027
6	Spain	-17,257		26	Chile	-991
7	Australia	-15,316		27	Egypt	-971
8	Portugal	-11,012		28	Panama	-933
9	Poland	-9,997		29	Uganda	-861
10	Greece	-9,820		30	Iceland	-849
11	Turkey	-9,819		31	Tunisia	-821
12	Argentina	-8,970		32	Serbia & Montenegro	-764
13	Italy	-5,670		33	Mozambique	-764
14	Austria	-5,205		34	West Bank and Gaza[b]	-748
15	India	-4,198		35	Bulgaria	-701
16	Lebanon	-3,065		36	Slovakia	-694
17	New Zealand	-2,734		37	Cuba	-687
18	Czech Republic	-2,236		38	Lithuania	-675
19	Peru	-1,628		39	Costa Rica[a]	-650
20	Hungary	-1,494		40	Congo[a]	-644

a 1999   b 1998

Largest surpluses as % of GDP
%

1	Kuwait	39.3		Finland	7.3
2	Qatar	37.4	26	Ecuador	6.8
3	Yemen	24.2	27	Syria	6.3
4	Singapore	23.6	28	Hong Kong	5.4
5	Russia	18.4		Luxembourg	5.4
6	Nigeria	17.0	30	Belgium	5.2
7	Oman	16.8	31	Indonesia	5.2
8	Algeria	16.7	32	Jordan	4.9
9	Guinea-Bissau	15.6		Libya[a]	4.9
10	Aruba	14.3	34	Ukraine	4.7
11	Norway	14.2	35	Kazakhstan	4.1
12	Switzerland	13.6	36	Suriname	3.8
13	Philippines	12.2	37	Netherlands	3.4
14	Iran	12.1	38	Vietnam	3.1
15	Venezuela	10.9	39	Taiwan	3.0
16	Namibia	10.3	40	Sweden	2.9
17	Botswana[a]	9.8	41	Canada	2.6
18	Mauritania	9.6	42	South Korea	2.5
19	Malaysia	9.4	43	Japan	2.4
	Turkmenistan	9.4		Uzbekistan	2.4
21	Saudi Arabia	8.3	45	China	1.9
22	Gabon	7.9	46	France	1.6
23	Thailand	7.7	47	Denmark	1.5
24	Bermuda	7.3	48	Bahrain	1.4

Largest deficits as % of GDP
%

1	Eritrea	-34.2	21	Iceland	-10.0
2	Malawi	-30.8	22	Panama	-9.4
3	Bhutan	-26.1	23	Niger	-9.2
4	Nicaragua	-21.1	24	Bahamas	-9.1
5	Mozambique	-20.3	25	Georgia	-8.9
6	Lebanon	-18.6		Serbia & Montenegro	-8.9
7	West Bank and Gaza[b]	-17.2	27	Benin	-8.8
8	Lesotho	-16.8	28	Greece	-8.7
9	Malta	-14.6	29	Honduras	-8.6
10	Armenia	-14.5	30	Sierra Leone[a]	-8.3
11	Uganda	-14.0	31	Liberia[b]	-8.1
12	Bosnia	-12.9		Netherlands Antilles	-8.1
13	Congo-Brazzaville[a]	-12.5	33	Ghana	-7.9
14	Kirgizstan	-12.1	34	Mali[c]	-7.8
15	Mongolia[a]	-11.6	35	Madagascar	-7.3
16	Gambia, The	-11.5	36	Burundi	-7.1
	Togo	-11.5		Laos[a]	-7.1
18	Chad	-11.2		Senegal	-7.1
19	Portugal	-10.5	39	Latvia	-6.9
20	Moldova	-10.2	40	Zambia[a]	-6.7

a 1999   b 1998   c 1997

Inflation

Highest inflation, 2000–01
% consumer price inflation

1	Angola	253.0	32	Kazakhstan	8.3
2	Suriname[a]	98.9	33	Laos	7.8
3	Zimbabwe	74.5	34	Guatemala	7.6
4	Belarus	61.1	35	Mongolia[a]	7.6
5	Turkey	54.5	36	Bulgaria	7.4
6	Ecuador	37.7		Nicaragua	7.4
7	Romania	34.5	38	Paraguay	7.3
8	Ghana	32.9		Slovakia	7.3
9	Malawi	27.2	40	Jamaica	7.0
10	Uzbekistan[b]	24.9	41	Kirgizstan	6.9
11	Russia	21.5		Nigeria[b]	6.9
12	Zambia	21.4	43	Bhutan[a]	6.8
13	Swaziland[b]	16.7		Brazil	6.8
14	Sudan[a]	16.0	45	Botswana	6.6
15	Haiti	14.2	46	Venezuela	6.5
	Sri Lanka	14.2	47	Iceland	6.4
17	Chad	12.4	48	Mexico	6.3
18	Madagascar[b]	12.0	49	Philippines	6.1
	Ukraine	12.0	50	Tanzania[b]	5.9
20	Indonesia	11.5	51	Estonia	5.8
21	Costa Rica	11.3	52	Poland	5.5
	Iran	11.3		Togo	5.5
23	Moldova	9.8		Trinidad & Tobago	5.5
24	Honduras	9.7	55	Mauritania	5.4
25	Slovenia	9.4		Mauritius	5.4
26	Burundi	9.3	57	Macedonia	5.2
	Papua New Guinea	9.3		Mali	5.2
28	Namibia[b]	9.2	59	Burkina Faso	4.9
29	Hungary	9.1	60	Croatia	4.7
30	Dominican Republic	8.9		Czech Republic	4.7
31	Colombia	8.7			

Highest inflation, 1996–2001
% average annual consumer price inflation

1	Angola	235.8	16	Ghana	22.3
2	Belarus	117.1	17	Moldova	19.3
3	Bulgaria	75.7	18	Indonesia	18.6
4	Turkey	68.4		Kirgizstan	18.6
5	Romania	63.2	20	Myanmar	18.4
6	Laos	49.6	21	Ukraine	17.7
7	Ecuador	48.8	22	Mongolia[c]	17.2
8	Zimbabwe	46.5	23	Iran	16.6
9	Suriname[c]	36.4	24	Burundi	15.7
10	Russia	31.9		Sierra Leone	15.7
11	Malawi	27.6	25	Mexico	13.7
12	Sudan[c]	25.8	27	Colombia	13.6
13	Zambia	24.7	28	Haiti	13.5
14	Uzbekistan	24.7	29	Honduras	13.2
15	Venezuela	23.2	30	Albania[d]	12.7

Lowest inflation, 2000–01

% consumer price inflation

1	Lesotho	-9.7	27	Cameroon[b]	1.2
2	Hong Kong	-1.6		Lithuania	1.2
3	Central African Rep[a]	-1.5	29	Malaysia	1.4
4	Argentina	-1.1	30	Bolivia	1.5
5	Armenia[b]	-0.8	31	Azerbaijan	1.6
	Sierra Leone[b]	-0.8		France	1.6
7	Bahrain[b]	-0.7		Kuwait	1.6
	Japan	-0.7	34	Qatar[b]	1.7
9	Syria[b]	-0.5		Thailand	1.7
10	Saudi Arabia	-0.4	36	Jordan	1.8
	Vietnam	-0.4		United Kingdom	1.8
12	Myanmar[b]	-0.1	38	Bahamas	2.0
13	Ethiopia[b]	0.0		Cyprus	2.0
	Taiwan	0.0		Mozambique[a]	2.0
15	Albania[b]	0.1		Peru	2.0
	Congo-Brazzaville	0.1	42	Denmark	2.3
17	Panama	0.4		Egypt	2.3
18	Cambodia	0.6	44	Germany	2.4
	Morocco	0.6		Latvia	2.4
20	China	0.7		Uganda	2.4
21	Gambia, The[b]	0.8	47	Belgium	2.5
	Kenya	0.8		Finland	2.5
23	Singapore	1.0	49	Austria	2.6
	Switzerland	1.0		Barbados	2.6
25	Fiji[b]	1.1		Canada	2.6
	Israel	1.1			

Lowest inflation, 1990–2000

% average annual consumer price inflation

1	Lesotho	-0.9	17	France	1.1
2	Azerbaijan	-0.6	18	Bahamas	1.3
	Central African Rep[c]	-0.6		Mali	1.3
	Saudi Arabia	-0.6	20	Morocco	1.4
5	Argentina	-0.4	21	Cameroon	1.5
6	Syria[d]	-0.3		Kuwait	1.5
7	Hong Kong	-0.2		New Zealand	1.5
8	Bahrain[d]	0.0		Senegal	1.5
9	Japan	0.1	25	Austria	1.6
10	China	0.3		Germany	1.6
11	Switzerland	0.8	27	Belgium	1.7
	Taiwan	0.8	28	Luxembourg	1.8
13	Congo-Brazzaville	0.9		Qatar	1.8
	Singapore	0.9	30	Canada	1.9
15	Panama	1.0		Finland	1.9
	Sweden	1.0			

a 1998–99 b 1999–2000 c 1996–99 d 1996–2000

Notes: Inflation is measured as the % increase in the consumer price index between two dates. The figures shown are based on the average level of the index during the relevant years.

Debt

Highest foreign debt[a]

$m

1	Brazil	237,953	25	Czech Republic	21,299
2	Russia	160,300	26	Morocco	17,944
3	Mexico	150,288	27	Sudan	15,741
4	China	149,800	28	Bangladesh	15,609
5	Argentina	146,172	29	Ecuador	13,281
6	Indonesia	141,803	30	Vietnam	12,787
7	South Korea	134,417	31	Ukraine	12,166
8	Turkey	116,209	32	Côte d'Ivoire	12,138
9	India	100,367	33	Croatia	12,120
10	Thailand	79,675	34	Serbia & Montenegro	11,960
11	Poland	63,561	35	Congo	11,645
12	Philippines	50,063	36	Tunisia	10,610
13	Malaysia	41,797	37	Lebanon	10,311
14	Venezuela	38,196	38	Romania	10,224
15	Chile	36,978	39	Angola	10,146
16	Nigeria	34,134	40	Bulgaria	10,026
17	Colombia	34,081	41	Slovakia	9,462
18	Pakistan	32,091	42	Sri Lanka	9,066
19	Hungary	29,415	43	Jordan	8,226
20	Egypt	28,957	44	Uruguay	8,196
21	Peru	28,560	45	Iran	7,953
22	Algeria	25,002	46	Cameroon	7,343
23	South Africa	24,861	47	Panama	7,056
24	Syria	21,657	48	Kazakhstan	6,664

Highest debt service[b]

$m

1	Brazil	62,788	21	South Africa	3,860
2	Mexico	58,259	22	Ukraine	3,661
3	Argentina	27,345	23	Iran	3,438
4	South Korea	23,205	24	Morocco	3,333
5	China	21,728	25	Pakistan	2,857
6	Turkey	21,136	26	Slovakia	2,590
7	Indonesia	18,772	27	Croatia	2,437
8	Thailand	14,017	28	Romania	2,341
9	Russia	11,671	29	Tunisia	1,900
10	Poland	10,290	30	Kazakhstan	1,840
11	India	9,921	31	Lebanon	1,821
12	Hungary	7,946	32	Egypt	1,813
13	Philippines	6,737	33	Uruguay	1,313
14	Chile	6,163	34	Vietnam	1,303
15	Malaysia	5,967	35	Ecuador	1,276
16	Venezuela	5,846	36	Angola	1,205
17	Colombia	5,171	37	Bulgaria	1,189
18	Czech Republic	4,774	38	Côte d'Ivoire	1,020
19	Algeria	4,467	39	Nigeria	1,009
20	Peru	4,305	40	Panama	928

a Foreign debt is debt owed to non-residents and repayable in foreign currency; the figures shown include liabilities of government, public and private sectors. Developed countries have been excluded.

Highest foreign debt burden
Foreign debt as % of GDP

1	Guinea-Bissau	321	23	Bulgaria	80
2	Nicaragua	283		Panama	80
3	Angola	270	25	Madagascar	79
4	Congo-Brazzaville	254		Moldova	79
5	Sudan	161	27	Togo	77
6	Zambia	153	28	Cameroon	70
7	Syria	136	29	Belarus	69
8	Congo	128		Guinea	69
9	Mauritania	126		Myanmar	69
10	Sierra Leone	121	32	Philippines	67
11	Côte d'Ivoire	117	33	Cambodia	66
12	Serbia & Montenegro	113		Thailand	66
13	Indonesia	111	35	Russia	64
14	Kirgizstan	106		Yemen	64
15	Gabon	96	37	Jamaica	63
16	Jordan	95	38	Estonia	62
17	Tajikistan	88		Gambia, The	62
18	Burundi	86		Hungary	62
19	Malawi	84	41	Croatia	61
	Nigeria	84		Lebanon	61
21	Laos	83		Papua New Guinea	61
22	Ecuador	82	44	Mongolia	60

Highest debt service ratios[b]
%

1	Brazil	97		Morocco	26
2	Argentina	75	24	Uganda	24
3	Bolivia	48	25	Cameroon	23
4	Peru	46		Honduras	23
5	Sierra Leone	43		Poland	23
6	Turkey	37	28	Kazakhstan	22
7	Mexico	36		Romania	22
8	Nicaragua	35	30	Angola	21
9	Burundi	33		Bosnia	21
	Lebanon	33		Mauritius	21
11	Colombia	32		Venezuela	21
12	Indonesia	30	34	Benin	20
	Kirgizstan	30		Côte d'Ivoire	20
	Rwanda	30		Ecuador	20
15	Chile	29		Tunisia	20
	Uruguay	29		Ukraine	20
17	Algeria	27		Zambia	20
	Hungary	27		Zimbabwe	20
	Pakistan	27	41	Ghana	19
	Uzbekistan	27		Slovakia	19
21	Croatia	26		Tanzania	19
	Mauritania	26			

b Debt service is the sum of interest and principal repayments (amortization) due on outstanding foreign debt. The debt service ratio is debt service expressed as a percentage of the country's exports of goods and services.

Aid

Largest bilateral and multilateral donors[a]

$m

1	Japan	13,508		13	Australia	987
2	United States	9,955		14	Switzerland	890
3	Germany	5,030		15	Belgium	820
4	United Kingdom	4,501		16	Austria	423
5	France	4,105		17	Finland	371
6	Netherlands	3,135		18	Saudi Arabia	295
7	Sweden	1,799		19	Portugal	271
8	Canada	1,744		20	Ireland	235
9	Denmark	1,664		21	Greece	226
10	Italy	1,376		22	South Korea	212
11	Norway	1,264		23	Kuwait	165
12	Spain	1,195		24	United Arab Emirates	150

Largest recipients of bilateral and multilateral aid

$m

1	China	1,735		34	French Polynesia	403
2	Indonesia	1,731		35	Peru	401
3	Vietnam	1,700		36	Cambodia	398
4	Russia	1,565		37	Nepal	390
5	India	1,487		38	Cameroon	380
6	Poland	1,396		39	Mali	360
7	Egypt	1,328		40	Côte d'Ivoire	352
8	Bangladesh	1,171		41	New Caledonia	350
9	Serbia & Montenegro	1,135		42	Burkina Faso	336
10	Tanzania	1,045		43	Turkey	325
11	Mozambique	876		44	Brazil	322
12	Uganda	819			Madagascar	322
13	Israel	800			Rwanda	322
14	Zambia	795		47	Albania	319
15	Bosnia	737		48	Bulgaria	311
16	Pakistan	703		49	Angola	307
17	Ethiopia	693		50	Laos	281
18	Thailand	641		51	Sri Lanka	276
19	West Bank and Gaza	636		52	Papua New Guinea	275
20	Ghana	609		53	Yemen	265
21	Philippines	578		54	Guatemala	264
22	Nicaragua	562		55	Hungary	252
23	Jordan	552			Macedonia	252
24	Ukraine	541		57	Benin	239
25	Kenya	512		58	Sudan	225
26	South Africa	488		59	Tunisia	223
27	Bolivia	477		60	Mongolia	217
28	Honduras	449		61	Armenia	216
29	Malawi	445		62	Kirgizstan	215
30	Czech Republic	438		63	Mauritania	212
31	Romania	432		64	Niger	211
32	Senegal	423		65	Haiti	208
33	Morocco	419		66	Lebanon	197

a China also provides aid, but does not disclose amounts.

Largest bilateral and multilateral donors[a]
% of GDP

1	Denmark	1.04	13	Germany	0.27
2	Netherlands	0.86	14	Portugal	0.26
3	Norway	0.85	15	Australia	0.25
4	Sweden	0.79		Canada	0.25
5	Luxembourg	0.68		Ireland	0.25
6	Kuwait	0.44	18	New Zealand	0.23
7	Switzerland	0.37		United Arab Emirates	0.23
8	Belgium	0.35	20	Austria	0.22
9	France	0.32		Spain	0.22
	United Kingdom	0.32	22	Saudi Arabia	0.21
11	Finland	0.31	23	Greece	0.20
12	Japan	0.29	24	Italy	0.13

Largest recipients of bilateral and multilateral aid
$ per head

1	French Polynesia	2,015	33	Czech Republic	43
2	New Caledonia	1,750	34	Rwanda	42
3	Netherlands Antilles	885	35	Sierra Leone	41
4	West Bank and Gaza	199	36	Bulgaria	39
5	Bosnia	184		Malawi	39
6	Israel	133	38	Benin	38
7	Namibia	127		Gambia, The	38
8	Macedonia	126		Latvia	38
9	Aruba	120	41	Fiji	36
10	Jordan	113		Poland	36
11	Nicaragua	110	43	Uganda	35
12	Serbia & Montenegro	107	44	Georgia	32
13	Albania	103		Ghana	32
14	Mongolia	87		Mali	32
15	Suriname	85	47	Slovenia	31
16	Bahrain	82	48	Cambodia	30
17	Mauritania	79		Tanzania	30
18	Zambia	76	50	Burkina Faso	29
19	Honduras	70		El Salvador	29
20	Cyprus	68		Moldova	29
21	Guinea-Bissau	67	53	Lithuania	27
22	Armenia	57	54	Cameroon	26
	Bolivia	57		Haiti	26
	Papua New Guinea	57	56	Bhutan	25
25	Lebanon	56		Hungary	25
26	Laos	53	58	Angola	23
	Malta	53		Guatemala	23
28	Eritrea	48		Liberia	23
	Mozambique	48		Tajikistan	23
30	Estonia	46		Tunisia	23
31	Senegal	45	63	Côte d'Ivoire	22
32	Kirgizstan	44		Vietnam	22

a China also provides aid, but does not disclose amounts.

Industry and services

Largest industrial output
$bn

1	United States	2,684	25	Poland		50
2	Japan	1,420	26	Thailand		49
3	China	549	27	Turkey		43
4	Germany	525	28	Malaysia		41
5	United Kingdom	359		Venezuela		41
6	France	302	30	Denmark		37
7	Italy	282	31	Finland		36
8	South Korea	195		Ireland		36
9	Canada	190	33	South Africa		35
10	Spain	154	34	Israel		34
11	Mexico	147	35	Egypt		32
12	Brazil	132		Singapore		32
13	Australia	127	37	Algeria		30
14	India	112	38	Portugal		28
15	Taiwan	100	39	Iran		24
16	Netherlands	98	40	Chile		23
17	Russia	96		Colombia		23
18	Switzerland	77		Philippines		23
19	Argentina	74	43	Hong Kong		22
20	Indonesia	72	44	Greece		20
21	Norway	61	45	Czech Republic		19
22	Austria	60	46	Nigeria		18
	Sweden	60	47	Peru		15
24	Belgium	54	48	Pakistan		13

Highest growth in industrial output
Average annual real % growth, 1990–2000[a]

1	Bosnia	23.3	12	Bangladesh	9.7
2	Vietnam	20.7	13	Lesotho	9.6
3	Laos	13.6	14	Malaysia	9.2
4	Cambodia	13.3	15	Bhutan	8.8
5	China	12.7	16	Congo-Brazzaville	8.7
6	El Salvador	11.9		West Bank and Gaza	8.7
7	Costa Rica	11.1	18	Mexico	8.5
8	Dominican Republic	11.0	19	Nicaragua	8.3
9	Ireland	10.7	20	Sri Lanka	8.1
10	Egypt	10.5	21	Peru	8.0
	Singapore	10.5	22	Argentina	7.8

Lowest growth in industrial output
Average annual real % growth, 1990–2000[a]

1	Moldova	-22.5	11	Cameroon	-5.4
2	Uzbekistan	-17.5	12	Romania	-5.2
3	Tajikistan	-16.2	13	Slovakia	-5.0
4	Bulgaria	-12.6	14	Burundi	-4.9
5	Latvia	-11.7	15	Belarus	-4.5
6	Ukraine	-10.9		Kazakhstan	-4.5
7	Kirgizstan	-10.8	17	Ethiopia	-4.3
8	Estonia	-9.5	18	Zimbabwe	-4.2
9	Zambia	-9.4	19	Burkina Faso	-3.4
10	Russia	-9.3	20	Hungary	-3.3

Largest manufacturing output

$bn

1	United States	1,570	21	Australia	44
2	Japan	1,123	22	Austria	42
3	Germany	431	23	Indonesia	40
4	China	373	24	Thailand	39
5	France	243	25	Poland	33
6	United Kingdom	224	26	Malaysia	29
7	Italy	214	27	Ireland	27
8	South Korea	144		Portugal	27
9	Russia[b]	132	29	Turkey	26
10	Canada	114	30	Denmark	24
11	Brazil	111		Singapore	24
12	Mexico	108	32	South Africa	21
13	Spain	93	33	Egypt	18
14	Taiwan	82	34	Iran	17
15	India	66		Norway	17
	Switzerland	66		Philippines	17
17	Netherlands	64	37	Venezuela	16
18	Sweden	57	38	Czech Republic	15
19	Argentina	47	39	Chile	11
20	Belgium	46	40	Colombia	10

Largest services output

$bn

1	United States	6,374	26	Norway	79
2	Japan	3,452	27	South Africa	75
3	Germany	1,138	28	Israel	74
4	United Kingdom	874	29	Finland	66
5	France	819		Venezuela	66
6	Italy	645	31	Greece	63
7	Canada	420	32	Iran	62
8	China	359	33	Singapore	61
9	Mexico	350	34	Thailand	60
10	Spain	332	35	Portugal	59
11	Brazil	296	36	Ireland	58
12	Netherlands	262	37	Indonesia	55
13	South Korea	241	38	Egypt	46
14	Australia	202	39	Colombia	42
15	India	200	40	Philippines	40
16	Argentina	182	41	Malaysia	39
17	Switzerland	156	42	Chile	38
18	Belgium	144	43	Peru	35
19	Sweden	143	44	New Zealand	31
20	Hong Kong	130	45	Pakistan	29
21	Austria	123	46	Czech Republic	25
	Russia	123	47	Bangladesh	24
23	Turkey	100	48	Morocco	18
24	Denmark	99	49	Romania	17
25	Poland	83	50	Algeria	16

a Or nearest available years.
b 1997

Agriculture

Most economically dependent on agriculture
% of GDP from agriculture

1	Myanmar[a]	60	25	Burkina Faso	35
2	Guinea-Bissau	59		Ghana	35
3	Congo[b]	58		Madagascar	35
4	Central African Rep	55		Uzbekistan	35
5	Laos	53	29	Bhutan	33
6	Ethiopia	52		Mongolia	33
7	Albania	51	31	Georgia	32
	Burundi	51		Nicaragua	32
9	Sierra Leone	47	33	Nigeria	30
10	Mali	46	34	Côte d'Ivoire	29
11	Tanzania	45	35	Haiti	28
12	Cameroon	44		Moldova	28
	Rwanda	44	37	Turkmenistan	27
14	Malawi	42		Zambia	27
	Uganda	42	39	Pakistan	26
16	Nepal	40		Papua New Guinea	26
17	Chad	39	41	Armenia	25
	Kirgizstan	39		Bangladesh	25
	Niger	39		India	25
20	Benin	38	44	Guinea	24
	Gambia, The	38		Mozambique	24
	Togo	38		Syria	24
23	Cambodia	37		Vietnam	24
	Sudan	37	48	Guatemala	23

Least economically dependent on agriculture
% of GDP from agriculture

1	Hong Kong	0.1	23	Australia	3.2
	Singapore	0.1		South Africa	3.2
3	Bahrain[a]	0.6	25	Slovenia	3.3
4	Luxembourg	0.7	26	Botswana	3.6
5	United Kingdom	1.0		Finland	3.6
6	Germany	1.2		Spain	3.6
7	United States	1.4	29	Poland	3.8
8	Belgium	1.5		Portugal	3.8
9	Japan	1.6	31	Ireland	4.0
	Switzerland	1.6	32	Czech Republic	4.1
	Trinidad & Tobago	1.6		Slovakia	4.1
12	Austria	1.8	34	Mexico	4.4
	Iceland	1.8	35	Latvia	4.5
14	Norway	1.9	36	South Korea	4.6
15	Sweden	2.0	37	Argentina	4.8
16	Taiwan	2.1	38	Venezuela	5.0
17	Jordan	2.3	39	Congo-Brazzaville	5.3
18	Canada	2.5	40	Angola	5.7
19	Denmark	2.7	41	Estonia	6.0
20	Netherlands[a]	2.8		Mauritius	6.0
21	France	2.9		Uruguay	6.0
	Italy	2.9	44	Barbados	6.3

a 1999 b 1997

Highest growth
Average annual real % growth, 1990–2000ᵃ

1	Sudan	8.8		10	Myanmar	4.9
2	Syria	6.3		11	Czech Republic	4.6
3	Cuba	6.1			Nicaragua	4.6
4	Malawi	6.0		13	Albania	4.5
5	Benin	5.3			Algeria	4.5
	Namibia	5.3			Angola	4.5
	Tunisia	5.3			Argentina	4.5
8	Bosnia	5.0			Armenia	4.5
	Laos	5.0			Yemen	4.5

Lowest growth
Average annual real % growth, 1990–2000ᵃ

1	Moldova	-10.4		9	Belarus	-4.6
2	Kazakhstan	-6.7		10	Hungary	-3.4
	West Bank and Gaza	-6.7			Japan	-3.4
4	Latvia	-6.4		12	Morocco	-2.8
5	Ukraine	-5.9		13	Croatia	-2.4
6	Estonia	-5.2		14	Turkmenistan	-2.1
	Tajikistan	-5.2		15	Lithuania	-1.9
8	Russia	-4.9		16	Haiti	-1.8

Biggest producers
'000 tonnes

Cereals

1	China	407,336		6	Indonesia	60,524
2	United States	344,118		7	Canada	51,315
3	India	235,494		8	Brazil	45,897
4	France	66,575		9	Germany	45,271
5	Russia	64,342		10	Argentina	38,785

Meat

1	China	62,817		6	Spain	4,853
2	United States	37,636		7	India	4,849
3	Brazil	14,680		8	Mexico	4,455
4	France	6,465		9	Russia	4,428
5	Germany	6,189		10	Italy	4,149

Fruit

1	China	65,178		6	Spain	16,125
2	India	44,298		7	Mexico	13,270
3	Brazil	32,718		8	France	11,155
4	United States	32,662		9	Iran	10,868
5	Italy	18,039		10	Turkey	10,610

Vegetables

1	China	278,340		6	Egypt	14,615
2	India	61,022		7	Russia	13,375
3	United States	37,698		8	Japan	12,714
4	Turkey	22,099		9	South Korea	12,113
5	Italy	16,048		10	Spain	11,795

a Or nearest available years.

Commodities

Wheat

Top 10 producers '000 tonnes		Top 10 consumers '000 tonnes	
1 EU15	104,400	1 China	115,400
2 China	99,700	2 EU15	91,200
3 India	75,800	3 India	63,100
4 United States	60,800	4 United States	36,300
5 Russia	34,500	5 Russia	35,100
6 Canada	26,800	6 Pakistan	20,600
7 Australia	22,200	7 Turkey	16,600
8 Pakistan	21,100	8 Iran	13,800
9 Turkey	17,500	9 Egypt	13,400
10 Argentina	16,500	10 Ukraine	11,000

Rice

Top 10 producers[a] '000 tonnes		Top 10 consumers[b] '000 tonnes	
1 China	187,909	1 China	134,319
2 India	127,319	2 India	83,500
3 Indonesia	51,899	3 Indonesia	35,877
4 Bangladesh	37,633	4 Bangladesh	25,790
5 Vietnam	31,020	5 Vietnam	16,958
6 Thailand	25,606	6 Thailand	9,400
7 Myanmar	18,571	7 Myanmar	9,350
8 Philippines	12,515	8 Japan	9,300
9 Japan	11,863	9 Philippines	8,750
10 Brazil	10,385	10 Brazil	7,995

Sugar[c]

Top 10 producers '000 tonnes		Top 10 consumers '000 tonnes	
1 India	22,000	1 India	16,500
2 EU15	17,900	2 EU15	14,100
3 Brazil	16,500	3 Brazil	9,700
4 United States	8,100	4 United States	9,000
5 China	7,600	5 China	8,600
6 Thailand	6,200	6 Russia	5,700
7 Mexico	4,800	7 Mexico	4,600
8 Australia	4,400	8 Indonesia	3,400
9 Cuba	4,100	9 Pakistan	3,300
10 South Africa	2,700	10 Japan	2,400

Coarse grains[d]

Top 5 producers '000 tonnes		Top 5 consumers '000 tonnes	
1 United States	273,200	1 United States	215,100
2 China	115,000	2 China	132,000
3 EU15	108,000	3 EU15	97,100
4 Brazil	42,600	4 Brazil	37,400
5 India	29,200	5 Mexico	36,000

Tea

| *Top 10 producers* | | *Top 10 consumers* | |
'000 tonnes		*'000 tonnes*	
1 India	846	1 India	653
2 China	683	2 China	456
3 Sri Lanka	307	3 Turkey	157
4 Kenya	236	4 Russia	151
5 Turkey	170	5 Japan	146
6 Indonesia	159	6 United Kingdom	134
7 Japan	89	7 Pakistan	111
8 Argentina	60	8 United States	88
9 Vietnam	59	9 Iran	85
10 Bangladesh	54	10 Egypt	63

Coffee

| *Top 10 producers* | | *Top 10 consumers* | |
'000 tonnes		*'000 tonnes*	
1 Brazil	1,920	1 United States	1,129
2 Vietnam	887	2 Brazil	780
3 Colombia	632	3 Germany	595
4 Indonesia	403	4 Japan	412
5 Mexico	308	5 France	324
6 India	291	6 Italy	314
7 Guatemala	282	7 Spain	178
8 Côte d'Ivoire	238	8 United Kingdom	149
9 Uganda	192	9 Netherlands	109
10 Ethiopia	166	10 Ethiopia	100

Cocoa

| *Top 10 producers* | | *Top 10 consumers* | |
'000 tonnes		*'000 tonnes*	
1 Côte d'Ivoire	1,409	1 United States	728
2 Ghana	437	2 Germany	274
3 Indonesia	410	3 France	214
4 Nigeria	165	4 United Kingdom	212
5 Brazil	124	5 Japan	144
6 Cameroon	115	6 Russia	141
7 Ecuador	95	7 Brazil	124
8 Papua New Guinea	47	8 Italy	90
9 Malaysia	45	9 Spain	82
10 Colombia	38	10 Canada	73

a Paddy (unmilled rice, in the husk).
b Milled rice.
c Raw.
d Includes: maize (corn), barley, sorghum, rye, oats and millet.

Copper

Top 10 producers[a]		*Top 10 consumers[b]*	
'000 tonnes		'000 tonnes	
1 Chile	4,602	1 United States	2,943
2 United States	1,473	2 China	1,928
3 Indonesia	1,006	3 Japan	1,349
4 Australia	832	4 Germany	1,310
5 Canada	634	5 South Korea	862
6 China	589	6 Italy	674
7 Russia	580	7 Taiwan	628
8 Peru	554	8 France	574
9 Poland	454	9 Mexico	464
10 Kazakhstan	430	10 Belgium	347

Lead

Top 10 producers[a]		*Top 10 consumers[b]*	
'000 tonnes		'000 tonnes	
1 Australia	678	1 United States	1,660
2 China	660	2 China	660
3 United States	447	3 Germany	390
4 Peru	271	4 Japan	343
5 Canada	149	5 South Korea	309
6 Mexico	138	6 United Kingdom	294
7 Sweden	107	7 Italy	279
8 South Africa	75	8 France	262
9 Morocco	72	9 Mexico	259
10 Ireland	58	10 Spain	226

Zinc

Top 10 producers[a]		*Top 10 consumers[c]*	
'000 tonnes		'000 tonnes	
1 China	1,780	1 China	1,402
2 Australia	1,420	2 United States	1,315
3 Canada	1,002	3 Japan	674
4 Peru	910	4 Germany	532
5 United States	829	5 South Korea	419
6 Mexico	401	6 Italy	385
7 Kazakhstan	322	7 France	365
8 Ireland	263	8 Taiwan	294
9 Spain	201	9 Belgium	275
10 India	190	10 India	224

Tin

Top 5 producers[a]		*Top 5 consumers[b]*	
'000 tonnes		'000 tonnes	
1 China	97.1	1 China	51.6
2 Indonesia	51.6	2 United States	50.7
3 Peru	37.4	3 Japan	25.2
4 Brazil	14.2	4 Germany	20.9
5 Bolivia	12.5	5 South Korea	15.2

Nickel

Top 10 producers[a] '000 tonnes		*Top 10 consumers*[b] '000 tonnes	
1 Russia	260.0	1 Japan	191.7
2 Canada	190.7	2 United States	146.9
3 Australia	167.0	3 Taiwan	105.9
4 New Caledonia	128.8	4 Germany	101.6
5 Cuba	71.4	5 South Korea	90.1
6 Indonesia	71.3	6 China	57.6
7 China	50.3	7 Italy	53.0
8 South Africa	36.6	8 France	52.8
9 Brazil	32.0	9 Finland	48.5
10 Dominican Republic	27.8	10 Russia	39.2

Aluminium

Top 10 producers[d] '000 tonnes		*Top 10 consumers*[e] '000 tonnes	
1 United States	3,668	1 United States	6,080
2 Russia	3,247	2 China	3,499
3 China	2,794	3 Japan	2,225
4 Canada	2,374	4 Germany	1,490
5 Australia	1,762	5 South Korea	823
6 Brazil	1,271	6 Canada	799
7 Norway	1,026	7 France	780
8 South Africa	683	Italy	780
9 India	649	9 Russia	748
10 Germany	644	10 India	602

Precious metals

Gold[a] Top 10 producers tonnes		*Silver*[a] Top 10 producers tonnes	
1 South Africa	428.5	1 Mexico	2,483
2 United States	337.7	2 Peru	2,438
3 Australia	296.4	3 Australia	2,060
4 China	175.0	4 United States	2,017
5 Canada	156.1	5 China	1,330
6 Russia	143.9	6 Chile	1,245
7 Peru	132.6	7 Canada	1,204
8 Indonesia	117.6	8 Poland	1,088
9 Uzbekistan	82.0	9 Kazakhstan	816
10 Papua New Guinea	73.3	10 Bolivia	434

a Mine production.
b Refined consumption.
c Slab consumption.
d Primary refined production.
e Primary refined consumption.

Rubber (natural and synthetic)

Top 10 producers		*Top 10 consumers*	
'000 tonnes		*'000 tonnes*	
1 Thailand	2,446	1 United States	3,382
2 United States	2,394	2 China	2,535
3 Japan	1,592	3 Japan	1,890
4 Indonesia	1,536	4 Germany	892
5 China	1,281	5 India	809
6 Germany	850	6 France	791
7 Russia	836	7 South Korea	713
8 India	689	8 Russia	575
9 South Korea	680	9 Brazil	530
10 Malaysia	615	10 Spain	450

Raw wool

Top 10 producers[a]		*Top 10 consumers[b]*	
'000 tonnes		*'000 tonnes*	
1 Australia	652	1 China	431
2 China	291	2 Italy	153
3 New Zealand	258	3 Russia	70
4 Russia	128	4 India	62
5 Iran	74	5 Turkey	61
6 Turkey	70	6 United Kingdom	42
7 Argentina	62	7 Iran	41
United Kingdom	62	South Korea	41
9 Uruguay	57	9 Japan	38
10 South Africa	50	10 United States	32

Cotton

Top 10 producers		*Top 10 consumers*	
'000 tonnes		*'000 tonnes*	
1 China	4,420	1 China	5,050
2 United States	3,742	2 India	2,924
3 India	2,380	3 United States	1,934
4 Pakistan	1,802	4 Pakistan	1,760
5 Uzbekistan	975	5 Turkey	1,150
6 Brazil	939	6 Brazil	900
7 Turkey	880	7 Indonesia	521
8 Australia	804	8 Mexico	435
9 Greece	421	9 Thailand	371
10 Syria	362	10 Russia	325

Major oil seeds[c]

Top 5 producers		*Top 5 consumers*	
'000 tonnes		*'000 tonnes*	
1 United States	84,530	1 United States	58,526
2 China	46,710	2 China	58,146
3 Brazil	40,754	3 EU 15	31,909
4 Argentina	30,951	4 Brazil	25,398
5 India	18,370	5 Argentina	22,090

Oil[d]

Top 15 producers
'000 barrels per day

1	Saudi Arabia[e]	9,145
2	United States	7,745
3	Russia	6,535
4	Iran[e]	3,770
5	Mexico	3,450
6	Norway	3,365
7	China	3,245
8	Venezuela[e]	3,235
9	Canada	2,710
10	United Kingdom	2,660
11	Iraq[e]	2,625
12	United Arab Emirates[e]	2,515
13	Kuwait[e]	2,150
14	Nigeria[e]	2,105
15	Algeria[e]	1,580

Top 15 consumers
'000 barrels per day

1	United States	18,745
2	Japan	5,525
3	China	4,840
4	Germany	2,760
5	Russia	2,475
6	South Korea	2,200
7	India	2,070
8	France	2,010
9	Italy	1,945
10	Mexico	1,840
11	Brazil	1,825
12	Canada	1,775
13	United Kingdom	1,675
14	Spain	1,455
15	Saudi Arabia[e]	1,335

Natural gas

Top 10 producers
Billion cubic metres

1	United States	555.6
2	Russia	545.0
3	Canada	167.8
4	United Kingdom	108.1
5	Algeria	89.3
6	Indonesia	63.9
7	Iran	60.2
8	Netherlands	57.3
9	Norway	52.4
10	Uzbekistan	52.2

Top 10 consumers
Billion cubic metres

1	United States	654.4
2	Russia	377.2
3	United Kingdom	95.7
4	Germany	79.2
5	Canada	77.8
6	Japan	76.2
7	Ukraine	68.5
8	Italy	63.8
9	Iran	62.9
10	Uzbekistan	49.8

Coal

Top 10 producers
Million tonnes oil equivalent

1	United States	570.7
2	China	498.0
3	Australia	155.6
4	India	154.3
5	South Africa	118.8
6	Russia	115.8
7	Poland	68.1
8	Germany	56.4
9	Indonesia	47.3
10	Ukraine	42.1

Top 10 consumers
Million tonnes oil equivalent

1	United States	564.1
2	China	480.1
3	India	163.4
4	Russia	110.4
5	Japan	98.9
6	Germany	82.7
7	South Africa	81.9
8	Poland	57.1
9	Australia	46.7
10	South Korea	42.9

a Greasy basis.
b Clean basis.
c Soybeans, sunflower seed, cottonseed, groundnuts and rapeseed.
d Includes crude oil, shale oil, oil sands and natural gas liquids.
e Opec members.

Energy

Largest producers

Million tonnnes coal equivalent, 1998

1	United States	2,377.5	16	South Africa	188.8
2	Russia	1,377.6	17	Germany	182.3
3	China	1,187.3	18	Kuwait	168.5
4	Saudi Arabia	714.8	19	France	165.0
5	Canada	515.6	20	Iraq	155.2
6	United Kingdom	400.4	21	Japan	147.8
7	India	356.6	22	Nigeria	147.1
8	Iran	334.7	23	Brazil	121.3
9	Venezuela	324.8	24	Poland	118.4
10	Mexico	314.8	25	Ukraine	116.2
11	Australia	306.2	26	Argentina	111.4
12	Indonesia	301.0	27	Libya	107.2
13	Norway	293.1	28	Malaysia	103.0
14	United Arab Emirates	220.0	29	Netherlands	96.7
15	Algeria	206.1	30	Colombia	96.2

Largest consumers

Million tonnes coal equivalent, 1998

1	United States	2,987.0	16	Iran	143.0
2	China	1,139.2	17	Saudi Arabia	140.8
3	Russia	829.8	18	Spain	140.4
4	Japan	659.7	19	South Africa	136.1
5	Germany	460.8	20	Poland	131.3
6	India	422.7	21	Netherlands	119.0
7	Canada	339.7	22	Indonesia	114.5
8	France	336.3	23	Venezuela	93.1
9	United Kingdom	332.2	24	Turkey	87.3
10	Italy	238.9	25	North Korea	85.7
11	Ukraine	209.7	26	Thailand	79.6
12	Mexico	187.6	27	Argentina	77.5
13	South Korea	187.5	28	Belgium	75.3
14	Brazil	170.4	29	Uzbekistan	70.5
15	Australia	150.8	30	Sweden	58.8

Energy efficiency

Most efficient		*Least efficient*	
GDP[a] per kg of energy, 1999, $		*GDP[a] per kg of energy, 1999, $*	
1 Costa Rica	10.84	1 Tanzania	1.09
2 Bangladesh	10.78	2 Uzbekistan	1.13
3 Albania	10.41	3 Ukraine	1.17
4 Morocco	9.99	4 Turkmenistan	1.20
5 Namibia	9.62	5 Zambia	1.21
6 Colombia	9.31	6 Nigeria	1.22
7 Uruguay	9.21	7 Trinidad & Tobago	1.32
8 Peru	8.93	8 Azerbaijan	1.56
9 Hong Kong	8.37	9 Bahrain	1.68
10 Sri Lanka	8.13	10 Kuwait	1.76
11 Italy	7.66	11 United Arab Emirates[b]	1.79
12 Tunisia	7.38	12 Russia	1.86

a At purchasing-power parity exchange rates.   b 1998

Largest exporters
Million tonnes coal equivalent, 1998

1	Russia	549.8		14	Netherlands	121.8
2	Saudi Arabia	543.9		15	Iraq	109.6
3	Canada	263.7		16	United States	108.4
4	Norway	262.8		17	Libya	87.0
5	Venezuela	228.9		18	China	68.9
6	Australia	182.6		19	South Africa	67.6
7	Iran	167.9		20	Turkey	65.4
8	United Arab Emirates	166.1		21	Colombia	62.1
9	Indonesia	157.8		22	Oman	61.0
10	United Kingdom	153.4		23	Singapore	60.1
11	Algeria	145.9		24	Malaysia	56.5
12	Mexico	136.9		25	Angola	50.0
13	Kuwait	127.6		26	South Korea	48.3

Largest importers
Million tonnes coal equivalent, 1998

1	United States	886.8		14	Canada	83.3
2	Japan	553.7		15	China	78.4
3	Germany	332.0		16	Brazil	72.9
4	South Korea	239.0		17	Thailand	52.0
5	Italy	233.9		18	Poland	43.6
6	France	226.9		19	Sweden	42.3
7	Netherlands	155.1		20	Belarus	38.4
8	Spain	134.0		21	Hong Kong	37.6
9	Singapore	119.7		22	Greece	34.6
10	United Kingdom	107.1		23	Philippines	32.7
11	Belgium	103.8		24	Australia	32.4
12	Ukraine	102.4		25	Russia	32.2
13	India	101.0		26	Austria	32.1

Largest consumption per head
Tonnes coal equivalent, 1998

1	Qatar	50.3		16	Netherlands	7.6
2	United Arab Emirates	21.5		17	Belgium	7.4
3	Bahrain	20.0		18	Finland	7.2
4	Kuwait	18.0		19	Saudi Arabia	7.0
5	Réunion	15.6		20	Sweden	6.6
6	Canada	11.1		21	New Zealand	5.8
7	United States	10.9		22	France	5.7
8	Brunei	10.8			United Kingdom	5.7
	Luxembourg	10.8		24	Germany	5.6
10	Singapore	10.4			Russia	5.6
11	Trinidad & Tobago	10.1		26	Czech Republic	5.4
12	Tunisia	9.2		27	Japan	5.2
13	Iceland	8.8		28	Estonia	5.0
14	Norway	8.6			Ireland	5.0
15	Australia	8.1		30	Switzerland	4.6

Note: Consumption data for small countries, especially oil producers, can be unreliable, often leading to unrealistically high consumption per head rates.

Workers of the world

Highest % of population in labour force

2000 or latest

1	Thailand	60.6	26	Norway	52.0
2	China	60.0	27	Lithuania	51.9
3	Iceland	56.4		Mozambique	51.9
4	Czech Republic	56.2	29	Macau	51.7
5	Estonia	55.7	30	Kenya	51.6
6	Denmark	55.1	31	Vietnam	51.5
7	Slovakia	54.8	32	Poland	51.4
8	Latvia	54.7		Tanzania	51.4
9	Bahamas	54.6		United States	51.4
10	Burundi	54.5	35	South Korea	51.1
11	Rwanda	54.2	36	Australia	51.0
12	Sweden	54.1	37	Bulgaria	50.9
13	Canada	53.8	38	Portugal	50.8
	Japan	53.8	39	Slovenia	50.7
	Switzerland	53.8		Ukraine	50.7
16	Qatar	53.6	41	Gambia, The	50.5
17	Russia	53.4	42	Finland	50.4
18	Barbados	53.2	43	Armenia	50.3
19	Myanmar	53.1		Moldova	50.3
20	Hong Kong	52.9	45	Eritrea	50.1
21	Bangladesh	52.8		Mongolia	50.1
22	Belarus	52.6		New Zealand	50.1
23	Jamaica	52.5		United Kingdom	50.1
24	Cambodia	52.4	49	Albania	49.9
	North Korea	52.4	50	Germany	49.8

Most male workforce

Highest % men in workforce

1	United Arab Emirates	85.2
2	Qatar	85.0
3	Saudi Arabia	83.9
4	Oman	82.9
5	Iraq	80.3
6	Bahrain	79.2
7	Libya	76.9
8	Jordan	75.4
9	Syria	73.0
10	Iran	72.9
11	Algeria	72.4
12	Malta	72.2
13	Ecuador	72.0
14	Yemen	71.9
15	Pakistan	71.4
16	Guatemala	71.1
17	Sudan	70.5
18	Lebanon	70.4
19	Paraguay	70.0
20	Egypt	69.6

Most female workforce

Highest % women in workforce

1	Cambodia	51.7
2	Ghana	50.5
	Latvia	50.5
4	Russia	49.2
5	Tanzania	49.1
6	Belarus	49.0
	Estonia	49.0
8	Ukraine	48.9
	Vietnam	48.9
10	Rwanda	48.8
11	Burundi	48.7
12	Armenia	48.6
	Malawi	48.6
	Moldova	48.6
15	Mozambique	48.4
16	Benin	48.3
17	Bulgaria	48.2
18	Finland	48.1
19	Lithuania	48.0
	Sweden	48.0

Lowest % of population in labour force
2000 or latest

1	Oman	26.5		Tunisia	39.6
2	Iraq	27.7	27	South Africa	39.7
3	Libya	28.6	28	Sudan	39.9
4	Jordan	29.8	29	Morocco	40.0
5	Iran	30.9	30	Costa Rica	40.0
6	Yemen	31.5		Côte d'Ivoire	40.0
7	Syria	31.9	32	Liberia	40.3
8	Saudi Arabia	32.9	33	Argentina	40.5
9	Algeria	33.7		Fiji	40.5
10	Belize	34.3		Kuwait	40.5
11	Lebanon	35.1		Nicaragua	40.5
12	Swaziland	36.7	37	Bolivia	40.7
13	Guatemala	36.9		Cameroon	40.7
14	Sierra Leone	37.2	39	Chile	40.8
15	Pakistan	37.5	40	Venezuela	40.9
16	Honduras	37.6	41	Congo	41.2
17	Paraguay	37.8		Lesotho	41.2
	Puerto Rico	37.8		Mexico	41.2
19	Peru	37.9		Namibia	41.2
	Suriname	37.9	45	Congo-Brazzaville	41.3
21	Malta	38.0		Malaysia	41.3
22	Egypt	38.1	47	Togo	41.4
23	Ecuador	39.1	48	Belgium	41.6
24	Tajikistan	39.3	49	Equatorial Guinea	41.7
25	Nigeria	39.6	50	Afghanistan	42.0

Highest rate of unemployment
% of labour force[a]

1	Lesotho	39.3	21	Georgia	13.8
2	Macedonia	34.5	22	Kazakhstan	13.7
3	Algeria	28.7	23	Nicaragua	13.3
4	South Africa	23.3	24	Jordan	13.2
5	Morocco	22.0	25	Trinidad & Tobago	13.1
6	Botswana	21.5	26	Argentina	12.8
7	Colombia	20.1	27	Ukraine	11.9
8	Slovakia	18.9	28	Panama	11.8
9	Albania	18.0	29	Ecuador	11.5
10	Netherlands Antilles	16.7	30	Russia	11.4
	Poland	16.7	31	Lithuania	11.1
12	Bulgaria	16.3		Moldova	11.1
13	Croatia	16.1	33	Greece	10.8
14	Dominican Republic	15.9		Italy	10.8
15	Jamaica	15.7		Romania	10.8
16	Zambia	15.0	36	Suriname	10.6
17	Venezuela	14.9	37	Philippines	10.1
18	Estonia	14.8		Puerto Rico	10.1
19	Spain	14.1	39	France	10.0
	West Bank and Gaza	14.1	40	Chile	9.9

a ILO definition.

The business world

Global competitiveness

Overall	Government	Trade blocks
1 United States	Singapore	Austria
2 Finland	Finland	Finland
3 Luxembourg	United States	Ireland
4 Netherlands	Hong Kong	Netherlands
5 Singapore	Ireland	Luxembourg
6 Denmark	Switzerland	Germany
7 Switzerland	Luxembourg	Denmark
8 Canada	Denmark	Belgium
9 Hong Kong	Australia	Mexico
10 Ireland	Canada	Spain
11 Sweden	Iceland	France
12 Iceland	Netherlands	Portugal
13 Austria	Chile	Sweden
14 Australia	Sweden	Hong Kong
15 Germany	Austria	Singapore
16 United Kingdom	New Zealand	Malaysia
17 Norway	Estonia	Canada
18 Belgium	Norway	Chile
19 New Zealand	Malaysia	United States
20 Chile	Spain	Greece
21 Estonia	Taiwan	Czech Republic
22 France	United Kingdom	Italy
23 Spain	Israel	United Kingdom
24 Taiwan	Hungary	China
25 Israel	South Korea	Hungary
26 Malaysia	Germany	Slovakia
27 South Korea	Thailand	Iceland
28 Hungary	Czech Republic	Estonia
29 Czech Republic	Belgium	Thailand
30 Japan	China	Switzerland
31 China	Japan	New Zealand
32 Italy	France	South Korea
33 Portugal	Mexico	Brazil
34 Thailand	Portugal	Turkey
35 Brazil	Slovakia	Taiwan
36 Greece	South Africa	Philippines
37 Slovakia	Philippines	Japan
38 Slovenia	Brazil	Slovenia
39 South Africa	Italy	Colombia
40 Philippines	Greece	Israel
41 Mexico	Colombia	Norway
42 India	Russia	Australia
43 Russia	Slovenia	Indonesia
44 Colombia	India	South Africa

Notes: Rankings reflect assessments for the ability of a country to achieve sustained high rates of GDP growth per head. Column 1 is based on 259 criteria covering: the openness of an economy, the role of the government, the development of financial markets, the quality of infrastructure, technology, business management and judicial and political institutions and labour-market flexibility. Column 2 looks at the extent to which government policies are conducive to competitiveness. Column 3 is based on the extent to which a country is integrated into regional trade blocks.

The business environment

		2002–06 score	1997–2001 score	1997–2001 ranking
1	Netherlands	8.84	8.67	2
2	United States	8.80	8.72	1
3	United Kingdom	8.75	8.62	4
4	Canada	8.74	8.59	5
5	Switzerland	8.65	8.40	7
6	Ireland	8.59	8.30	8
7	Finland	8.57	8.27	9
8	Singapore	8.56	8.47	6
9	Sweden	8.52	8.11	10
10	Germany	8.51	7.93	13
	Hong Kong	8.51	8.64	3
12	Denmark	8.50	8.00	12
13	Belgium	8.30	7.92	14
14	Australia	8.27	7.89	15
15	France	8.26	7.76	16
16	New Zealand	8.17	8.06	11
17	Norway	8.09	7.58	18
18	Taiwan	8.06	7.37	21
19	Austria	8.04	7.59	17
20	Spain	8.00	7.42	19
21	Chile	7.88	7.40	20
22	Italy	7.85	6.87	23
23	Portugal	7.60	7.00	22
24	Israel	7.54	6.75	25
25	South Korea	7.38	6.33	29
26	Japan	7.36	6.73	26
27	Hungary	7.26	6.42	28
28	Thailand	7.25	6.29	30
29	Greece	7.15	6.12	33
30	Poland	7.07	6.22	31
31	Mexico	7.02	6.09	34
32	Czech Republic	7.01	6.18	32
33	Argentina	6.99	6.54	27
34	Malaysia	6.88	6.80	24
35	Slovakia	6.57	5.46	37
36	South Africa	6.49	5.51	36
37	Brazil	6.44	5.44	38
	Philippines	6.44	5.52	35
39	India	6.42	5.19	45
40	Peru	6.17	5.40	41
41	China	6.15	5.33	44
42	Saudi Arabia	6.13	5.43	40
43	Colombia	6.12	5.35	43
44	Egypt	6.07	5.44	39
45	Sri Lanka	5.97	5.02	47
46	Turkey	5.94	5.35	42

Note: Scores reflect the opportunities for, and hindrances to, the conduct of business, measured by countries' rankings in ten categories including market potential, tax and labour-market policies, infrastructure, skills and the political environment. Scores reflect average and forecast average over given date range.

Business creativity and research

Innovation index[a]

1	Canada	6.51	23	Ireland	4.43
2	United States	6.50	24	Iceland	4.35
3	Taiwan	6.37	25	Greece	3.95
4	Finland	6.12	26	Estonia	3.94
5	Australia	5.96	27	Slovenia	3.80
6	South Korea	5.46	28	Russia	3.72
7	Norway	5.27	29	Hong Kong	3.67
8	Belgium	5.19	30	Argentina	3.61
9	Sweden	5.17	31	Portugal	3.58
10	New Zealand	5.11	32	Costa Rica	3.51
11	United Kingdom	5.02	33	Ukraine	3.48
12	France	5.01	34	Chile	3.41
13	Germany	4.98	35	Hungary	3.30
14	Netherlands	4.88	36	Latvia	3.29
15	Denmark	4.83	37	Panama	3.24
16	Austria	4.81	38	Czech Republic	3.24
17	Japan	4.74	39	Bulgaria	3.19
18	Israel	4.71	40	South Africa	3.10
19	Singapore	4.48	41	Uruguay	3.03
	Spain	4.48	42	Venezuela	3.01
21	Italy	4.47	43	Poland	2.98
22	Switzerland	4.44	44	Slovakia	2.97

Information and communications technology index[b]

1	Finland	6.58	23	Israel	5.83
2	Iceland	6.47	24	Japan	5.82
3	Sweden	6.45	25	Portugal	5.68
4	Singapore	6.40	26	Spain	5.63
5	United States	6.34	27	Italy	5.55
6	Norway	6.28	28	Slovenia	5.47
7	Denmark	6.25	29	Czech Republic	5.45
8	Canada	6.23	30	Hungary	5.30
9	Netherlands	6.20	31	Slovakia	5.26
10	Hong Kong	6.19	32	Chile	5.20
11	Australia	6.15	33	Malaysia	5.16
12	Switzerland	6.10	34	Uruguay	5.15
13	Austria	6.09	35	Greece	5.14
	United Kingdom	6.09	36	Latvia	5.02
15	Germany	6.01	37	Poland	4.90
	Taiwan	6.01	38	Brazil	4.86
17	New Zealand	5.99	39	Argentina	4.84
18	Ireland	5.97	40	South Africa	4.80
19	Belgium	5.90	41	Maurutius	4.77
20	Estonia	5.88	42	Costa Rica	4.69
21	France	5.87	43	Lithuania	4.67
	South Korea	5.87	44	Trinidad & Tobago	4.64

a The innovation index is a measure of human resources skills, market incentive structures and interaction between business and scientific sectors.
b The information and communications technology (ICT) index is a measure of ICT usage and includes per capita measures of telephone lines, Internet usage, personal computers and mobile phone users.

Total expenditure on R&D
% of GDP

1	Sweden	3.8		23	Czech Republic	1.4
2	Finland	3.3		24	New Zealand	1.1
3	Japan	3.1			Russia	1.1
4	Israel	2.8		26	China	1.0
5	South Korea	2.7			Italy	1.0
	Switzerland	2.7		28	Brazil	0.9
	United States	2.7			Spain	0.9
8	Iceland	2.6		30	Hungary	0.8
9	Germany	2.5			Portugal	0.8
10	Denmark	2.1		32	Greece	0.7
	France	2.1			Estonia	0.7
12	Belgium	2.0			Poland	0.7
	Netherlands	2.0			Slovakia	0.7
	Taiwan	2.0			South Africa	0.7
15	Singapore	1.9		37	Chile	0.6
16	Austria	1.8			India	0.6
	Canada	1.8			Turkey	0.6
	United Kingdom	1.8		40	Argentina	0.5
19	Norway	1.7			Hong Kong	0.5
20	Australia	1.6			Malaysia	0.5
	Ireland	1.6		43	Colombia	0.4
22	Slovenia	1.5			Mexico	0.4

Patents

No. of patents granted to residents
Total, 1999

| | | | | *No. of patents in force* | | |
				Per 100,000 inhabitants, 1999		
1	Japan	133,960		1	Luxembourg	7,094
2	United States	83,907		2	Switzerland	1,221
3	South Korea	43,314		3	Sweden	1,106
4	Germany	18,811		4	Belgium	835
5	Taiwan	18,052		5	Japan	794
6	Russia	15,362		6	Netherlands	764
7	France	11,500		7	Canada	687
8	Italy	6,481		8	Ireland	619
9	United Kingdom	4,465		9	France	585
10	China	3,097		10	Taiwan	577
11	Netherlands	2,960		11	Denmark	555
12	Sweden	2,526		12	Australia	466
13	Spain	1,843		13	Singapore	458
14	Switzerland	1,455		14	United States	456
15	Canada	1,347		15	Spain	454
16	Austria	1,284		16	Germany	453
17	Australia	1,239		17	Finland	394
18	Belgium	1,050		18	Norway	354
19	Poland	1,022		19	Portugal	225
20	Finland	964		20	Israel	197

Business costs and corruption

Business operating costs[a]
2001, 100 = highest

1	Japan	100.0	17	Singapore	22.4
2	United States	66.3	18	Venezuela	21.3
3	Germany	66.0	19	Russia	21.0
4	United Kingdom	64.0	20	Mexico	19.6
5	Belgium	58.7	21	Brazil	15.7
6	Sweden	54.5	22	South Africa	15.0
7	France	54.4	23	Czech Republic	13.4
8	Netherlands	54.0	24	Poland	13.1
9	Canada	45.6	25	Malaysia	11.1
10	Italy	45.5	26	Chile	10.4
11	Spain	39.5	27	China	8.7
12	Australia	38.3	28	India	7.7
13	Argentina	36.8	29	Thailand	7.3
14	Hong Kong	27.3	30	Indonesia	1.7
15	South Korea	27.1	31	Hungary	1.0
16	Taiwan	26.6			

Business software piracy
2001, % of software that is pirated

1	Vietnam	97	22	Singapore	50
2	China	94	23	Italy	46
3	Indonesia	89	24	Slovakia	45
	Ukraine	89	25	Czech Republic	43
5	Russia	88	26	Portugal	42
6	Pakistan	83	27	Ireland	41
7	Thailand	79	28	France	40
8	Bulgaria	78		Netherlands	40
9	Romania	77	30	Austria	37
10	Greece	66		Japan	37
	Malaysia	66	32	Norway	35
12	Croatia	63		Sweden	35
	India	63	34	Switzerland	34
14	Philippines	61	35	Australia	33
	Slovenia	61		Belgium	33
16	Hong Kong	57	37	Finland	29
17	South Korea	56	38	Germany	28
18	Poland	54		New Zealand	28
19	Taiwan	53	40	Denmark	26
20	Hungary	51		United Kingdom	26
	Spain	51			

Bribe payers index
10 = least likely to pay bribes

1	Australia	8.5	9	Germany	6.3
2	Sweden	8.4		Singapore	6.3
	Switzerland	8.4	11	Spain	5.8
4	Austria	8.2	12	France	5.5
5	Canada	8.1	13	Japan	5.3
6	Belgium	7.8		United States	5.3
	Netherlands	7.8	15	Hong Kong	4.3
8	Britain	6.9		Malaysia	4.3

Corruption perceptions index[b]

2001, 10 = least corrupt

1	Finland	9.9	47	Bulgaria	3.9
2	Denmark	9.5		Croatia	3.9
3	New Zealand	9.4		Czech Republic	3.9
4	Iceland	9.2	50	Colombia	3.8
	Singapore	9.2	51	Mexico	3.7
6	Sweden	9.0		Panama	3.7
7	Canada	8.9		Slovakia	3.7
8	Netherlands	8.8	54	Egypt	3.6
9	Luxembourg	8.7		El Salvador	3.6
10	Norway	8.6		Tunisia	3.6
11	Australia	8.5	57	Argentina	3.5
12	Switzerland	8.4		China	3.5
13	United Kingdom	8.3	59	Ghana	3.4
14	Hong Kong	7.9		Latvia	3.4
15	Austria	7.8	61	Malawi	3.2
16	Israel	7.6		Tanzania	3.2
	United States	7.6	63	Dominican Republic	3.1
18	Chile	7.5		Moldova	3.1
	Ireland	7.5	65	Guatemala	2.9
20	Germany	7.4		Philippines	2.9
21	Japan	7.1		Senegal	2.9
22	Spain	7.0		Zimbabwe	2.9
23	France	6.7	69	Romania	2.8
24	Belgium	6.6		Venezuela	2.8
25	Portugal	6.3	71	Honduras	2.7
26	Botswana	6.0		India	2.7
27	Syria	5.9		Kazakhstan	2.7
28	Estonia	5.6		Uzbekistan	2.7
29	Italy	5.5	75	Vietnam	2.6
30	Namibia	5.4		Zambia	2.6
31	Hungary	5.3	77	Côte d'Ivoire	2.4
	Thailand	5.3		Nicaragua	2.4
	Trinidad & Tobago	5.3	79	Ecuador	2.3
34	Slovenia	5.2		Pakistan	2.3
35	Uruguay	5.1		Russia	2.3
36	Malaysia	5.0	82	Taiwan	2.2
37	Jordan	4.9	83	Ukraine	2.1
38	Lithuania	4.8	84	Azerbaijan	2.0
	South Africa	4.8		Bolivia	2.0
40	Costa Rica	4.5		Cameroon	2.0
	Mauritius	4.5		Kenya	2.0
42	Greece	4.2	88	Indonesia	1.9
	South Korea	4.2		Turkey	1.9
44	Peru	4.1	90	Nigeria	1.0
	Poland	4.1	91	Bangladesh	0.4
46	Brazil	4.0			

a These costs include labour, business travel, taxes, rents, telecommunications and transport.
b This index ranks countries based on how much corruption is perceived to exist among politicians and public officials.

Businesses and banks

Largest businesses
By sales, $bn

1	Exxon Mobil	United States	210.4
2	Wal-Mart Stores	United States	193.3
3	General Motors	United States	184.7
4	Ford Motor	United States	180.6
5	DaimlerChrysler	United States	150.1
6	Royal Dutch/Shell Group	United Kingdom/Netherlands	149.1
7	BP	United Kingdom	148.1
8	General Electric	United States	129.9
9	Mitsubishi	Japan	126.6
10	Toyota Motor	Japan	121.4
11	Mitsui	Japan	118.0
12	Citigroup	United States	111.8
13	Itochu	Japan	109.8
14	Total Fina Elf	France	105.9
15	Nippon Telegraph & Telephone[a]	Japan	103.2
16	Enron	United States	100.8
17	AXA	France	92.8
18	Sumitomo	Japan	91.2
19	Intl. Business Machines	United States	88.4
20	Marubeni	Japan	85.4
21	Volkswagen	Germany	78.9
22	Hitachi	Japan	76.1
23	Siemens	Germany	74.9
24	ING Group	Netherlands	71.2
25	Allianz	Germany	71.0
26	Matsushita Electric Industrial	Japan	69.5
27	E. ON	Germany	68.4
28	Nippon Life Insurance	Japan	68.1
29	Deutsche Bank	Germany	67.1
30	Sony	Japan	66.2
31	AT&T	United States	66.0
32	Verizon Communications	United States	64.7
33	U.S. Postal Service[a]	United States	64.6
34	Philip Morris	United States	63.3
35	CGNU	United Kingdom	61.5
36	J.P. Morgan Chase	United States	60.1
37	Carrefour	France	59.9
38	Credit Suisse	Switzerland	59.3
39	Nissho Iwai	Japan	58.6
40	Honda Motor	Japan	58.5
41	Bank of America Corp	United States	57.7
42	BNP Paribas	France	57.6
43	Nissan Motor	Japan	55.1
44	Toshiba	Japan	53.8
45	PDVSA	Venezuela	53.7

a Government owned.

Notes: Industrial and service corporations. Figures refer to the year ended December 31, 2000, except for Japanese companies, where figures refer to year ended March 31, 2001. They include sales of consolidated subsidiaries but exclude excise taxes, thus differing, in some instances, from figures published by the companies themselves.

Largest banks
By capital, $m

1	Citigroup	United States	54,498
2	Mizuho Financial Group	Japan	50,502
3	Bank of America Corp	United States	40,667
4	J.P. Morgan Chase	United States	37,581
5	HSBC Holdings	United Kingdom	34,620
6	Crédit Agricole Groupe	France	26,383
7	Industrial and Commercial Bank of China	China	22,792
8	Deutsche Bank	Germany	20,076
9	Bank of Tokyo-Mitsubishi	Japan	20,050
10	Sakura Bank	Japan	20,035
11	Bank One Corp	United States	19,824
12	HypoVereinsbank	Germany	19,806
13	UBS	Switzerland	19,488
14	BNP Paribas	France	18,889
15	Sumitomo Bank	Japan	18,124
16	Royal Bank of Scotland	United Kingdom	18,011
17	ABN-Amro Bank	Netherlands	17,689
18	Bank of China	China	17,086
19	Credit Suisse Group	Switzerland	16,566
20	Wells Fargo & Co.	United States	16,096
21	Agricultural Bank of China	China	15,971
22	Sanwa Bank	Japan	15,953
23	Barclays Bank	United Kingdom	15,737
24	ING Bank	Netherlands	14,702
25	FleetBoston Financial Corp	United States	14,334
26	Banco Santander Central Hispano	Spain	14,150
27	Banco Bilbao Vizcaya Argentaria	Spain	14,066
28	First Union Corp	United States	13,952
29	China Construction Bank	China	13,875
30	Société Générale	France	13,679
31	Rabobank Nederland	Netherlands	13,635
32	Norinchukin Bank	Japan	13,239
33	Banca Intesa	Italy	12,765
34	Tokai Bank	Japan	12,500
35	Commerzbank	Germany	11,653
36	Lloyds TSB Group	United Kingdom	11,432
37	Dresdner Bank	Germany	11,209
38	Crédit Mutuel	France	10,880
39	Fortis Bank	Belgium	10,758
40	Abbey National	United Kingdom	10,749
41	Groupe Caisse d'Epargne	France	10,000
42	Ashai Bank	Japan	9,877
43	Halifax	United Kingdom	9,396
44	Royal Bank of Canada	Canada	8,884
45	Scotiabank	Canada	8,779
46	Westdeutsche Landesbank Girozentrale	Germany	8,762

Notes: Capital is essentially equity and reserves.
Figures for Japanese banks refer to the year ended March 31, 2001. Figures for all other countries refer to the year ended December 31, 2000.

Stockmarkets

Largest market capitalisation
$m, end 2000

1	United States	15,104,037		27	Ireland	81,882
2	Japan	3,157,222		28	Turkey	69,659
3	United Kingdom	2,576,992		29	Saudi Arabia	67,171
4	France	1,446,634		30	Norway	65,034
5	Germany	1,270,243		31	Israel	64,081
6	Canada	841,385		32	Portugal	60,681
7	Switzerland	792,316		33	Chile	60,401
8	Italy	768,364		34	Philippines	51,554
9	Netherlands	640,456		35	Russia	38,922
10	Hong Kong	623,398		36	Iran	34,041
11	China	580,991		37	Luxembourg	34,016
12	Spain	504,219		38	Poland	31,279
13	Australia	372,794		39	Austria	29,935
14	Sweden	328,339		40	Thailand	29,489
15	Finland	293,635		41	Egypt	28,741
16	Taiwan	247,602		42	Indonesia	26,834
17	Brazil	226,152		43	United Arab Emirates	23,262
18	South Africa	204,952		44	Kuwait	20,772
19	Belgium	182,481		45	New Zealand	18,613
20	South Korea	171,587		46	Hungary	12,021
21	Argentina	166,068		47	Cyprus	11,516
22	Singapore	152,827		48	Czech Republic	11,002
23	India	148,064		49	Morocco	10,899
24	Malaysia	116,935		50	Peru	10,562
25	Greece	110,839		51	Colombia	9,560
26	Denmark	107,666		52	Venezuela	8,128

Highest growth in market capitalisation, $ terms
% increase, 1990–2000

1	China[a]	28,548			Lithuania[b]	911
2	Poland[a]	21,622		22	Ireland[c]	872
3	Russia[a]	15,852		23	Iceland[c]	817
4	Latvia[b]	5,530		24	Cyprus[a]	793
5	Argentina	4,982		25	Philippines	770
6	Malta[c]	3,763		26	Armenia[f]	733
7	Hungary[a]	2,280		27	Hong Kong	648
8	Romania[c]	1,956		28	Greece	628
9	Israel	1,828		29	Colombia	575
10	Paraguay[d]	1,663		30	Ghana[a]	561
11	Egypt	1,528		31	Portugal	560
12	Namibia[e]	1,381		32	Trinidad & Tobago	522
13	Brazil	1,283		33	Barbados	499
14	Peru	1,201		34	Netherlands	434
15	Finland	1,192		35	Croatia[c]	433
16	Zambia[b]	1,142		36	Tunisia	431
17	Panama[e]	1,136		37	Italy	416
18	Morocco	1,028		38	Switzerland	395
19	Ecuador[b]	920		39	United States	394
20	Bulgaria[b]	911		40	Bolivia[g]	383

Highest growth in value traded, $ terms
% increase, 1990–2000

1	China[a]	87,892	23	Italy	1,729
2	Poland[a]	52,154	24	United States	1,719
3	Hungary[a]	31,874	25	Brazil	1,709
4	Panama[e]	15,300	26	Morocco	1,665
5	Pakistan	14,174	27	Netherlands	1,585
6	Cyprus[a]	14,148	28	Peru	1,436
7	Bangladesh	12,700	29	Bulgaria[b]	1,350
8	Iceland[c]	12,400	30	South Korea	1,306
9	Egypt	8,725	31	Luxembourg	1,285
10	Romania[c]	7,767	32	Mauritius	1,150
11	Russia[c]	7,479	33	Hong Kong	991
12	Malta[c]	6,067	34	South Africa	850
13	Finland	5,154	35	France	827
14	Tunisia	3,195	36	Canada	790
15	Portugal	3,123	37	Switzerland	785
16	Turkey	2,968	38	Denmark	724
17	Greece	2,324	39	Chile	677
18	Spain	2,306	40	Saudi Arabia[a]	661
19	Nigeria	2,291	41	Slovakia[c]	647
20	India	2,226	42	Argentina	599
21	Sweden	2,120	43	Philippines	574
22	Latvia[h]	1,800	44	United Kingdom	558

Highest growth in number of listed companies
% increase, 1990–2000

1	Romania[c]	138,775	24	Malaysia	182
2	China[a]	7,657	25	Singapore	179
3	Peru	7,567	26	Hong Kong	174
4	Croatia[e]	3,100	27	Iceland[c]	171
5	Bulgaria[c]	3,044	28	Taiwan	167
6	Poland	2,400	29	Malta[c]	150
7	Russia[a]	1,815	30	Germany	147
8	Paraguay[d]	1,733	31	India	144
9	Bolivia[g]	800	32	Spain	139
10	Swaziland	500	33	Oman	138
11	Zambia[b]	350	34	Indonesia	132
12	Namibia[e]	333	35	Greece	127
13	Lithuania[c]	315	36	Fiji[g]	125
14	Lebanon[b]	300	37	Panama[e]	123
15	Latvia[b]	276	38	Finland	111
16	Canada	248	39	South Korea	96
17	Tunisia	238	40	Egypt	88
18	Iran[a]	213	41	Côte d'Ivoire	78
19	Mauritius	208	42	Botswana[a]	78
20	Israel	203		Honduras[a]	78
21	Cyprus[a]	200		Thailand	77
22	Turkey	186	45	Norway	71
	Hungary[a]	186	46	Ghana[a]	69

a 1991–2000 b 1995–2000 c 1994–2000 d 1993–1999
e 1992–2000 f 1995–1999 g 1994–1999 h 1996–2000

Transport: *roads and cars*

Longest road networks
Km, 2000 or latest

1	United States	6,304,193	21	Argentina	215,471
2	India	3,319,644	22	Sweden	212,402
3	Brazil	1,724,929	23	Bangladesh	207,486
4	China	1,402,698	24	Philippines	201,994
5	Japan	1,161,894	25	Austria	200,000
6	Canada	901,903	26	Romania	198,603
7	France	894,000	27	Nigeria	194,394
8	Australia	811,603	28	Hungary	188,203
9	Spain	663,795	29	Ukraine	169,491
10	Italy	654,676	30	Iran	167,157
11	Russia	532,393	31	Congo	157,000
12	Ireland	479,688	32	Saudi Arabia	151,470
13	Turkey	385,960	33	Belgium	148,216
14	United Kingdom	371,913	34	Greece	117,000
15	Poland	364,656	35	Netherlands	116,500
16	South Africa	362,099	36	Colombia	112,988
17	Indonesia	342,700	37	Algeria	104,000
18	Mexico	329,532	38	Sri Lanka	96,695
19	Pakistan	254,410	39	Venezuela	96,155
20	Germany	230,735	40	Vietnam	93,300

Densest road networks
Km of road per km² land area, 2000 or latest

1	Macau	15.94	21	United Kingdom	1.53
2	Malta	7.13	22	Sri Lanka	1.47
3	Ireland	6.83	23	Bangladesh	1.44
4	Belgium	4.86	24	Spain	1.32
5	Singapore	4.80	25	Cyprus	1.20
6	Bahrain	4.72	26	Poland	1.17
7	Barbados	4.17	27	Latvia	1.15
8	Japan	3.08		Lithuania	1.15
9	Netherlands	2.81	29	Estonia	1.14
10	Austria	2.39	30	India	1.01
11	Italy	2.17	31	Slovenia	1.00
12	Hungary	2.02	32	Taiwan	0.99
13	Luxembourg	2.01	33	Mauritius	0.94
14	Switzerland	1.72	34	Greece	0.89
15	Hong Kong	1.70	35	South Korea	0.88
	Jamaica	1.70	36	Slovakia	0.87
17	Denmark	1.66	37	Romania	0.84
18	France	1.64	38	Israel	0.78
19	Trinidad & Tobago	1.62	39	Portugal	0.77
20	Puerto Rico	1.58	40	Czech Republic	0.70

Most crowded road networks
Number of vehicles per km of road network, 2000 or latest

1	Hong Kong	287	26	Luxembourg	55
2	United Arab Emirates	232	27	Italy	54
3	Macau	201		Switzerland	54
4	Germany	194	29	Russia	48
5	Lebanon	191	30	Mexico	47
6	Singapore	169	31	Slovenia	46
7	Kuwait	156	32	Guatemala	45
8	Qatar	154	33	Croatia	44
9	Taiwan	150	34	Jordan	40
10	South Korea	138		Tunisia	40
11	Israel	107	36	Barbados	39
12	Malta	103	37	France	38
13	Thailand	97	38	Greece	37
14	Malaysia	75	39	El Salvador	36
15	Puerto Rico	74	40	Macedonia	35
16	Brunei	73		Belgium	35
17	Czech Republic	67		Serbia & Montenegro	35
18	Bahrain	65	43	Cyprus	34
19	Mauritius	64		Slovakia	34
20	Japan	63		United States	34
	Portugal	63	46	Poland	33
	Uruguay	63	47	Cambodia	31
23	United Kingdom	62		Denmark	31
24	Bulgaria	60		Finland	31
25	Netherlands	58	50	Argentina	30

Most used road networks
'000 vehicle-km per year per km of road network, 2000 or latest

1	Indonesia	8,134.1	16	Luxembourg	739.8
2	Hong Kong	5,888.0	17	Czech Republic	693.2
3	Taiwan	2,780.3	18	Greece	678.4
4	Germany	2,554.9	19	Japan	658.5
5	Israel	2,202.8	20	Denmark	630.9
6	Bahrain	1,434.5	21	China	599.5
7	Portugal	1,396.9	22	Finland	590.6
8	Malta	1,245.8	23	France	581.0
9	United Kingdom	1,243.3	24	Cambodia	563.2
10	Belgium	1,067.9	25	Croatia	489.4
11	Netherlands	943.8	26	Macedonia	489.1
12	Pakistan	859.9	27	Slovenia	458.2
13	South Korea	773.3	28	El Salvador	423.2
14	Tunisia	770.4	29	United States	420.8
15	Switzerland	753.5	30	Ecuador	393.0

Highest car ownership
Number of cars per 1,000 people, 2000 or latest

1	Lebanon	732		Kuwait	359
2	New Zealand	578	27	Ireland	349
3	Brunei	576	28	Estonia	339
3	Luxembourg	576	29	Czech Republic	335
5	Iceland	561	30	Portugal	321
6	Italy	542	31	Lithuania	317
7	Germany	516	32	Poland	259
8	Austria	506	33	Greece	254
9	Malta	494	34	Bahrain	250
10	Switzerland	493	35	Croatia	247
11	Australia	488	36	Hungary	237
12	United States	481	37	Slovakia	236
13	France	477	38	Latvia	235
14	Canada	458	39	Bulgaria	234
15	Sweden	450	40	Israel	233
16	Belgium	444	41	Puerto Rico	230
17	Slovenia	426	42	Qatar	219
18	Japan	413	43	Taiwan	212
19	Norway	411	44	South Korea	171
20	Spain	408	45	Bahamas	161
21	Finland	403	46	Libya	154
22	Cyprus	400		Uruguay	154
23	Netherlands	384	48	Belarus	145
23	United Kingdom	384		Malaysia	145
25	Denmark	359		Serbia & Montenegro	145

Lowest car ownership
Number of cars per 1,000 people, 2000 or latest

1	Somalia	0.1	17	Liberia	2.6
	Tajikistan	0.1	18	Burundi	2.8
3	Armenia	0.3	19	Mali	2.9
	Central African Rep	0.3	20	Chad	3.2
	Mozambique	0.3	21	Laos	3.4
6	Bangladesh	0.5	22	Burkina Faso	3.6
7	Myanmar	0.6	23	Niger	3.8
8	Tanzania	0.8	24	Sierra Leone	3.9
9	Ethiopia	0.9	25	Madagascar	4.1
10	Guatemala	1.0	26	Haiti	4.4
11	Afghanistan	1.4	27	Ghana	4.7
	Rwanda	1.4	28	Pakistan	5.0
13	Eritrea	1.5	29	India	5.2
14	Uganda	1.8	30	Guinea-Bissau	5.7
15	Guinea	2.0		Lesotho	5.7
16	Malawi	2.3			

Most accidents
Number of people injured per 100m vehicle-km, 2000 or latest

1	Malawi	2,730	26	Mongolia	90
2	Rwanda	1,764	27	Saudi Arabia	89
3	South Korea	510	28	Philippines	86
4	Costa Rica	406	29	Germany	81
5	Kenya	363		Macedonia	81
6	India	333	31	United States	74
7	Honduras	317	32	Spain	73
8	Turkey	228	33	Mexico	66
9	Egypt	222	34	Iceland	61
10	Sri Lanka	205	35	Bahrain	60
11	Portugal	194	36	Yemen	59
12	Morocco	183	37	Hungary	57
13	Hong Kong	176	38	Senegal	56
14	Kirgizstan	134	39	Switzerland	54
15	Japan	133	40	Iran	53
16	Colombia	126		Oman	53
17	Latvia	125	42	Malta	42
18	Italy	122	43	Thailand	40
19	Canada	121	44	Slovakia	39
20	Czech Republic	113	45	Ireland	38
21	Israel	110	46	Norway	34
22	Belgium	108	47	Mauritius	32
23	South Africa	100		Zimbabwe	32
24	Slovenia	98	49	France	31
25	United Kingdom	94		Sweden	31

Most deaths
Number of people killed per 100m vehicle-km, 2000 or latest

1	Malawi	1,117		Saudi Arabia	11
2	India	65		Yemen	11
3	Egypt	44	18	Mexico	10
4	Kenya	41	19	Turkey	9
5	Latvia	25	20	Albania	8
6	Kirgizstan	24	21	South Africa	7
7	Sri Lanka	23		Suriname	7
8	Mongolia	22	23	Portugal	6
9	Colombia	17		Romania	6
	Morocco	17	25	Czech Republic	5
	South Korea	17		Ecuador	5
12	Honduras	16		Iran	5
13	Philippines	14	28	Macedonia	4
14	Thailand	13		Oman	4
15	Costa Rica	11		Senegal	4

Transport: *planes and trains*

Most air travel
Million passenger-km[a] per year

1	United States	1,056,767		16	Mexico	32,004
2	United Kingdom	259,979		17	Australia	30,292
3	Japan	169,019		18	India	26,481
4	Germany	165,224		19	Russia	25,841
5	China[b]	134,961		20	Turkey	20,948
6	France	110,508		21	Israel	16,683
7	Singapore	71,841		22	Austria	15,344
8	Canada	68,482		23	United Arab Emirates	12,887
9	South Korea	63,784		24	Finland	12,683
10	Spain	62,513		25	Pakistan	12,055
11	Netherlands	60,726		26	Argentina	11,530
12	Brazil[c]	50,404		27	Portugal	11,317
13	Thailand	42,395		28	Norway	10,753
14	Malaysia	37,939		29	Sweden	10,285
15	Switzerland	36,781		30	Indonesia	10,132

Busiest airports

Total passengers, m			*International passengers, m*		
1	Atlanta, Hartsfield	75.8	1	London, Heathrow	56.9
2	Chicago, O'Hare	66.8	2	Paris, Charles de Gaulle	42.5
3	Los Angeles, Intl.	61.0	3	Frankfurt, Main	40.3
4	London, Heathrow	60.7	4	Amsterdam, Schipol	40.2
5	Tokyo, Haneda	58.7	5	Hong Kong, Intl.	32.1
6	Dallas, Ft. Worth	55.2	6	London, Gatwick	29.0
7	Frankfurt, Main	48.6	7	Singapore, Changi	27.0
8	Paris, Charles de Gaulle	48.0	8	Tokyo, Narita	24.0
9	Amsterdam, Schipol	39.5	9	Brussels, Zaventem	21.5
10	Denver, Intl	36.1	10	Zurich	21.2
11	Phoenix, Skyharbor Intl.	35.5	11	Bangkok, Intl.	21.0
12	Las Vegas, McCarran Intl.	35.2	12	New York, Kennedy	18.6

Average daily aircraft movements, take-offs and landings

1	Chicago, O'Hare	2,492		12	Houston, George Bush	
2	Atlanta, Hartsfield	2,439			Intercont.	1,290
3	Dallas, Ft. Worth	2,147			Miami, Intl	1,290
4	Los Angeles, Intl.	2,022		14	Philadelphia, Intl	1,279
5	Phoenix, Skyharbor Intl.	1,537		15	London, Heathrow	1,270
6	Paris, Charles de Gaulle	1,432		16	Charlotte/Douglas,	
7	Detroit, Metro	1,430			Intl.	1,264
8	Minneapolis, St Paul	1,370		17	Frankfurt, Main	1,251
9	Las Vegas, McCarran Intl.	1,353		18	Boston, Logan Intl.	1,246
10	Denver, Intl.	1,327		19	Pittsburgh, Intl.	1,238
11	St Louis, Lambert	1,299		20	Newark, Intl.	1,195

a Air passenger–km data refer to the distance travelled by each aircraft of national origin.
b Includes Hong Kong
c 1999

Longest railway networks
'000 km

1	United States	230.7		21	Australia	9.5
2	Canada	93.4		22	Czech Republic	9.4
3	Russia	86.1		23	Turkey	8.7
4	India	62.8		24	Hungary	8.5
5	China	58.7		25	Pakistan	7.8
6	Germany	36.7		26	Iran	6.7
7	Argentina	34.2		27	Finland	5.9
8	France	32.5		28	Austria	5.8
9	Mexico	26.5		29	Belarus	5.5
10	South Africa	22.7		30	Egypt	5.0
11	Poland	22.6		31	Philippines	4.9
12	Ukraine	22.3		32	Cuba	4.8
13	Brazil	22.1		33	Sudan	4.6
14	Japan	20.2		34	North Korea	4.5
15	United Kingdom	17.1		35	Bulgaria	4.3
16	Italy	16.5			Serbia & Montenegro	4.3
17	Spain	13.9		37	Indonesia	4.2
18	Kazakhstan	13.5			Norway	4.2
19	Romania	11.4		39	New Zealand	3.9
20	Sweden	9.9		40	Algeria	3.8

Most rail passengers
Km per person per year

1	Japan	1,900		11	Russia	898
2	Switzerland	1,798		12	Luxembourg	790
3	Belarus	1,737		13	Italy	783
4	France	1,177		14	Belgium	722
5	Ukraine	1,025		15	Czech Republic	712
6	Denmark	1,015		16	Hungary	705
7	Austria	1,001		17	United Kingdom	691
8	Egypt	992		18	Sweden	675
9	Netherlands	934		19	Finland	655
10	Germany	905		20	Kazakhstan	631

Most rail freight
Million tonnes-km per year

1	United States	2,140,192		11	Poland	54,015
2	China	1,333,606		12	Australia	34,050
3	Russia	1,197,495		13	Belarus	31,425
4	India	305,201		14	Italy	22,826
5	Canada	295,982		15	Japan	22,313
6	Ukraine	172,840		16	United Kingdom	19,115
7	Kazakhstan	124,983		17	Sweden	18,982
8	South Africa	100,434		18	Czech Republic	17,220
9	Germany	76,906		19	Romania	16,401
10	France	55,448		20	Austria	16,311

Transport: *sail away*

Largest merchant fleets
Number of vessels not less than 100 GRT and built before end of 2001[a]
By country of :

		registration	ownership			registration	ownership
1	Japan	7,924	2,979	46	Iceland	324	65
2	Panama	6,245	4	47	Portugal	321	75
3	United States	5,824	1,465	48	Bangladesh	317	30
4	Russia	4,727	2,511	49	Nigeria	293	38
5	China	3,280	2,234	50	Finland	284	148
6	Indonesia	2,528	605	51	Azerbaijan	283	151
7	South Korea	2,426	872	52	Saudi Arabia	274	121
8	Norway	2,363	1,708	53	Venezuela	268	63
9	Singapore	1,729	714	54	Croatia	243	109
10	Philippines	1,697	334	55	Romania	240	107
11	Liberia	1,566	0	56	Syria	215	67
12	Spain	1,545	324	57	Ghana	212	18
13	Greece	1,529	3,151	58	Georgia	201	5
14	Italy	1,476	645	59	Kuwait	200	35
15	UK	1,462	825	60	South Africa	197	24
16	Malta	1,421	15	61	Ireland	193	52
17	Cyprus	1,407	75	62	Estonia	191	88
18	Netherlands	1,337	810	63	Senegal	188	2
19	Bahamas	1,312	17	64	Belgium	185	167
20	Honduras	1,183	4	65	Netherlands Antilles	176	0
	Hong Kong	1,183	555		North Korea	176	100
22	Turkey	1,146	562	67	Ecuador	175	28
23	Denmark	1,054	726		Lithuania	175	67
24	India	1,018	407	69	Bulgaria	172	107
25	Germany	906	2,212	70	Latvia	160	104
26	Malaysia	882	312	71	New Zealand	159	44
27	Canada	875	298	72	Algeria	143	71
28	Ukraine	838	395	73	Mauritania	141	0
29	Peru	717	23	74	Libya	140	17
30	Vietnam	700	150	75	Mozambique	131	1
31	France	699	283	76	Bermuda	127	0
32	Taiwan	656	542	77	Myanmar	124	34
33	Mexico	633	99	78	Angola	123	13
34	Australia	622	87	79	Bahrain	121	14
35	Sweden	578	346		Namibia	121	3
36	Thailand	568	258	81	Papua New Guinea	114	17
37	Cambodia	564	0	82	Colombia	105	22
38	Morocco	485	43	83	Madagascar	104	11
39	Chile	480	90	84	Lebanon	99	49
40	Argentina	478	87	85	Cuba	92	62
41	Brazil	475	179	86	Iraq	91	34
42	Poland	393	131	87	Uruguay	90	19
43	Iran	389	163				
44	Egypt	364	126				
45	UAE	341	185				

a Gross Tonnage (GRT) = total volume within the hull and above deck. 1 GRT=100 cu ft.

Tourism

Most tourist arrivals
Number of arrivals, '000

1	France	75,500	21	Thailand	9,509
2	United States	50,891	22	Macau	6,682
3	Spain	48,201	23	Ireland	6,584
4	Italy	41,182	24	Singapore	6,569
5	China	31,229	25	Belgium	6,496
6	United Kingdom	25,191	26	South Africa	6,001
7	Russia	21,169	27	South Korea	5,322
8	Mexico	20,643	28	Brazil	5,313
9	Canada	20,423	29	Indonesia	5,064
10	Germany	18,983	30	Tunisia	5,057
11	Austria	17,982	31	Australia	4,946
12	Poland	17,400	32	Japan	4,757
13	Hungary	15,571	33	Czech Republic	4,666
14	Hong Kong	13,059	34	Norway	4,416
15	Greece	12,500	35	Morocco	4,113
16	Portugal	12,037	36	Puerto Rico	3,341
17	Switzerland	11,400	37	Argentina	2,991
18	Malaysia	10,222	38	Dominican Republic	2,977
19	Netherlands	10,200	39	India	2,641
20	Turkey	9,587	40	Sweden	2,612

Biggest tourist spenders
$m

1	United States	62,153	9	Canada	12,733
2	Germany	48,107	10	Netherlands	11,339
3	United Kingdom	36,384	11	China	8,640
4	Japan	35,629	12	Belgium	8,600
5	Spain	24,658	13	Switzerland	7,037
6	France	18,381	14	Taiwan	6,679
7	Italy	17,712	15	Poland	6,566
8	Austria	13,537	16	Russia	6,318

Largest tourist receipts
$m

1	United States	85,153	16	Netherlands	7,536
2	Spain	36,426	17	Thailand	7,119
3	France	33,401	18	Switzerland	6,945
4	Italy	27,468	19	Turkey	6,859
5	United Kingdom	23,148	20	South Korea	6,609
6	Austria	17,995	21	Indonesia	5,749
7	Germany	16,309	22	Portugal	5,595
8	China	16,231	23	Belgium	5,471
9	Greece	13,073	24	Sweden	4,608
10	Canada	10,768	25	Malaysia	4,563
11	Poland	8,708	26	Russia	4,454
12	Australia	8,442	27	Brazil	4,228
13	Mexico	8,295	28	Ireland	3,667
14	Hong Kong	7,886	29	Taiwan	3,605
15	Singapore	7,799	30	Czech Republic	3,482

Education

Highest primary enrolment
Number enrolled as % of relevant age group, 1998 or latest available

1	Brazil	154	16	Cambodia	119
	Gabon	154		Tunisia	119
	Uganda	154	18	Netherlands Antilles	117
4	Libya	153		Philippines	117
5	Haiti	152		Swaziland	117
6	Ireland	141	21	Paraguay	115
7	Malawi	134	22	Mexico	114
8	Dominican Republic	133		Myanmar	114
9	South Africa	127		Nepal	114
10	Namibia	126		Rwanda	114
	Peru	126	26	Ecuador	113
12	Portugal	124		Indonesia	113
	Togo	124		Uruguay	113
14	Bangladesh	122	29	Colombia	112
15	Argentina	120		Fiji	112

Lowest primary enrolment
Number enrolled as % of relevant age group, 1998 or latest available

1	Bhutan	21	15	Chad	67
	Niger	31	16	Jordan	69
3	Burkina Faso	42		Serbia & Montenegro	69
4	Congo	46	18	Senegal	70
5	Burundi	51	19	Mozambique	71
6	Eritrea	53		Saudi Arabia	71
	Mali	53	21	Oman	75
8	Sudan	56	22	Kuwait	77
9	Central African Rep	57	23	Côte d'Ivoire	78
	Congo-Brazzaville	57		Uzbekistan	78
11	Guinea	59		Yemen	78
12	Guinea-Bissau	62	26	Ghana	79
13	Ethiopia	63	27	Gambia, The	81
14	Tanzania	65	28	Ukraine	82

Highest tertiary enrolment[a]
Number enrolled as % of relevant age group, 1998 or latest available

1	Finland	83	11	Libya	57
2	Australia	80	12	Spain	56
3	United States	77	13	Denmark	55
4	South Korea	68	14	Slovenia	53
5	Norway	65	15	France	51
6	New Zealand	63		Latvia	51
	Sweden	63	17	Austria	50
8	Belgium	59		Greece	50
9	Canada	58	19	Israel	49
	United Kingdom	58		Netherlands	49

Notes: The gross enrolment ratios shown are the actual number enrolled as a percentage of the number of children in the official primary age group. They may exceed 100 when children outside the primary age group are receiving primary education either because they have not moved on to secondary education or because they have started primary education early.

Least literate
% adult literacy rate, 1998 or latest available

1	Niger	15.9	17	Mozambique	44.0
2	Burkina Faso	23.9	18	Bhutan	44.2
3	Afghanistan	33.4	19	Yemen	46.3
4	Sierra Leone	34.3	20	Central African Rep	46.7
5	Gambia, The	36.6	21	Côte d'Ivoire	46.8
6	Benin	37.4	22	Burundi	48.0
	Senegal	37.4	23	Laos	48.7
8	Guinea	37.9	24	Morocco	48.9
9	Guinea-Bissau	38.5	25	Haiti	49.8
10	Ethiopia	39.1	26	Liberia	54.0
11	Mauritania	40.2	27	Egypt	55.3
12	Bangladesh	41.4	28	Eritrea	55.7
13	Mali	41.5	29	Iraq	55.9
14	Nepal	41.8	30	India	57.2
15	Chad	42.6		Togo	57.2
16	Pakistan	43.2			

Highest education spending
% of GDP, 1998 or latest available

1	Lesotho	13.0		New Zealand	7.2
2	Zimbabwe	10.8	15	Denmark	6.9
3	Moldova	10.6	16	Estonia	6.8
4	Botswana	9.1		Jordan	6.8
5	Namibia	8.1		Latvia	6.8
6	Sweden	8.0	19	Cuba	6.7
7	Israel	7.7		Yemen	6.7
	Norway	7.7	21	Kenya	6.6
	Uzbekistan	7.7	22	Kuwait	6.5
10	Tunisia	7.6	23	Lithuania	6.4
11	Finland	7.5	24	Austria	6.3
	Saudi Arabia	7.5		Jamaica	6.3
13	Barbados	7.2			

Lowest education spending
% of GDP, 1998 or latest available

1	Nigeria	0.7	13	Lebanon	2.1
2	Sierra Leone	1.0		Tanzania	2.1
3	Myanmar	1.2	15	Bangladesh	2.2
4	Indonesia	1.4		Tajikistan	2.2
5	Uganda	1.6		Turkey	2.2
6	Chad	1.7	18	China	2.3
7	Guinea	1.8		Dominican Republic	2.3
8	Central African Rep	1.9		Zambia	2.3
	Madagascar	1.9	21	Laos	2.4
	United Arab Emirates	1.9	22	El Salvador	2.5
11	Armenia	2.0		Nepal	2.5
	Guatemala	2.0		Uruguay	2.5

a Tertiary education includes all levels of post-secondary education including courses
  leading to awards not equivalent to a university degree, courses leading to a first
  university degree and postgraduate courses.

Life: *the chances*

Highest life expectancy
Years, 2000–05

1	Japan	81.5		New Zealand	78.0
2	Sweden	80.1	27	Luxembourg	77.9
3	Hong Kong	79.9	28	United States	77.5
4	Iceland	79.4	29	Barbados	77.2
5	Macau	79.3	30	Bermuda[a]	77.1
6	Australia	79.2	31	Ireland	77.0
	Israel	79.2	32	Costa Rica	76.7
8	Martinique	79.1	33	Denmark	76.6
	Switzerland	79.1	34	Kuwait	76.5
10	Canada	79.0	35	Cuba	76.4
	France	79.0	36	Brunei	76.3
12	Norway	78.9		Netherlands Antilles	76.3
13	Belgium	78.8	38	Portugal	76.2
	Spain	78.8	39	Slovenia	76.1
15	Italy	78.7	40	Jamaica	75.7
16	Austria	78.5	41	Chile	75.6
	Greece	78.5		Puerto Rico	75.6
	Malta	78.5	43	South Korea	75.5
19	Cyprus	78.3	44	Czech Republic	75.4
	Guadeloupe	78.3		United Arab Emirates	75.4
	Netherlands	78.3	46	Taiwan[b]	75.3
22	Germany	78.2	47	Uruguay	75.0
	United Kingdom	78.2	48	Réunion	74.9
24	Singapore	78.1	49	Trinidad & Tobago	74.8
25	Finland	78.0	50	Panama	74.5

Highest male life expectancy
Years, 2000–05

1	Japan	77.8		Norway	76.0
2	Sweden	77.6	11	Greece	75.9
3	Hong Kong	77.3		Malta	75.9
4	Iceland	77.1		Singapore	75.9
	Israel	77.1		Switzerland	75.9
6	Macau	76.9	15	Martinique	75.8
7	Australia	76.4	16	Belgium	75.7
8	Canada	76.2		United Kingdom	75.7
9	Cyprus	76.0	18	Netherlands	75.6

Highest female life expectancy
Years, 2000–05

1	Japan	85.0		Italy	81.9
2	France	82.8		Norway	81.9
	Hong Kong	82.8	12	Canada	81.8
4	Sweden	82.6		Iceland	81.8
5	Martinique	82.3	14	Guadeloupe	81.7
	Spain	82.3	15	Macau	81.6
	Switzerland	82.3	16	Austria	81.5
8	Australia	82.0		Finland	81.5
9	Belgium	81.9	18	Greece	81.2

a 2001   b 2000

Lowest life expectancy
Years, 2000–05

1	Botswana	36.1	26	Kenya	49.3
2	Mozambique	38.0	27	Cameroon	50.0
3	Swaziland	38.1	28	Tanzania	51.1
4	Malawi	39.3	29	Congo-Brazzaville	51.6
5	Lesotho	40.2	30	Congo	52.1
6	Sierra Leone	40.5		Mali	52.1
7	Burundi	40.6		Nigeria	52.1
8	Rwanda	40.9	33	Togo	52.2
9	Zambia	42.2	34	Eritrea	52.4
10	Zimbabwe	42.9	35	Mauritania	52.5
11	Afghanistan	43.2	36	Gabon	52.9
12	Ethiopia	43.3	37	Haiti	53.3
13	Central African Rep	44.3	38	Madagascar	53.6
	Namibia	44.3	39	Benin	54.0
15	Guinea-Bissau	45.4	40	Senegal	54.3
16	Angola	45.8	41	Laos	54.5
17	Uganda	46.0	42	Liberia	55.6
18	Niger	46.2	43	Cambodia	56.2
19	Chad	46.3		Myanmar	56.2
20	Gambia, The	47.1	45	Sudan	57.0
21	South Africa	47.4	46	Ghana	57.2
22	Côte d'Ivoire	47.9	47	Papua New Guinea	57.7
23	Burkina Faso	48.1	48	Nepal	59.8
24	Guinea	48.5	49	Bangladesh	60.7
25	Somalia	48.9	50	Pakistan	61.0

Lowest male life expectancy
Years, 2000–05

1	Botswana	36.5	10	Central African Rep	42.7
2	Mozambique	37.3	11	Ethiopia	42.8
3	Swaziland	38.1	12	Afghanistan	43.0
4	Sierra Leone	39.2	13	Zimbabwe	43.3
5	Malawi	39.6	14	Guinea-Bissau	44.0
6	Burundi	39.8	15	Namibia	44.3
7	Rwanda	40.2	16	Angola	44.5
8	Lesotho	40.9	17	Chad	45.1
9	Zambia	42.6	18	Uganda	45.3

Lowest female life expectancy
Years, 2000–05

1	Botswana	35.6	10	Zimbabwe	42.4
2	Swaziland	38.1	11	Afghanistan	43.5
3	Mozambique	38.6	12	Ethiopia	43.8
4	Malawi	39.0	13	Namibia	44.1
5	Lesotho	39.6	14	Central African Rep	46.0
6	Burundi	41.4	15	Niger	46.5
7	Rwanda	41.7	16	Uganda	46.8
	Zambia	41.7	17	Guinea-Bissau	46.9
9	Sierra Leone	41.8	18	Angola	47.1

Death: *the chances*

Highest death rates
Number of deaths per 1,000 population, 2000–05

#	Country	Rate	#	Country	Rate
1	Botswana	24.5		Moldova	12.3
2	Mozambique	23.9	50	Liberia	12.2
3	Sierra Leone	23.3	51	Myanmar	11.6
4	Swaziland	23.0		Senegal	11.6
5	Malawi	22.6	53	Croatia	11.3
6	Lesotho	21.9		Denmark	11.3
7	Afghanistan	21.4	55	Lithuania	11.2
8	Burundi	20.8	56	Sudan	11.1
9	Rwanda	20.6	57	Italy	10.9
10	Ethiopia	19.4	58	Czech Republic	10.8
11	Guinea-Bissau	19.3		Germany	10.8
12	Niger	19.1		Portugal	10.8
13	Angola	19.0	61	Serbia & Montenegro	10.7
14	Zambia	18.8	62	Cambodia	10.6
15	Central African Rep	18.6		Sweden	10.6
	Chad	18.6	64	United Kingdom	10.5
17	Namibia	17.8	65	Ghana	10.4
	Zimbabwe	17.8		Greece	10.4
19	Mali	17.3	67	Kazakhstan	10.1
20	Uganda	17.2	68	Belgium	10.0
21	South Africa	17.1		Norway	10.0
22	Gambia, The	17.0	70	Austria	9.9
	Somalia	17.0		Georgia	9.9
24	Guinea	16.8		Nepal	9.9
25	Burkina Faso	15.9		North Korea	9.9
26	Ukraine	15.4		Poland	9.9
27	Côte d'Ivoire	15.3		Slovenia	9.9
	Russia	15.3	76	Finland	9.8
29	Gabon	15.2		Slovakia	9.8
30	Bulgaria	15.1		Spain	9.8
31	Cameroon	14.6		Switzerland	9.8
32	Mauritania	14.2	80	Pakistan	9.7
33	Belarus	14.1	81	Papua New Guinea	9.6
34	Congo-Brazzaville	14.0	82	France	9.4
35	Kenya	13.7	83	Uruguay	9.3
36	Congo	13.6	84	Luxembourg	9.1
37	Hungary	13.5	85	Netherlands	9.0
38	Latvia	13.4	86	Bangladesh	8.7
39	Eritrea	13.3	87	Bhutan	8.6
	Estonia	13.3	88	India	8.4
	Nigeria	13.3		Macedonia	8.4
42	Madagascar	13.2		United States	8.4
	Togo	13.2	91	Japan	8.3
44	Tanzania	13.1		Yemen	8.3
45	Romania	12.8	93	Bolivia	8.2
46	Haiti	12.6		Ireland	8.2
47	Laos	12.6	95	Bosnia	8.1
48	Benin	12.3			

Note: Both death and, in particular, infant mortality rates can be underestimated in certain countries where not all deaths are officially recorded.

Highest infant mortality
Number of deaths per 1,000 live births, 2000–05

1	Afghanistan	161.3	21	Madagascar	91.5
2	Sierra Leone	146.3	22	Laos	88.0
3	Malawi	130.1	23	Myanmar	87.2
4	Mozambique	127.7	24	Burkina Faso	86.6
5	Niger	125.7	25	Pakistan	86.5
6	Guinea-Bissau	121.2	26	Eritrea	82.4
7	Mali	120.5	27	Côte d'Ivoire	80.8
8	Rwanda	119.2	28	Benin	80.6
9	Angola	117.7	29	Gabon	80.0
10	Chad	116.1	30	Zambia	79.6
11	Gambia, The	115.0	31	Cameroon	79.3
12	Guinea	114.4		Liberia	79.3
13	Somalia	112.7	33	Nigeria	78.5
14	Burundi	111.5	34	Sudan	77.7
15	Lesotho	111.2	35	Congo	77.2
16	Ethiopia	106.1	36	Togo	74.8
17	Mauritania	96.7	37	Tanzania	72.7
18	Uganda	93.9	38	Cambodia	72.5
19	Central African Rep	93.3	39	Nepal	70.9
20	Swaziland	91.7	40	Botswana	67.2

Lowest death rates
No. deaths per 1,000 pop., 2000–05

1	Kuwait	2.7
2	Brunei	3.2
3	Bahrain	3.7
4	Costa Rica	4.0
	Syria	4.0
	United Arab Emirates	4.0
7	Oman	4.1
	Qatar	4.1
	Saudi Arabia	4.1
10	Jordan	4.3
	West Bank and Gaza	4.3
12	Macau	4.6
13	Malaysia	4.7
	Venezuela	4.7
15	Libya	4.8
16	Iran	5.0
17	Mexico	5.1
	Panama	5.1
	Paraguay	5.1
20	Nicaragua	5.2
	Philippines	5.2
22	Algeria	5.3
	Singapore	5.3
24	Albania	5.4
	Lebanon	5.4
26	Fiji	5.5

Lowest infant mortality
No. deaths per 1,000 live births, 2000–05

1	Japan	3.3
2	Sweden	3.4
3	Finland	4.0
4	Hong Kong	4.1
5	Belgium	4.2
6	Iceland	4.5
	Netherlands	4.5
	Norway	4.5
9	Germany	4.6
	Singapore	4.6
11	Austria	4.7
12	Switzerland	4.8
13	Denmark	5.0
	France	5.0
15	Australia	5.2
16	Spain	5.3
17	Canada	5.4
	Czech Republic	5.4
	Italy	5.4
	United Kingdom	5.4
21	Luxembourg	5.6
	Slovenia	5.6
23	Israel	5.9
24	Ireland	6.0
25	Portugal	6.1
26	New Zealand	6.2

Death and diseases

Cancer[a]
%

1	Netherlands	25.3
2	Belgium	24.6
	Canada	24.6
	France	24.6
5	Italy	24.0
6	Australia	23.9
7	United Kingdom	23.6
8	Ireland	22.9
9	Germany	22.7
10	Austria	22.5
	Norway	22.5
12	Singapore	22.3
13	United States	22.2
14	Spain	22.0
15	Israel	21.7
16	Slovenia	21.4
17	Hungary	21.2
18	Sweden	21.0
19	Costa Rica	20.7
20	Chile	19.9

Heart attack[a]
%

1	Azerbaijan	44.8
2	Lithuania	38.4
3	Macedonia	36.8
4	Austria	36.5
5	Estonia	34.6
6	Sweden	33.7
7	Israel	32.8
8	United States	32.7
9	Argentina	32.3
	Finland	32.3
11	Germany	32.1
12	Ireland	31.9
13	Australia	31.7
14	Kazakhstan	31.6
15	Moldova	31.4
16	Latvia	30.9
	Romania	30.9
18	Greece	30.6
19	Cuba	29.9
20	Mauritius	29.4
	Norway	29.4

Infectious disease[a]
%

1	Ecuador	6.7
2	Venezuela	4.8
3	Tajikistan	4.1
4	Argentina	3.4
5	Mexico	3.3
6	Kazakhstan	2.6
	Singapore	2.6
8	Chile	2.5
9	Azerbaijan	2.3
	Kirgizstan	2.3
11	Colombia	2.2
12	Costa Rica	2.0
13	Mauritius	1.8
14	Cuba	1.6
	Israel	1.6
16	France	1.4
	United States	1.4
18	Trinidad & Tobago	1.3
19	Latvia	1.2
	Russia	1.2

Motor accident[a]
%

1	Ecuador	2.1
2	Venezuela	2.0
3	Costa Rica	1.9
4	Colombia	1.7
	Greece	1.7
	Latvia	1.7
	Portugal	1.7
8	Estonia	1.5
	Mexico	1.5
	Slovenia	1.5
11	Cuba	1.4
	Mauritius	1.4
13	Lithuania	1.3
	Poland	1.3
	Russia	1.3
16	United States	1.2
17	Belgium	1.1
	Chile	1.1
	France	1.1
	Hungary	1.1
	Italy	1.1
	Moldova	1.1
	Spain	1.1

a Data refer to the chances a newborn baby has of eventually dying from one of the causes shown. Statistics are available for only a limited number of countries and many less developed countries are excluded. Latest available.

Measles immunisation

Lowest % of children under 12 months[b]

1	Congo-Brazzaville	23.0
2	Somalia	26.0
3	Ethiopia	27.0
4	Chad	29.7
5	North Korea	34.0
6	Niger	35.5
7	Central African Rep	39.0
8	Afghanistan	40.0
9	Nigeria	40.5
10	Togo	43.0
11	Angola	46.0
12	India	50.0
13	Guinea	52.0
14	Sudan	52.7
15	Burkina Faso	53.0
16	Uganda	53.1
17	Pakistan	54.0
18	Gabon	54.8
19	Madagascar	55.1
20	Cambodia	55.4

DPT[a] immunisation

Lowest % of children under 12 months[b]

1	Somalia	18.0
2	Chad	20.7
3	Ethiopia	21.0
4	Angola	22.0
5	Nigeria	26.3
6	Niger	28.1
7	Congo-Brazzaville	29.0
8	Central African Rep	33.0
9	Afghanistan	35.0
10	Gabon	37.0
	North Korea	37.0
12	Guinea-Bissau	37.8
13	Mauritania	39.9
14	Togo	41.0
15	Burkina Faso	42.0
16	Haiti	43.0
17	Guinea	46.0
	Sierra Leone	46.0
19	Cameroon	48.0
20	Cambodia	48.8

AIDS

Cases per 100,000 population[c]

1	Namibia	1,485.3	21	Trinidad & Tobago	261.5
2	Congo-Brazzaville	1,346.7	22	Ghana	245.7
3	Bahamas	1,150.7	23	Uganda	239.7
4	Lesotho	719.4	24	Jamaica	215.2
5	Bermuda	667.7	25	Guadeloupe	189.0
6	Botswana	660.5	26	Central African Rep	188.8
7	Zimbabwe	592.2	27	Eritrea	187.8
8	Malawi	535.6	28	Honduras	183.7
9	Swaziland	517.5	29	Chad	169.8
10	Barbados	449.1	30	Congo	167.0
11	Gabon	440.9	31	Ethiopia	159.5
12	Zambia	431.3	32	Spain	152.9
13	Burundi	399.0	33	Burkina Faso	148.1
14	Tanzania	371.3	34	Mozambique	136.8
15	Côte d'Ivoire	349.4	35	Suriname	131.9
16	Rwanda	296.9	36	Cameroon	127.6
17	Thailand	289.0	37	Brazil	126.6
18	United States	284.6	38	Panama	123.5
19	Togo	266.1	39	Martinique	113.8
20	Kenya	265.7	40	Haiti	109.3

a Diptheria, whooping cough (pertussis) and tetanus.
b 1999 or latest year.
c AIDS data refer to the total number of cases reported to the World Health Organisation up to November 25 2001. The number of cases diagnosed and reported depends on the quality of medical practice and administration and is likely to be under-recorded in a number of countries.

Health

Highest health spending
As % of GDP[a]

1	United States	12.9
2	Nicaragua	12.5
3	Lebanon	12.2
4	Germany	10.5
5	Switzerland	10.4
6	Israel	9.5
7	Colombia	9.4
8	Canada	9.3
	France	9.3
	Uruguay	9.3
11	Norway	9.2
12	Belgium	8.8
13	Iceland	8.7
	Netherlands	8.7
15	Australia	8.6
	Honduras	8.6
17	Argentina	8.4
	Denmark	8.4
	Greece	8.4
	United Arab Emirates	8.4
21	Austria	8.2
	Italy	8.2
23	New Zealand	8.1
	Zimbabwe	8.1
25	Jordan	8.0
26	Sweden	7.9
27	Kenya	7.8
28	Portugal	7.7
29	Slovenia	7.6
30	Panama	7.3

Lowest health spending
As % of GDP[a]

1	Indonesia	1.6
2	Myanmar	1.8
3	Antigua and Barbuda	1.9
4	Madagascar	2.1
5	Laos	2.5
	Malaysia	2.5
	Syrian Arab Republic	2.5
8	Niger	2.6
	Togo	2.6
10	Belize	2.7
11	Georgia	2.8
	Nigeria	2.8
13	Chad	2.9
14	Central African Republic	3.0
	Tanzania	3.0
16	Gabon	3.1
17	Papua New Guinea	3.2
	Singapore	3.2
19	Albania	3.3
	Benin	3.3
21	Mauritius	3.4
22	Mozambique	3.5
	Oman	3.5
	Sri Lanka	3.5
	Swaziland	3.5
26	Algeria	3.6
	Bangladesh	3.6
	Ecuador	3.6
	Philippines	3.6

Highest population per doctor
Latest available year

1	Niger	33,333
2	Nepal	25,000
3	Papua New Guinea	14,286
4	Senegal	11,111
5	Yemen	5,000
6	Cambodia	3,333
	Myanmar	3,333
8	Sri Lanka	2,500
9	Vietnam	2,000
	West Bank and Gaza	2,000
11	Iraq	1,667
12	Costa Rica	1,111
13	Algeria	1,000
14	Turkey	833
15	Albania	769
	Oman	769
	South Korea	769
	Syria	769
19	Bosnia	714
20	Singapore	613
21	China	595
22	Mexico	588
23	Romania	556
	United Kingdom	556
25	Japan	526
26	Tajikistan	500
27	Canada	476
28	Croatia	435
	Ireland	435
	New Zealand	435
	Poland	435
	Slovenia	435

Most hospital beds
Beds per 1,000 pop.

1	Switzerland	18.1	31	New Zealand	6.2
2	Japan	16.4	32	Israel	6.0
3	Iceland	14.8	33	Slovenia	5.7
4	Norway	14.4	34	Italy	5.5
5	Belarus	12.2		South Korea	5.5
6	Russia	12.1	36	Malta	5.4
7	Moldova	12.0	37	Grenada	5.3
8	Ukraine	11.8	38	Cuba	5.1
9	Netherlands	11.3		Poland	5.1
10	Latvia	10.3		Trinidad and Tobago	5.1
11	Azerbaijan	9.7	41	Greece	5.0
12	Kirgizstan	9.5	42	Georgia	4.8
13	Germany	9.3	43	Macedonia	4.7
14	Lithuania	9.2	44	Denmark	4.5
15	Austria	8.7	45	Uruguay	4.4
	Czech Republic	8.7	46	Libya	4.3
17	Bulgaria	8.6	47	Canada	4.1
18	Australia	8.5		United Kingdom	4.1
	France	8.5	49	Portugal	4.0
	Kazakhstan	8.5	50	Bahamas	3.9
21	Uzbekistan	8.4		Spain	3.9
22	Hungary	8.3	52	Ireland	3.7
23	Luxembourg	8.0		Suriname	3.7
24	Barbados	7.6		Sweden	3.7
	Romania	7.6	55	United States	3.6
26	Finland	7.5	56	Argentina	3.3
27	Estonia	7.4		Puerto Rico	3.3
28	Belgium	7.3	58	Albania	3.2
29	Slovakia	7.1	59	Brazil	3.1
30	Netherlands Antilles	6.5	60	Bahrain	2.9

Lowest population per doctor
Latest available year

1	Italy	169		Hungary	313
2	Belarus	227		Portugal	313
	Georgia	227	19	Finland	323
4	Russia	238	20	Luxembourg	323
5	Lithuania	250		Netherlands	323
6	Israel	256		Spain	323
7	Belgium	263		Sweden	323
8	Azerbaijan	278		Uzbekistan	323
9	Bulgaria	286	25	Austria	333
	Germany	286		Czech Republic	333
	Kazakhstan	286		Estonia	333
	Moldova	286		France	333
	Slovakia	286		Kirgizstan	333
14	Switzerland	294		Ukraine	333
15	Denmark	294	31	Latvia	357
16	Armenia	313		Norway	357

a Latest available year.

Till death us do part

Highest marriage rates[a]
Number of marriages per 1,000 population

#	Country	Rate	#	Country	Rate
1	Bermuda	15.7	33	Nicaragua	6.3
2	Barbados	13.5	34	Réunion	6.2
3	Cyprus	11.1	35	Brunei	6.1
	Iraq	11.1		Japan	6.1
5	United Kingdom	10.6	37	Kazakhstan	6.0
6	Egypt	10.1		Kirgizstan	6.0
7	Fiji	9.9		Malta	6.0
8	Bangladesh	9.7		Moldova	6.0
9	Bahamas	9.3		Mongolia	6.0
	Denmark	9.3		Ukraine	6.0
	Sri Lanka	9.3	43	Romania	5.9
12	Puerto Rico	8.7	44	Croatia	5.8
13	Mauritius	8.6		Turkmenistan	5.8
14	United States	8.5	46	Bahrain	5.7
15	Turkey	8.1	47	Greece	5.6
16	Taiwan	7.9		Iceland	5.6
17	Iran	7.8		Trinidad & Tobago	5.6
18	Syria	7.5	50	Algeria	5.5
19	Jamaica	7.4		Ecuador	5.5
20	Belarus	7.1		Suriname	5.5
21	Macedonia	7.0		Uruguay	5.5
22	Australia	6.9	54	Cuba	5.4
	Costa Rica	6.9		Germany	5.4
	Mexico	6.9		Jordan	5.4
	Philippines	6.9		Netherlands	5.4
	Thailand	6.9		Tunisia	5.4
27	Albania	6.8	59	Norway	5.3
28	Indonesia	6.7	60	Netherlands Antilles	5.2
	South Korea	6.7		Spain	5.2
30	China	6.6	62	Chile	5.1
	Portugal	6.6		Guatemala	5.1
32	Singapore	6.5		Macau	5.1

Lowest marriage rates[a]
Number of marriages per 1,000 population

#	Country	Rate	#	Country	Rate
1	Ireland	2.1	11	Estonia	3.5
2	Rwanda	2.7		United Arab Emirates	3.5
3	Qatar	2.9	13	Georgia	3.6
4	Armenia	3.0		Poland	3.6
	Saudi Arabia	3.0	15	Belgium	3.7
6	Malaysia	3.1		Slovenia	3.7
7	Colombia	3.3	17	Argentina	3.8
	Dominican Republic	3.3		Venezuela	3.8
	Latvia	3.3	19	Bulgaria	4.0
10	Panama	3.4		Honduras	4.0

a Latest available year.

Note: Marriage rates refer to registered marriages only and, therefore, reflect the customs surrounding registry and efficiency of administration. The data are based on latest available figures and hence will be affected by the population age structure at the time.

Highest divorce rates[a]
Number of divorces per 1,000 population

1	United States	4.6	33	Romania	1.9
2	Belarus	4.4	34	Iceland	1.8
3	Puerto Rico	3.9		Japan	1.8
4	Bermuda	3.7		Kirgizstan	1.8
5	Cuba	3.5		Luxembourg	1.8
	Ukraine	3.5		Singapore	1.8
7	Lithuania	3.3		Taiwan	1.8
8	Estonia	3.2	40	Hong Kong	1.7
	New Zealand	3.2	41	Egypt	1.6
	United Kingdom	3.2		Portugal	1.6
11	Czech Republic	3.1		Slovakia	1.6
	Russia	3.1	44	Kuwait	1.5
13	Moldova	3.0		South Korea	1.5
14	Australia	2.7		Tajikistan	1.5
15	Belgium	2.6		Uzbekistan	1.5
	Finland	2.6	48	Bahamas	1.4
	Hungary	2.6		Barbados	1.4
	Netherlands Antilles	2.6		Cyprus	1.4
	Switzerland	2.6		Georgia	1.4
20	Denmark	2.5	52	Guadeloupe	1.3
	Latvia	2.5		Jordan	1.3
22	Germany	2.4		Réunion	1.3
	Norway	2.4		Turkmenistan	1.3
24	Sweden	2.3	56	Bahrain	1.2
25	Austria	2.2		Bulgaria	1.2
	Canada	2.2		Dominican Republic	1.2
	Kazakhstan	2.2		Poland	1.2
	Uruguay	2.2	60	Costa Rica	1.1
29	France	2.0		Slovenia	1.1
	Israel	2.0		Thailand	1.1
	Netherlands	2.0		Tunisia	1.1
	Suriname	2.0		United Arab Emirates	1.1

Lowest divorce rates[a]
Number of divorces per 1,000 population

1	Colombia	0.2	16	Azerbaijan	0.7
	Guatemala	0.2		Ecuador	0.7
	Honduras	0.2		Iran	0.7
	Nicaragua	0.2		Martinique	0.7
	Sri Lanka	0.2		Mauritius	0.7
6	Jamaica	0.3		Panama	0.7
7	Armenia	0.4		Qatar	0.7
	Bosnia	0.4		Syria	0.7
	El Salvador	0.4	24	Albania	0.8
	Macedonia	0.4		Brazil	0.8
	Mongolia	0.4		Brunei	0.8
12	Chile	0.5		Iraq	0.8
	Mexico	0.5		Italy	0.8
14	Libya	0.6		Spain	0.8
	Turkey	0.6			

Households and prices

Biggest households[a]
Population per dwelling

1	Saudi Arabia	7.6		27	Bangladesh	5.4
2	Gabon	7.1			Central African Rep	5.4
3	Bosnia	6.5			Guinea	5.4
	Pakistan	6.5			India	5.4
5	Algeria	6.4			Laos	5.4
6	United Arab Emirates	6.3			Sri Lanka	5.4
7	Congo-Brazzaville	6.1		33	Fiji	5.3
	North Korea	6.1			Gambia, The	5.3
	Sudan	6.1			Guinea-Bissau	5.3
	Swaziland	6.1			Iran	5.3
11	Jordan	6.0			Morocco	5.3
	Kuwait	6.0			Tanzania	5.3
	Togo	6.0			Uganda	5.3
14	Burundi	5.8		40	Chad	5.2
	Niger	5.8			Iraq	5.2
	Papua New Guinea	5.8			Kirgizstan	5.2
	Réunion	5.8		43	Afghanistan	5.1
	Rwanda	5.8			Haiti	5.1
	Uzbekistan	5.8			Madagascar	5.1
20	Ghana	5.7			Netherlands Antilles	5.1
	Malawi	5.7			Turkmenistan	5.1
	Senegal	5.7		48	Armenia	5.0
	Sierra Leone	5.7			Mauritius	5.0
24	Yemen	5.6			Mongolia	5.0
25	Lesotho	5.5			Panama	5.0
	Mozambique	5.5			Philippines	5.0

Highest cost of living[b]
December 2001, USA=100

1	Japan	137		17	Austria	86
2	Hong Kong	117		18	Finland	84
3	Norway	104			Russia	84
4	Gabon	102		20	Iceland	83
	United Kingdom	102			Jordan	83
6	United States	100		22	Netherlands	82
7	Singapore	98		23	Nigeria	80
8	China	96		24	Bahrain	79
9	France	93		25	Côte d'Ivoire	78
	Israel	93			Germany	78
	Switzerland	93			Sweden	78
12	Denmark	91		28	Venezuela	77
	Taiwan	91		29	Belgium	76
14	Argentina	90			Ireland	76
	Mexico	90			United Arab Emirates	76
	South Korea	90				

a Latest available year.
b The cost of living index shown is compiled by The Economist Intelligence Unit for use
by companies in determining expatriate compensation: it is a comparison of the cost
of maintaining a typical international lifestyle in the country rather than a
comparison of the purchasing power of a citizen of the country. The index is based on
typical urban prices an international executive and family will face abroad. The prices

Smallest households[a]
Population per dwelling

1	Sweden	2.0			Portugal	2.7
2	Denmark	2.1			Slovakia	2.7
3	Finland	2.2		29	Belarus	2.8
	Germany	2.2			Czech Republic	2.8
	Norway	2.2			Russia	2.8
6	Iceland	2.3		32	Cyprus	2.9
	Netherlands	2.3			Greece	2.9
	Switzerland	2.3			Luxembourg	2.9
9	Austria	2.4			Poland	2.9
	Belgium	2.4			Romania	2.9
	Hungary	2.4		37	Slovenia	3.0
	United Kingdom	2.4		38	Malta	3.1
13	Canada	2.5			Myanmar	3.1
	Estonia	2.5		40	Hong Kong	3.2
	France	2.5			Ireland	3.2
	Latvia	2.5			Macau	3.2
	United States	2.5			South Korea	3.3
18	Australia	2.6			Spain	3.3
	Croatia	2.6			Taiwan	3.3
	Italy	2.6		46	Albania	3.4
	Lithuania	2.6			Brazil	3.4
	Ukraine	2.6			Serbia & Montenegro	3.4
	Uruguay	2.6		49	Argentina	3.5
24	Bulgaria	2.7			Israel	3.5
	Japan	2.7			Nicaragua	3.5
	New Zealand	2.7			Singapore	3.5

Lowest cost of living[b]
December 2001, USA=100

1	Iran	28		17	Thailand	54
2	India	39		18	Bangladesh	55
3	Pakistan	41		19	Costa Rica	56
4	Philippines	42			Zambia	56
	Serbia & Montenegro	42		21	Chile	57
6	Libya	43			Czech Republic	57
	Romania	43		23	Colombia	60
8	South Africa	44			Kenya	60
9	Turkey	47			Malaysia	60
10	Paraguay	49			Morocco	60
11	Brazil	50		27	New Zealand	62
	Hungary	50			Poland	62
13	Algeria	52		29	Ukraine	63
	Tunisia	52		30	Croatia	64
15	Sri Lanka	53			Senegal	64
	Uzbekistan	53				

are for products of international comparable quality found in a supermarket or department store. Prices found in local markets and bazaars are not used unless the available merchandise is of the specified quality and the shopping area itself is safe for executive and family members. New York City prices are used as the base, so United States = 100.

Consumer goods: *ownership*

TV
Colour TVs per 100 households

1	Taiwan	99.4	26	Norway	91.7
2	United States	99.3	27	Australia	91.4
3	Belgium	99.2		Jordan	91.4
	Hong Kong	99.2	29	Greece	91.0
	Ireland	99.2	30	Venezuela	90.4
6	Japan	99.1	31	Malaysia	90.3
7	Canada	98.7	32	Slovenia	89.4
8	Singapore	98.5	33	Mexico	88.7
9	Netherlands	98.3	34	Argentina	88.1
10	Spain	98.2	35	Hungary	87.9
	United Kingdom	98.2	36	Slovakia	87.7
12	Finland	98.1	37	Kuwait	87.4
13	Austria	97.7	38	Czech Republic	87.1
	Saudi Arabia	97.7	39	Tunisia	86.4
15	Portugal	97.4	40	Croatia	86.3
16	Sweden	97.3	41	Brazil	86.1
17	Switzerland	97.2	42	Colombia	84.8
18	Germany	97.0	43	Estonia	84.0
	New Zealand	97.0	44	Poland	82.4
20	France	95.9	45	Thailand	80.2
21	United Arab Emirates	95.4	46	Russia	79.8
22	Israel	95.1	47	Belarus	78.2
23	Italy	94.9	48	Ukraine	73.7
24	South Korea	92.5	49	Lithuania	72.0
25	Denmark	92.1	50	Algeria	68.6

Telephone
Telephone lines per 100 people

1	Bermuda	87.2	23	Israel	47.6
2	Luxembourg	78.3		South Korea	47.6
3	Sweden	73.9	25	Singapore	47.2
4	Denmark	72.3	26	Italy	47.1
5	Norway	72.0		New Zealand	47.1
6	Switzerland	71.8	28	Austria	46.8
7	United States	66.5	29	Barbados	46.3
8	Iceland	66.4	30	Guadeloupe	44.9
9	Cyprus	64.3	31	Spain	43.1
10	Germany	63.5	32	Martinique	43.0
11	Netherlands	62.1	33	Portugal	42.4
12	Japan	59.7	34	Slovenia	40.1
13	Hong Kong	58.1	35	Bahamas	40.0
14	United Kingdom	57.8	36	United Arab Emirates	39.7
15	France	57.4	37	Macau	39.4
16	Taiwan	57.3	38	Czech Republic	37.4
17	Finland	54.8		Hungary	37.4
18	Malta	53.0	40	Croatia	36.5
19	Greece	52.9	41	Bulgaria	35.9
20	Australia	52.0	42	Estonia	35.2
21	Belgium	49.3	43	Aruba	35.0
22	Ireland	48.5	44	Puerto Rico	33.6

Video cassette recorder

VCRs per 100 households

1	Canada	90.3	13	Switzerland	74.4
2	United Kingdom	86.7	14	Belgium	74.3
3	Denmark	83.7	15	Hong Kong	72.6
4	United States	83.2	16	Finland	68.8
5	New Zealand	80.6	17	South Korea	67.9
6	Singapore	79.8	18	Italy	67.5
7	Ireland	79.5	19	Malaysia	66.8
8	Netherlands	78.1	20	Israel	66.3
8	Sweden	78.1	21	Germany	65.9
10	Australia	78.0	22	Spain	65.5
11	Japan	77.2	23	France	60.5
12	Poland	75.4	24	Austria	58.6

Computer

Computers per 100 people

1	United States	62.3	18	Japan	34.9
2	Sweden	56.1	19	Belgium	34.5
3	Australia	51.7	20	France	33.7
4	Luxembourg	51.5	21	Germany	33.6
5	Norway	50.8	22	Austria	28.0
	Singapore	50.8	23	Slovenia	27.6
7	Switzerland	50.0	24	Cyprus	25.1
8	Bermuda	49.5		South Korea	25.1
9	Denmark	43.2	26	Israel	24.6
10	Netherlands	42.9	27	Malta	23.0
11	Finland	42.4	28	Taiwan	22.3
12	Iceland	41.8	29	Guadeloupe	21.7
13	Ireland	39.1	30	Italy	19.5
14	Canada	39.0	31	Macau	17.9
15	New Zealand	38.6	32	Estonia	17.5
16	Hong Kong	38.5	33	Spain	16.8
17	United Kingdom	36.6	34	Qatar	16.4

Mobile telephone

Subscribers per 100 people

1	Luxembourg	96.7	16	Netherlands	73.9
2	Taiwan	96.6	17	Denmark	73.7
3	Hong Kong	84.4	18	Ireland	72.9
4	Italy	83.9	19	Switzerland	72.4
5	Norway	82.5	20	United Arab Emirates	72.0
6	Iceland	82.0	21	Martinique	71.5
7	Israel	80.8	22	Singapore	69.2
8	Austria	80.7	23	Germany	68.3
9	United Kingdom	78.3	24	Czech Republic	65.9
10	Finland	77.8	25	Spain	65.5
11	Portugal	77.4	26	Guadeloupe	63.6
12	Sweden	77.1	27	New Zealand	62.1
13	Slovenia	75.9	28	South Korea	60.8
14	Greece	75.1	29	France	60.5
15	Belgium	74.7	30	Australia	57.8

Books and newspapers

Book sales

	$m				Per head, $	
1	United States	26,165		1	Japan	182
2	Japan	23,111		2	Norway	115
3	Germany	8,334		3	Germany	102
4	United Kingdom	4,326		4	Singapore	100
5	Mexico	2,839		5	United States	92
6	China	2,652		6	Finland	81
7	France	2,293		7	Belgium	80
8	Italy	2,194			Switzerland	80
9	Spain	1,997		9	Sweden	74
10	Canada	1,574		10	United Kingdom	73
11	Australia	1,078		11	Denmark	61
12	Belgium	812		12	New Zealand	59
13	South Korea	794		13	Australia	56
14	India	747		14	Canada	51
15	Colombia	712		15	Ireland	50
16	Argentina	683			Spain	50
17	Sweden	648		17	France	39
18	Taiwan	631		18	Italy	38
19	Venezuela	620		19	Austria	37
20	Switzerland	572		20	Portugal	30
21	Norway	515		21	Mexico	29
22	Finland	421		22	Taiwan	28
23	Singapore	400		23	Israel	27
24	Poland	358		24	Venezuela	26
25	Chile	356		25	Chile	23
26	Vietnam	345		26	Netherlands	22
27	Netherlands	344		27	Greece	20
28	South Africa	336		28	Argentina	18
29	Denmark	323		29	Colombia	17
30	Portugal	305			South Korea	17
				31	Czech Republic	16

Daily newspapers

Copies per '000 population, latest year

1	Norway	526	16	Portugal	70
2	Sweden	464	17	Slovakia	65
3	Finland	444	18	Bolivia	62
4	Japan	424	19	India	61
5	Switzerland	319	20	Ecuador	59
6	United Kingdom	312	21	Philippines	49
7	Netherlands	286	22	Brazil	44
8	Denmark	284	23	Pakistan	40
9	Singapore	279	24	Italy	38
10	Thailand	219	25	China	36
11	United States	193	26	Poland	32
12	Belgium	174	27	Colombia	27
13	Canada	169	28	Argentina	26
14	Malaysia	123		Indonesia	26
15	Greece	99	30	South Africa	25

Music and the Internet

Music sales[a]

$m, 2001			$ per head		
1	United States	13,412	1	Norway	48
2	Japan	5,254	2	United States	47
3	United Kingdom	2,809		United Kingdom	47
4	Germany	2,129	4	Japan	41
5	France	1,828	5	Switzerland	38
6	Canada	660	6	Iceland	37
7	Spain	613	7	Denmark	36
8	Mexico	566	8	Ireland	33
9	Italy	525		Sweden	33
10	Australia	523	10	Austria	31
11	Netherlands	436		France	31
12	Brazil	424	12	Australia	27
13	Sweden	287		Netherlands	27
14	Switzerland	274	14	Germany	26
15	South Korea	266	15	Belgium	23
16	Austria	253	16	Finland	22
17	Belgium	233		New Zealand	22
18	India	229	18	Canada	21
19	Russia	223	19	Cyprus	18
20	Norway	216	20	Spain	15
21	Denmark	193	21	Hong Kong	14
22	Taiwan	170	22	Portugal	13

Internet hosts

By country, January 2002			Per 1,000 pop., January 2002		
1	United States[b]	97,635,222	1	United States	344.8
2	Japan	7,118,333	2	Iceland	205.6
3	Canada	2,890,273	3	Finland	181.7
4	Germany	2,681,325	4	Norway	139.9
5	United Kingdom	2,462,915	5	Denmark	133.4
6	Australia	2,288,584	6	Sweden	129.7
7	Italy	2,282,457	7	Netherlands	124.7
8	Netherlands	1,983,102	8	Australia	119.8
9	Taiwan	1,712,539	9	New Zealand	107.4
10	France	1,670,694	10	Canada	93.8
11	Brazil	1,644,575	11	Bermuda	86.0
12	Spain	1,497,450	12	Switzerland	85.3
13	Sweden	1,141,093	13	Austria	81.1
14	Finland	944,670	14	Taiwan	75.8
15	Mexico	918,288	15	Belgium	65.5
16	Denmark	707,141	16	Hong Kong	56.2
17	Belgium	668,508	17	Japan	56.0
18	Austria	657,173	18	Singapore	49.5
19	Poland	654,198	19	Estonia	49.1
20	Norway	629,669	20	Luxembourg	41.8
21	Switzerland	613,918	21	United Kingdom	41.5
22	Argentina	465,359	22	Italy	39.7
23	South Korea	439,859	23	Spain	37.5

a Vinyl, tape and compact disc sales.
b Includes all hosts ending ".com", ".net" and ".org", which exaggerates the numbers.

Nobel prize winners: *1901–2001*

Peace

1	United States	16
2	United Kingdom	11
3	France	9
4	Sweden	5
5	Germany	4
	Belgium	4
7	Norway	3
	South Africa	3
9	Argentina	2
	Austria	2
	Israel	2
	Russia	2
	Switzerland	2

Economics[a]

1	United States	25
2	United Kingdom	8
3	Norway	2
	Sweden	2
5	France	1
	Germany	1
	Netherlands	1
	Russia	1

Literature

1	France	14
2	United States	12
3	United Kingdom	9
4	Germany	7
5	Spain	6
	Sweden	6
7	Italy	5
8	Norway	3
	Poland	3
	Russia	3

Physiology or medicine

1	United States	46
2	United Kingdom	19
3	Germany	14
4	Sweden	7
5	France	6
	Switzerland	6
7	Austria	5
	Denmark	5
9	Belgium	3
	Italy	3

Physics

1	United States	43
2	United Kingdom	19
3	Germany	17
4	France	8
5	Netherlands	6
6	Russia	5
7	Sweden	4
	Switzerland	4
9	Austria	3
	Italy	3
	Japan	3

Chemistry

1	United States	37
2	United Kingdom	22
3	Germany	14
4	France	6
5	Sweden	5
	Switzerland	5
7	Canada	4
8	Japan	3
9	Argentina	1
	Austria	1
	Belgium	1
	Czech Republic	1
	Denmark	1
	Finland	1
	Italy	1
	Netherlands	1
	Norway	1
	Russia	1

a Since 1969.
Prizes by country of residence at time awarded. When prizes have been shared in the same field, one credit given to each country. Only top rankings in each field are included.

Olympic medal winners

Summer games, 1896–2000

		Gold	Silver	Bronze
1	United States	872	659	581
2	Soviet Union[a]	517	423	382
3	Germany	374	392	417
4	France	189	195	216
5	United Kingdom	188	243	232
6	Italy	179	144	155
7	Hungary	150	134	158
8	Sweden	138	157	176
9	Australia	103	110	139
10	Finland	101	81	114
11	Japan	98	97	103
12	China	80	79	64
13	Romania	74	83	108
14	Netherlands	61	66	85
15	Cuba	57	47	41
16	Poland	56	72	113
17	Canada	52	80	99
18	Bulgaria	48	82	65
19	Switzerland	47	74	62
20	Denmark	41	63	58

Winter games, 1924–2002

		Gold	Silver	Bronze
1	Germany	108	105	87
2	Norway	94	94	75
3	Soviet Union[a]	87	63	67
4	United States	69	72	52
5	Finland	42	51	49
6	Austria	41	57	63
7	Sweden	39	30	29
8	Switzerland	32	33	38
9	Italy	31	31	27
10	Canada	31	28	37
11	Russia	27	20	13
12	Netherlands	22	28	19
13	France	22	22	28
14	South Korea	11	5	4
15	Japan	8	10	13
16	United Kingdom	8	4	15
17	Croatia	3	1	0
18	China	2	12	8
19	Czech Republic	2	1	2
20	Australia	2	0	1

a Includes unified team in 1992.

Drinking and smoking

Beer drinkers
Retail sales per head, litres

1	Czech Republic	84.9
2	Austria	79.4
3	Germany	77.6
4	South Africa	76.1
5	Australia	70.4
6	United States	65.5
7	Finland	57.2
8	New Zealand	57.0
9	Netherlands	56.8
10	Venezuela	52.8
11	Slovakia	51.6
12	Denmark	51.3
13	Poland	51.2
14	Canada	49.7
15	Colombia	49.5
16	Sweden	47.3
17	Hungary	45.8
18	Luxembourg	45.3
19	Latvia	44.9
20	Japan	41.6
21	Estonia	39.3
22	Belgium	38.4
23	Norway	37.5

Wine drinkers
Retail sales per head, litres

1	Italy	48.5
2	France	34.4
3	Argentina	32.8
4	Switzerland	29.8
5	Hungary	29.4
6	Denmark	26.6
7	Luxembourg	22.1
8	Slovenia	20.5
9	Greece	20.4
10	Germany	19.9
11	Belgium	18.8
12	Netherlands	17.7
13	New Zealand	17.1
14	Australia	17.0
	Portugal	17.0
16	Spain	16.8
17	Romania	16.5
18	Austria	16.1
19	Chile	15.0
20	United Kingdom	13.8
21	Slovakia	13.6
22	Sweden	12.9
23	Latvia	11.9

Alcoholic drinks
$ per head

1	Ireland	1,254.5
2	United Kingdom	871.5
3	Finland	412.7
4	Norway	384.0
5	Denmark	364.5
6	Sweden	315.7
7	New Zealand	313.4
8	Switzerland	274.7
9	Canada	273.8
10	United States	262.9
11	Germany	235.6
12	Australia	223.0
13	France	196.7
14	Belgium	187.0
15	Austria	182.5
16	Japan	180.9
17	Portugal	164.1
18	Lithuania	157.8
19	Netherlands	157.4
20	Poland	148.6
21	Slovenia	146.0
22	Hungary	134.1
23	South Africa	122.2
24	Russia	110.3

Smokers
Av. ann. consumption of cigarettes per head per day

1	Greece	8.5
2	Bulgaria	7.7
3	Japan	7.0
4	Bosnia	6.4
	Spain	6.4
6	Albania	6.2
	Slovenia	6.2
8	Cyprus	5.9
	South Korea	5.9
10	Russia	5.8
11	Hungary	5.6
	Latvia	5.6
	Switzerland	5.6
14	Poland	5.3
15	Macedonia	5.2
16	Austria	5.1
17	Belgium	5.0
	Taiwan	5.0
19	Belarus	4.8
	Ireland	4.8
	Turkey	4.8
22	Germany	4.7
	Italy	4.7

Crime and punishment

Serious assault[a]

No. per 100,000 pop., 1999

1	Australia	708.5
2	Dominican Republic	682.4
3	South Africa	595.6
4	Namibia	533.6
5	Israel	491.8
6	Swaziland	471.7
7	Ghana	418.9
8	Lebanon	209.7
9	Zimbabwe	198.4
10	Tunisia	165.0
11	France	162.7
12	Uruguay	162.5
13	Barbados	161.9
14	Lesotho	156.9
15	Canada	140.2
16	Germany	139.6
17	Hong Kong	117.1
18	Rwanda	114.3
19	Turkey	112.0
20	Puerto Rico	101.8

Theft[a]

No. per 100,000 pop., 1999

1	Denmark	7,687.6
2	Australia	6,215.0
3	Dominican Republic	4,779.3
4	Norway	4,577.1
5	Canada	3,968.9
6	Germany	3,894.4
7	Switzerland	3,886.4
8	France	3,849.2
9	South Africa	3,407.2
10	Iceland	3,374.9
11	Luxembourg	3,079.9
12	Estonia	2,917.0
13	Austria	2,649.5
14	Finland	2,618.5
15	Hungary	2,591.0
16	Puerto Rico	2,214.3
17	Barbados	2,182.5
18	Swaziland	1,954.7
19	Zimbabwe	1,827.6
20	Slovenia	1,803.2

Prisoners

Total prison pop., latest available year

1	United States	2,071,686
2	China	1,428,126
3	Russia	977,700
4	India	381,147
5	Brazil	233,859
6	Ukraine	219,955
7	Thailand	217,697
8	South Africa	176,588
9	Iran	158,000
10	Mexico	144,261
11	Rwanda	143,021
12	Kazakhstan	84,000
13	Poland	80,004
14	Germany	79,348
15	Pakistan	78,938
16	United Kingdom	76,958
17	Turkey	71,860
18	Philippines	70,383
19	Uzbekistan	63,900
20	Indonesia	62,886
21	South Korea	62,732
22	Japan	61,242

Per 100,000 pop., latest available year

1	United States	732
2	Russia	676
3	Belarus	554
4	Kazakhstan	522
5	Bahamas	478
6	Bermuda	447
7	Suriname	437
8	Ukraine	436
9	Kirgizstan	426
10	South Africa	403
11	Botswana	396
12	Puerto Rico	372
13	Latvia	368
14	Netherlands Antilles	364
15	Singapore	359
16	Trinidad & Tobago	351
17	Thailand	342
18	Estonia	337
19	Azerbaijan	323
20	Lithuania	303
	Panama	303
22	Cuba	297

a Crime statistics are based on offences recorded by the police. The number will therefore depend partly on the efficiency of police administration systems, the definition of offences, and the proportion of crimes reported, and therefore may not be strictly comparable.

Stars...

Space missions
Firsts and selected events

1957 Man-made satellite
Dog in space, Laika

1961 Human in space, Yuri Gagarin
Entire day in space, Gherman Titov

1963 Woman in space, Valentina Tereshkova

1964 Space crew, one pilot and two passengers

1965 Space walk, Alexei Leonov
Computer guidance system
Eight days in space achieved (needed to travel to moon and back)

1966 Docking between space craft and target vehicle
Autopilot re-entry and landing

1968 Live television broadcast from space
Moon orbit

1969 Astronaut transfer from one craft to another in space
Moon landing

1971 Space station, Salyut
Drive on the moon

1973 Space laboratory, Skylab

1978 Non-Amercian, non-Soviet, Vladimir Remek (Czechoslovakia)

1982 Space shuttle, Columbia (first craft to carry four crew members)

1983 Five crew mission

1984 Space walk, untethered
Capture, repair and redeployment of satellite in space
Seven crew mission

1986 Space shuttle explosion, Challenger
Mir space station activated

1990 Hubble telescope deployed

2001 Dennis Tito, first paying space tourist

Astronauts
Longest time in space, hours

United States		Yuri Ramanenko	10,344
John Blaha	3,864	Alexandr Volkov	9,384
Norman Thagard	3,360	Leonid Kizim	9,024
Andrew Thomas	3,268	**Other nations**	
David Wolf	3,216	Jean-Loup Chrétien	784
Edward Gibson	2,017	Ulf Merbold	441
William Pogue	2,017	Pedro Duque	381
Russia		Claude Andre-Deshays	379
Musa Manarov	12,984	Jean-François Clervoy	262
Sergi Krikalev	11,064		

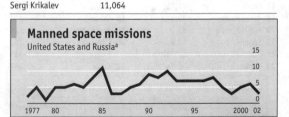

Manned space missions
United States and Russia[a]

15
10
5
0

1977   80   85   90   95   2000 02

...and Wars

Defence spending
As % of GDP

1	Eritrea	31.5	22	Cambodia	6.1
2	Angola	19.2		Sudan	6.1
3	North Korea	13.9		Zimbabwe	6.1
4	Afghanistan	13.0	25	United Arab Emirates	5.9
5	Qatar	11.7	26	Brunei	5.8
6	Saudi Arabia	10.1		Pakistan	5.8
7	Oman	10.0	28	Bhutan	5.6
	Serbia & Montenegro	10.0		Burundi	5.6
9	Kuwait	9.8		Liberia	5.6
10	Iraq	9.7		Syria	5.6
11	Israel	8.9		Taiwan	5.6
12	Congo-Brazzaville	8.4	33	Botswana	5.5
13	Armenia	8.0	34	China	5.3
	Uzbekistan	8.0		Sri Lanka	5.3
15	Yemen	7.8	36	Turkey	5.2
16	Iran	7.5	37	Morocco	5.1
17	Jordan	6.9	38	Russia	5.0
18	Algeria	6.8	39	Greece	4.9
	Ethiopia	6.8		Singapore	4.9
20	Tajikistan	6.5	41	Cyprus	4.8
21	Bahrain	6.4	42	Rwanda	4.7

Armed forces
'000

		Regulars	Reserves			Regulars	Reserves
1	China	2,810.0	600.0	20	Indonesia	297.0	400.0
2	Russia	1,520.0	2,400.0	21	France	294.4	419.0
3	United States	1,365.8	1,211.5	22	Brazil	287.6	1,115.0
4	India	1,303.0	528.4	23	Italy	250.6	65.2
5	North Korea	1,055.0	4,700.0	24	Japan	236.7	49.2
6	South Korea	683.0	4,500.0	25	Germany	221.1	364.3
7	Pakistan	612.0	513.0	26	Poland	217.3	406.0
8	Turkey	609.7	378.7	27	United Kingdom	212.5	302.8
9	Iran	513.0	350.0	28	Romania	207.0	470.0
10	Vietnam	484.0	3,000.0	29	Saudi Arabia	201.5	20.0
11	Egypt	448.5	254.0	30	Eritrea	200.0	120.0
12	Iraq	429.0	650.0	31	Morocco	198.5	150.0
13	Afghanistan	400.0		32	Mexico	192.8	300.0
14	Taiwan	370.0	1,657.5	33	Israel	172.5	400.0
15	Ethiopia	352.5		34	Spain	166.0	447.9
16	Myanmar	343.8		35	Greece	159.2	291.0
17	Syria	316.0	396.0	36	Colombia	152.0	60.7
18	Ukraine	303.8	1,000.0	37	Cambodia	140.0	
19	Thailand	301.0	200.0	38	Bangladesh	137.0	
				39	Algeria	124.0	150.0
				40	Peru	115.0	188.0

a Previously Soviet Union; United States only from 1994; up to May 2002.

Environment

Environmental sustainability index[a]

Highest			Lowest		
1	Finland	73.9	1	Kuwait	23.9
2	Norway	73.0	2	United Arab Emirates	25.7
3	Sweden	72.6	3	North Korea	32.3
4	Canada	70.6	4	Iraq	33.2
5	Switzerland	66.5	5	Saudi Arabia	34.2
6	Uruguay	66.0	6	Haiti	34.8
7	Austria	64.2	7	Ukraine	35.0
8	Iceland	63.9	8	South Korea	35.9
9	Costa Rica	63.2	9	Sierra Leone	36.5
10	Latvia	63.0	10	Nigeria	36.7
11	Hungary	62.7	11	Somalia	37.1
12	Croatia	62.5	12	Turkmenistan	37.3
13	Botswana	61.8	13	Liberia	37.7
14	Slovakia	61.6	14	China	38.5
15	Argentina	61.5	15	Guinea-Bissau	38.8
16	Australia	60.3		Madagascar	38.8
17	Estonia	60.0	17	Mauritania	38.9
	Panama	60.0	18	Belgium	39.1
19	New Zealand	59.9	19	Libya	39.3
20	Brazil	59.6	20	Niger	39.4

Sulphur dioxide emissions
'000 tons per populated sq km

1	Belgium	21.39	12	Netherlands	4.19
2	South Korea	19.43	13	Egypt	4.09
3	Jamaica	17.05	14	Poland	3.90
4	Czech Republic	7.98	15	Israel	3.31
5	North Korea	7.64	16	Libya	3.22
6	Kuwait	7.12	17	Denmark	2.86
7	United Kingdom	5.37	18	Australia	2.84
8	Germany	5.10	19	Canada	2.79
9	Slovakia	4.85		Italy	2.79
10	Bulgaria	4.61	21	Jordan	2.71
11	Chile	4.38	22	China	2.68

Carbon dioxide emissions
Tons of carbon per person

1	United Arab Emirates	10.23	12	Finland	2.82
2	Kuwait	7.40	13	Denmark	2.76
3	United States	5.43	14	Germany	2.75
4	Australia	4.88		Israel	2.75
5	Trinidad	4.76	16	Belgium	2.73
6	Canada	4.17	17	Russia	2.66
7	Saudi Arabia	3.83	18	North Korea	2.64
8	Estonia	3.25	19	United Kingdom	2.51
9	Czech Republic	3.14	20	Japan	2.45
10	Netherlands	2.85	21	South Africa	2.38
11	Ireland	2.84	22	Oman	2.32

a Based on 20 key indicators, including: environmental systems and stresses; human
  vulnerability to environmental risks; institutional capacities on environmental issues;
  shared resources

Fertiliser consumption
Hundreds of grams per hectare of arable land

1	Iceland	31,000	15	Vietnam	3,416
2	Costa Rica	8,796	16	Lebanon	3,360
3	Switzerland	7,928	17	United Kingdom	3,325
4	United Arab Emirates	7,900	18	Slovenia	3,316
5	Malaysia	7,726	19	Japan	3,131
6	Ireland	5,210	20	Colombia	3,016
7	Netherlands	5,132	21	China	2,826
8	South Korea	5,117	22	Sri Lanka	2,683
9	New Zealand	4,254	23	France	2,631
10	Egypt	3,926	24	Papua New Guinea	2,500
11	Oman	3,750	25	Germany	2,474
12	Belgium	3,744	26	Norway	2,258
13	Kuwait	3,500	27	Chile	2,256
14	Israel	3,450	28	Italy	2,104

Petrol prices
Litre of premium gasoline, ratio to world average

Highest			Lowest		
1	Uruguay	1.95	1	Turkmenistan	0.03
2	United Kingdom	1.92	2	Iraq	0.05
3	Israel	1.87	3	Iran	0.08
4	Argentina	1.75	4	Venezuela	0.20
5	Finland	1.74	5	Indonesia	0.28
	Japan	1.74	6	Ghana	0.33
7	Iceland	1.72	7	Kuwait	0.34
8	Netherlands	1.69	8	Saudi Arabia	0.39
9	Burundi	1.66	9	Libya	0.41
	Denmark	1.66		United Arab Emirates	0.41
11	Zambia	1.64	11	Egypt	0.43
12	Central African Rep	1.62	12	Algeria	0.44
	France	1.62		Nigeria	0.44
14	Italy	1.59	14	Malaysia	0.46
15	Belgium	1.57		Sudan	0.46
16	Sweden	1.54	16	Angola	0.49
17	Brazil	1.51	17	Ecuador	0.51
18	South Korea	1.51		Oman	0.51
19	Germany	1.49	19	Russia	0.54
20	North Korea	1.46	20	Kazakhstan	0.59
	Rwanda	1.46	21	Philippines	0.61
22	Turkey	1.44		Ukraine	0.61
23	Uganda	1.41	23	Mongolia	0.62
24	Guinea	1.39		Vietnam	0.62
	Zimbabwe	1.39	25	Thailand	0.64
26	Austria	1.34		Trinidad & Tobago	0.64
	Morocco	1.34	27	China	0.66
	Sierra Leone	1.34	28	Laos	0.67
29	Hungary	1.33	29	Belarus	0.68
30	Bolivia	1.31	30	Botswana	0.69
	Peru	1.31			

Land area under protected status

Highest, %		Lowest, %	
1 Venezuela	60.72	1 Kuwait	1.04
2 Saudi Arabia	34.17	2 Liberia	1.16
3 Zambia	30.09	3 Turkey	1.20
4 Austria	29.23	4 Ukraine	1.34
5 Tanzania	27.74	5 Papua New Guinea	1.49
6 Germany	25.24	6 Moldova	1.50
7 Denmark	23.96	7 Uzbekistan	1.83
8 New Zealand	23.84	8 Madagascar	2.07
9 Slovakia	21.64	9 Sierra Leone	2.12
10 Bhutan	21.40	10 Philippines	2.17
11 Uganda	20.78	11 Algeria	2.44
12 United States	20.13	12 Russia	2.46
13 Guatemala	19.90	13 North Korea	2.58
14 Costa Rica	19.21	14 Gabon	2.70
15 Panama	19.08	Kazakhstan	2.70
16 Chile	18.74	16 Belgium	2.81
17 Switzerland	18.04	17 Vietnam	2.93
18 United Kingdom	17.73	18 Jordan	3.10

Mammals under threat

% of species threatened

1 New Zealand	80.00	10 South Korea	26.53
2 Iceland	54.55	11 Papua New Guinea	26.13
3 Cuba	35.48	12 Dominican Republic	25.00
4 Madagascar	35.46	13 Australia	24.23
5 Philippines	31.65	14 United Kingdom	24.00
6 Indonesia	30.63	15 Chile	23.08
7 Spain	29.27	16 Sri Lanka	22.73
8 India	27.22	17 Jamaica	20.83
9 Portugal	26.98	18 Romania	20.24

Environmental quality of life

Highest cities, New York = 100		Lowest cities, New York = 100	
1 Calgary, Canada	166.0	1 Mexico city, Mexico	29.5
2 Honolulu, US	161.5	2 Baku, Azerbaijan	31.5
3 Helsinki, Finland	158.0	3 Dacca, Bangladesh	35.0
Katsuyama, Japan	158.0	4 Bombay, India	41.5
5 Minneapolis, US	154.0	5 Almaty, Kazakhstan	44.5
Ottawa, Canada	154.0	6 New Delhi, India	50.0
7 Victoria, Seychelles	152.5	7 Antananarivo, Madag.	52.0
Wellington, New Zea.	152.5	8 Novosibirsk, Russia	52.5
9 Auckland, New Zea.	150.0	9 Belgrade, Yugoslavia	53.0
10 Kobe, Japan	149.5	10 Bangkok, Thailand	58.0
Omuta, Japan	149.5	Rayong, Thailand	58.0
Oslo, Norway	149.5	12 Quito, Ecuador	60.0
Perth, Australia	149.5	13 Port au Prince, Haiti	61.0
Stockholm, Sweden	149.5	14 Bangalore, India	62.0
Tsukuba, Japan	149.5	15 Ndjamena, Chad	62.5
Zurich, Switzerland	149.5	16 Bamako, Mali	64.0

Country
profiles

ALGERIA

Area	2,381,741 sq km	Capital	Algiers
Arable as % of total land	3	Currency	Algerian dinar (AD)

People

Population	30.3m	Life expectancy: men		68.7 yrs
Pop. per sq km	13		women	71.8 yrs
Av. ann. growth		Adult literacy		66.7%
in pop. 1995–2000	1.82%	Fertility rate (per woman)		2.79
Pop. under 15	34.8%	Urban population		60.3%
Pop. over 65	4.1%			per 1,000 pop.
No. of men per 100 women	103	Crude birth rate		23.5
Human Development Index	69.3	Crude death rate		5.3

The economy

GDP	AD4,012bn	GDP per head	$1,750
GDP	$53.3bn	GDP per head in purchasing	
Av. ann. growth in real		power parity (USA=100)	14.8
GDP 1990–2000	1.6%	Economic freedom index	3.10

Origins of GDP[a]		**Components of GDP**[a]	
	% of total		% of total
Agriculture	11.7	Private consumption	28.7
Industry, of which:	47.7	Public consumption	20.9
manufacturing	4.3	Investment	18.7
Services	40.6	Exports	44.3
		Imports	-13.6

Structure of employment[b]

	% of total		% of labour force
Agriculture	25	Unemployed 1997	28.0
Industry	26	Av. ann. rate 1990–97	24.5
Services	49		

Energy

	m TCE		
Total output	206.1	% output exported	70.8
Total consumption	53.4	% consumption imported	2.1
Consumption per head,			
kg coal equivalent	1,774		

Inflation and finance

Consumer price		*av. ann. increase 1995–2000*	
inflation 2001	3.5%	Narrow money (M1)	14.9%
Av. ann. inflation 1996–2001	3.2%	Broad money	15.7%
Money market rate, 2001	3.35%		

Exchange rates

	end 2001		December 2001
AD per $	77.82	Effective rates	1995 = 100
AD per SDR	97.80	– nominal	88.54
AD per euro	69.69	– real	113.94

Trade

Principal exports		Principal imports	
	$bn fob		*$bn cif*
Other energy & products	9.4	Capital goods	2.8
Natural gas	6.8	Food	2.4
Crude oil	4.8		
Total including others	**21.7**	Total incl. others	**9.3**

Main export destinations[a]		Main origins of imports[a]	
	% of total		*% of total*
Italy	21.6	France	32.0
France	11.7	Italy	9.0
United States	11.7	Germany	6.4
Spain	9.9	Spain	5.7

Balance of payments, reserves and debt, $bn

Visible exports fob	21.7	Overall balance[c]	1.2
Visible imports fob	-9.3	Change in reserves	7.4
Trade balance	12.3	Level of reserves	
Invisibles inflows	1.3	end Dec.	13.6
Invisibles outflows	-5.5	No. months of import cover	11.0
Net transfers	0.8	Foreign debt	25.0
Current account balance	8.9	– as % of GDP	54
– as % of GDP	16.7	Debt service paid	4.5
Capital balance[c]	-2.3	Debt service ratio	27

Health and education

Health spending, % of GDP	3.6	Education spending, % of GDP	6.0
Doctors per 1,000 pop.	1.0	Enrolment, %: primary	109
Hospital beds per 1,000 pop.	2.1	secondary	67
Improved-water source access,		tertiary	15
% of pop.	94		

Society

No. of households	4.6m	Colour TVs per 100 households	68.6
Av. no. per household	6.4	Telephone lines per 100 pop.	6.0
Marriages per 1,000 pop.	5.5	Mobile telephone subscribers	
Divorces per 1,000 pop.	...	per 100 pop.	0.3
Cost of living, Dec. 2001		Computers per 100 pop.	0.7
New York = 100	52	Internet hosts per 1,000 pop.	...

a 1999
b 1996
c 1997

ARGENTINA

Area	2,766,889 sq km	Capital	Buenos Aires
Arable as % of total land	9	Currency	Peso (P)

People

Population	37.0m	Life expectancy: men	70.6 yrs
Pop. per sq km	13	women	77.7 yrs
Av. ann. growth		Adult literacy	96.8%
in pop. 1995–2000	1.2%	Fertility rate (per woman)	2.4
Pop. under 15	27.7%	Urban population	89.9%
Pop. over 65	9.7%		per 1,000 pop.
No. of men per 100 women	96.3	Crude birth rate	19.0
Human Development Index	84.2	Crude death rate	7.8

The economy

GDP	P285bn	GDP per head	$7,700
GDP	$285bn	GDP per head in purchasing	
Av. ann. growth in real		power parity (USA=100)	35.3
GDP 1990–2000	3.9%	Economic freedom index	2.50

Origins of GDP		**Components of GDP**	
	% of total		% of total
Agriculture	5.3	Consumption	83.1
Industry, of which:	25.4	Investment	15.9
manufacturing	16.0	Exports	10.8
Services	69.3	Imports	-11.4

Structure of employment[a]

	% of total		% of labour force
Agricultural	1	Unemployed 1998	12.8
Industry	25	Av. ann. rate 1990–98	11.7
Services	74		

Energy

	m TCE		
Total output	111.350	% output exported	28.7
Total consumption	77.529	% consumption imported	10.1
Consumption per head			
kg coal equivalent	2,146		

Inflation and finance

Consumer price		*av. ann. increase 1995–2000*	
inflation 2001	-1.1%	Narrow money (M1)	3.6%
Av. ann. inflation 1996–2001	-0.4%	Broad money	11.7%
Money market rate, 2001	24.90%		

Exchange rates

	end 2001		December 2001
P per $	1.00	Effective rates	1995 = 100
P per SDR	1.26	– nominal	...
P per euro	0.90	– real	...

Trade

Principal exports		Principal imports	
	$bn fob		*$bn cif*
Manufactures	8.1	Intermediate goods	8.4
Agricultural products	7.9	Capital goods	5.9
Fuels	4.8	Consumer goods	4.6
Total incl. others	**26.3**	Total incl. others	**25.2**

Main export destinations		Main origins of imports	
	% of total		*% of total*
Brazil	26.5	Brazil	25.1
United States	11.8	United States	18.7
Chile	10.6	Germany	5.0
Spain	3.5	China	4.6

Balance of payments, reserves and debt, $bn

Visible exports fob	26.4	Overall balance	-1.2
Visible imports fob	-23.9	Change in reserves	-1.2
Trade balance	2.6	Level of reserves	
Invisibles inflows	11.9	end Dec.	25.2
Invisibles outflows	-23.8	No. months of import cover	6.3
Net transfers	0.3	Foreign debt	146.2
Current account balance	-9.0	– as % of GDP	55
– as % of GDP	-3.1	Debt service paid	27.3
Capital balance	8.2	Debt service ratio	75

Health and education

Health spending, % of GDP	8.4	Education spending, % of GDP[b]	3.5
Doctors per 1,000 pop.	2.7	Enrolment, %: primary	120
Hospital beds per 1,000 pop.	3.3	secondary	89
Improved-water source access,		tertiary	47
% of pop.	79		

Society

No. of households	16.1m	Colour TVs per 100 households	88.1
Av. no. per household	3.5	Telephone lines per 100 pop.	21.6
Marriages per 1,000 pop.	3.8	Mobile telephone subscribers	
Divorces per 1,000 pop.	...	per 100 pop.	18.6
Cost of living, Dec. 2001		Computers per 100 pop.	5.3
New York = 100	90	Internet hosts per 1,000 pop.	12.6

a 1998
b 1997

AUSTRALIA

Area	7,682,300 sq km	Capital	Canberra
Arable as % of total land	6	Currency	Australian dollar (A$)

People

Population	19.1m	Life expectancy: men		76.4 yrs
Pop. per sq km	2		women	82.0 yrs
Av. ann. growth		Adult literacy		99.0%
in pop. 1995–2000	1.1%	Fertility rate (per woman)		1.7
Pop. under 15	20.5%	Urban population		84.7%
Pop. over 65	12.3%			per 1,000 pop.
No. of men per 100 women	98.7	Crude birth rate		12.7
Human Development Index	93.6	Crude death rate		7.4

The economy

GDP	A$673bn	GDP per head	$20,340
GDP	$390bn	GDP per head in purchasing	
Av. ann. growth in real		power parity (USA=100)	73.2
GDP 1990–2000	3.3%	Economic freedom index	1.85

Origins of GDP		**Components of GDP**	
	% of total		% of total
Agriculture & mining	7.8	Private consumption	59.4
Industry, of which:	20.4	Public consumption	18.8
manufacturing	15.0	Investment	22.9
Services	71.8	Exports	21.8
		Imports	-22.9

Structure of employment[a]

	% of total		% of labour force
Agriculture	5	Unemployed 2000	6.4
Industry	21	Av. ann. rate 1990–2000	8.5
Services	74		

Energy

	m TCE		
Total output	306.166	% output exported	59.6
Total consumption	150.758	% consumption imported	21.5
Consumption per head,			
kg coal equivalent	8,140		

Inflation and finance

Consumer price		*av. ann. increase 1995–2000*	
inflation 2001	4.4%	Narrow money (M1)	10.4%
Av. ann. inflation 1996–2001	2.3%	Broad money	8.3%
Treasury bill rate, 2001	5.06%		

Exchange rates

	end 2001		December 2001
A$ per $	1.96	Effective rates	1995 = 100
A$ per SDR	2.46	– nominal	87.9
A$ per euro	1.76	– real	92.4

Trade

Principal exports		Principal imports	
	$bn fob		$bn cif
Minerals & metals	26.7	Intermediate & other goods	32.1
Rural goods	15.2	Consumption goods	22.0
Manufacturing goods	14.6	Capital goods	17.5
Other goods	7.3	Fuels & lubricants	5.4
Total incl. others	**63.8**	Total incl. others	**71.5**

Main export destinations		Main origins of imports	
	% of total		% of total
Japan	19.3	EU15	22.1
Asean[b]	13.2	United States	21.0
EU15	12.4	Asean[b]	14.2
United States	9.9	Japan	12.8

Balance of payments, reserves and aid, $bn

Visible exports fob	64.0	Capital balance	14.6
Visible imports fob	-68.8	Overall balance	-1.4
Trade balance	-4.7	Change in reserves	-3.1
Invisibles inflows	27.0	Level of reserves	
Invisibles outflows	-37.5	end Dec.	18.8
Net transfers	-0.0	No. months of import cover	2.1
Current account balance	-15.3	Aid given	0.99
– as % of GDP	-3.9	– as % of GDP	0.25

Health and education

Health spending, % of GDP	8.6	Education spending, % of GDP	4.8
Doctors per 1,000 pop.	2.5	Enrolment, %: primary[d]	101
Hospital beds per 1,000 pop.	8.5	secondary[cd]	153
Improved-water source access,		tertiary[d]	80
% of pop.	100		

Society

No. of households	7.3m	Colour TVs per 100 households	91.4
Av. no. per household	2.6	Telephone lines per 100 pop.	52.0
Marriages per 1,000 pop.	6.9	Mobile telephone subscribers	
Divorces per 1,000 pop.	2.7	per 100 pop.	57.8
Cost of living, Dec. 2001		Computers per 100 pop.	51.7
New York = 100	73	Internet hosts per 1,000 pop.	119.8

a 1999
b Brunei, Indonesia, Laos, Malaysia, Myanmar, Philippines, Singapore, Thailand, Vietnam.
c Includes training for unemployed.
d 1997

AUSTRIA

Area	83,855 sq km	Capital	Vienna
Arable as % of total land	17	Currency	Euro (€)

People

Population	8.1m	Life expectancy: men		75.4 yrs
Pop. per sq km	96	women		81.5 yrs
Av. ann. growth		Adult literacy		99.0%
in pop. 1995–2000	0.08%	Fertility rate (per woman)		1.24
Pop. under 15	16.6%	Urban population		64.7%
Pop. over 65	15.6%			per 1,000 pop.
No. of men per 100 women	95	Crude birth rate		8.3
Human Development Index	92.1	Crude death rate		9.9

The economy

GDP	ASch2,823bn	GDP per head	$23,310
GDP	$189bn	GDP per head in purchasing	
Av. ann. growth in real		power parity (USA=100)	77.2
GDP 1990–2000	2.5%	Economic freedom index	2.10

Origins of GDP		**Components of GDP**	
	% of total		% of total
Agriculture	1.8	Private consumption	56.7
Industry, of which:	30.0	Public consumption	19.4
manufacturing	...	Investment	23.8
Services	68.2	Exports	48.7
		Imports	-49.2

Structure of employment[a]

	% of total		% of labour force
Agriculture	7	Unemployed 1999	4.3
Industry	30	Av. ann. rate 1990–99	4.7
Services	63		

Energy

	m TCE		
Total output	8.906	% output exported	37.0
Total consumption	35.759	% consumption imported	89.8
Consumption per head,			
kg coal equivalent	4,393		

Inflation and finance

Consumer price		av. ann. increase 1995–2000	
inflation 2001	2.6%	Euro area:	
Av. ann. inflation 1996–2001	1.6%	Narrow money (M1)	7.8%
Interbank rate, 2001	4.26%	Broad money	4.5%

Exchange rates

	end 2001		July 2001
			1995 = 100
Euro per $	1.13	Effective rates	
Euro per SDR	1.43	– nominal	93.7
		– real	82.9

Trade

Principal exports		Principal imports	
	$bn fob		*$bn cif*
Machinery & transport		Machinery & transport	
equipment	29.9	equipment	30.1
Base metals & manufactures	7.2	Chemicals	8.2
Chemicals	6.5	Base metals & manufactures	6.3
Wood, paper & manufactures	5.6	Food, drink & tobacco	3.7
Food, drink & tobacco	3.1	Fuel	3.7
Textiles	3.1	Wood, paper & manufactures	3.1
Total incl. others	**66.5**	Total incl. others	**71.5**

Main export destinations		Main origins of imports	
	% of total		*% of total*
Germany	33.3	Germany	43.6
Italy	8.9	Italy	6.8
Switzerland	6.7	Switzerland	4.8
Hungary	5.0	Hungary	4.6
EU15	61.7	EU15	68.6

Balance of payments, reserves and aid, $bn

Visible exports fob	64.7	Capital balance	3.9
Visible imports fob	-67.4	Overall balance	-0.7
Trade balance	-2.7	Change in reserves	-1.3
Invisibles inflows	42.1	Level of reserves	
Invisibles outflows	-43.3	end Dec.	17.6
Net transfers	-1.2	No. months of import cover	1.9
Current account balance	-5.2	Aid given	0.42
– as % of GDP	-2.8	– as % of GDP	0.22

Health and education

Health spending, % of GDP	8.2	Education spending, % of GDP	6.3
Doctors per 1,000 pop.	3.0	Enrolment, %: primary	100
Hospital beds per 1,000 pop.	8.7	secondary	96
Improved-water source access,		tertiary	50
% of pop.	100		

Society

No. of households	3.3m	Colour TVs per 100 households	97.7
Av. no. per household	2.4	Telephone lines per 100 pop.	46.8
Marriages per 1,000 pop.	4.8	Mobile telephone subscribers	
Divorces per 1,000 pop.	2.2	per 100 pop.	80.7
Cost of living, Dec. 2001		Computers per 100 pop.	28.0
New York = 100	86	Internet hosts per 1,000 pop.	81.1

a 1999

BANGLADESH

Area	143,998 sq km	Capital	Dhaka
Arable as % of total land	62	Currency	Taka (Tk)

People

Population	137.4m	Life expectancy:	men	60.6 yrs
Pop. per sq km	954		women	60.8 yrs
Av. ann. growth		Adult literacy		41.4%
in pop. 1995–2000	2.12%	Fertility rate (per woman)		3.56
Pop. under 15	38.7%	Urban population		24.5%
Pop. over 65	3.1%			per 1,000 pop.
No. of men per 100 women	106	Crude birth rate		29.9
Human Development Index	47.0	Crude death rate		8.7

The economy

GDP	Tk2,371bn	GDP per head	$360
GDP	$47.1bn	GDP per head in purchasing	
Av. ann. growth in real		power parity (USA=100)	4.7
GDP 1990–2000	5.0%	Economic freedom index	3.70

Origins of GDP[a]		Components of GDP[a]	
	% of total		% of total
Agriculture	34	Private consumption	76.7
Industry, of which:	19	Public consumption	4.5
manufacturing	12	Investment	23.6
Services	47	Exports	14.6
		Imports	-20.1

Structure of employment[b]

	% of total		% of labour force
Agriculture	63	Unemployed 1996	2.5
Industry	10	Av. ann. rate 1990–96	2.2
Services	27		

Energy

	m TCE		
Total output	10.141	% output exported	0.0
Total consumption	13.799	% consumption imported	31.5
Consumption per head,			
kg coal equivalent	111		

Inflation and finance

		av. ann. increase 1995–2000	
Consumer price			
inflation 2000	4.0%	Narrow money (M1)	10.1%
Av. ann. inflation 1996–2000	5.5%	Broad money	13.3%
Deposit rate, 2001	8.50%		

Exchange rates

	end 2001		December 2001
Tk per $	57.00	Effective rates	1995 = 100
Tk per SDR	71.63	– nominal	...
Tk per euro	51.04	– real	...

Trade

Principal exports[a]	$bn fob	Principal imports[a]	$bn cif
Clothing	3.8	Machinery & transport	
Fish & fish products	0.4	equipment	2.5
Leather	0.3	Textiles & yarn	2.1
Jute goods	0.2	Fuels	0.8
		Iron & steel	0.5
		Cereal & dairy products	0.3
Total incl. others	**6.0**	Total incl. others	**9.4**

Main export destinations	% of total	Main origins of imports	% of total
United States	33.4	India	9.8
Germany	10.9	Japan	9.4
United Kingdom	7.1	Singapore	8.4
France	5.2	China	7.0
Italy	4.0	Hong Kong	5.4

Balance of payments, reserves and debt, $bn

Visible exports fob	6.4	Overall balance	-0.0
Visible imports fob	-8.1	Change in reserves	-0.1
Trade balance	-1.7	Level of reserves	
Invisibles inflows	0.9	end Dec.	1.5
Invisibles outflows	-2.0	No. months of import cover	1.8
Net transfers	2.4	Foreign debt	15.6
Current account balance	-0.3	– as % of GDP	21
– as % of GDP	-0.6	Debt service paid	0.8
Capital balance	-0.0	Debt service ratio	10

Health and education

Health spending, % of GDP	3.6	Education spending, % of GDP[c]	2.2
Doctors per 1,000 pop.	0.2	Enrolment, %: primary	122
Hospital beds per 1,000 pop.	0.3	secondary	47
Improved-water source access,		tertiary	5
% of pop.	97		

Society

No. of households	23.7m	Colour TVs per 100 households	0.6
Av. no. per household	5.4	Telephone lines per 100 pop.	0.4
Marriages per 1,000 pop.	9.7	Mobile telephone subscribers	
Divorces per 1,000 pop.	...	per 100 pop.	0.4
Cost of living, Dec. 2001		Computers per 100 pop.	0.2
New York = 100	55	Internet hosts per 1,000 pop.	...

a Fiscal year ending June 30 2001.
b Fiscal year ending June 30 1996.
c 1997

BELGIUM

Area	30,520 sq km	Capital	Brussels
Arable as % of total land	25	Currency	Euro (€)

People

Population	10.2m	Life expectancy: men	75.7 yrs
Pop. per sq km	336	women	81.9 yrs
Av. ann. growth		Adult literacy	99.0%
in pop. 1995–2000	0.2%	Fertility rate (per woman)	1.48
Pop. under 15	17.3%	Urban population	97.3%
Pop. over 65	17.0%		per 1,000 pop.
No. of men per 100 women	96.0	Crude birth rate	9.7
Human Development Index	93.5	Crude death rate	10.0

The economy

GDP	BFr9,924bn	GDP per head	$22,110
GDP	$227bn	GDP per head in purchasing	
Av. ann. growth in real		power parity (USA=100)	80.6
GDP 1990–2000	2.2%	Economic freedom index	2.10

Origins of GDP		**Components of GDP**	
	% of total		% of total
Agriculture	1.4	Private consumption	53.8
Industry, of which:	24.0	Public consumption	21.3
manufacturing	...	Investment	21.6
Services	74.6	Exports	88.1
		Imports	-84.7

Structure of employment[a]

	% of total		% of labour force
Agriculture	2	Unemployed 2000	7.0
Industry	27	Av. ann. rate 1990–2000	8.3
Services	71		

Energy

	m TCE		
Total output	17.627	% output exported[b]	189.3
Total consumption	75.266	% consumption imported[b]	137.9
Consumption per head,			
kg coal equivalent	7,422		

Inflation and finance

Consumer price		av. ann. increase 1995–2000	
inflation 2001	2.5%	Euro area:	
Av. ann. inflation 1996–2001	1.7%	Narrow money (M1)	7.8%
Interbank rate, 2001	4.26%	Broad money	4.5%

Exchange rates

	end 2001		July 2001
Euro per $	1.13	Effective rates	1995 = 100
Euro per SDR	1.43	– nominal	90.6
		– real	86.4

Trade

Principal exports		Principal imports	
	$bn fob		*$bn cif*
Machinery & transport equip.	55.2	Machinery & transport	52.8
Manufactured materials	44.0	Manufactures	36.1
Chemicals	38.2	Chemicals	28.7
Food & animals	14.6	Mineral fuels	15.1
Total incl. others	**185.6**	Total incl. others	**172.4**

Main export destinations		Main origins of imports	
	% of total		*% of total*
France	17.6	Netherlands	17.3
Germany	16.8	Germany	16.5
Netherlands	12.5	France	12.7
United Kingdom	10.0	United Kingdom	8.5
EU15	74.2	EU15	68.4

Balance of payments[c], reserves and aid, $bn

Visible exports fob	167.0	Capital balance	-11.3
Visible imports fob	-164.2	Overall balance	-1.0
Trade balance	2.8	Change in reserves	-1.1
Invisibles inflows	119.8	Level of reserves	
Invisibles outflows	-106.5	end Dec.	12.3
Net transfers	-3.8	No. months of import cover	0.5
Current account balance	11.8	Aid given	0.82
– as % of GDP	5.2	– as % of GDP	0.35

Health and education

Health spending, % of GDP	8.8	Education spending, % of GDP[e]	3.1
Doctors per 1,000 pop.	3.8	Enrolment, %: primary[e]	103
Hospital beds per 1,000 pop.	7.3	secondary[de]	146
Improved-water source access, % of pop.	...	tertiary[e]	57

Society

No. of households	4.2m	Colour TVs per 100 households	99.2
Av. no. per household	2.4	Telephone lines per 100 pop.	49.3
Marriages per 1,000 pop.	3.7	Mobile telephone subscribers	
Divorces per 1,000 pop.	2.6	per 100 pop.	74.7
Cost of living, Dec. 2001		Computers per 100 pop.	34.5
New York = 100	76	Internet hosts per 1,000 pop.	68.5

a 1998
b Energy trade data are distorted by transitory and oil refining activities.
c Including Luxembourg.
d Includes training for unemployed.
e 1997

BRAZIL

Area	8,511,965 sq km	Capital	Brasilia
Arable as % of total land	6	Currency	Real (R)

People

Population	170.4m	Life expectancy: men	64.7 yrs
Pop. per sq km	20	women	72.6 yrs
Av. ann. growth		Adult literacy	85.2%
in pop. 1995–2000	1.3%	Fertility rate (per woman)	2.15
Pop. under 15	28.8%	Urban population	81.3%
Pop. over 65	5.1%		per 1,000 pop.
No. of men per 100 women	97.6	Crude birth rate	19.2
Human Development Index	75.0	Crude death rate	7.0

The economy

GDP	R1,090bn	GDP per head	$3,490
GDP	$596bn	GDP per head in purchasing	
Av. ann. growth in real		power parity (USA=100)	21.4
GDP 1990–2000	2.0%	Economic freedom index	3.10

Origins of GDP		**Components of GDP**	
	% of total		% of total
Agriculture	7.7	Private consumption	60.6
Industry, of which:	37.5	Public consumption	19.3
manufacturing	...	Investment	20.3
Services	57.1	Exports	10.8
		Imports	-12.4

Structure of employment[a]

	% of total		% of labour force
Agriculture	23	Unemployed 1999	9.6
Industry	20	Av. ann. rate 1990–99	7.0
Services	57		

Energy

	m TCE		
Total output	121.332	% output exported	4.7
Total consumption	170.418	% consumption imported	42.8
Consumption per head,			
kg coal equivalent	1,028		

Inflation and finance

		av. ann. increase 1995–2000	
Consumer price			
inflation 2001	6.8%	Narrow money (M1)	18.2%
Av. ann. inflation 1996–2001	5.8%	Broad money	10.4%
Money market rate, 2001	17.47%		

Exchange rates

	end 2001		December 2001
R per $	2.32	Effective rates	1995 = 100
R per SDR	2.92	– Nominal	...
R per euro	2.08	– Real	...

Trade

Principal exports	$bn fob	Principal imports	$bn fob
Transport equipment & parts	9.2	Machines & electrical	
Metal goods	5.9	equipment	18.1
Soyabeans etc.	4.4	Chemical products	9.3
Chemical products	4.1	Oil derivatives	7.6
Iron ore	2.4	Transport equipment & parts	4.9
Total incl. others	**55.1**	Total incl. others	**55.8**

Main export destinations	% of total	Main origins of imports	% of total
United States	23.8	United States	23.1
Argentina	11.1	Argentina	12.2
Netherlands	5.0	Germany	7.9
Germany	4.5	Japan	5.3

Balance of payments, reserves and debt, $bn

Visible exports fob	55.1	Overall balance	8.0
Visible imports fob	-55.8	Change in reserves	-2.7
Trade balance	-0.7	Level of reserves	
Invisibles inflows	13.0	end Dec.	33.0
Invisibles outflows	-38.5	No. months of import cover	4.2
Net transfers	1.5	Foreign debt	238.0
Current account balance	-24.6	– as % of GDP	36
– as % of GDP	-4.1	Debt service paid	62.8
Capital balance	29.6	Debt service ratio	97

Health and education

Health spending, % of GDP	6.5	Education spending, % of GDP	4.6
Doctors per 1,000 pop.	1.3	Enrolment, %: primary	154
Hospital beds per 1,000 pop.	3.1	secondary	83
Improved-water source access,		tertiary	14
% of pop.	87		

Society

No. of households	47.3m	Colour TVs per 100 households	86.1
Av. no. per household	3.4	Telephone lines per 100 pop.	21.7
Marriages per 1,000 pop.	4.5	Mobile telephone subscribers	
Divorces per 1,000 pop.	0.8	per 100 pop.	16.7
Cost of living, Dec. 2001		Computers per 100 pop.	6.3
New York = 100	50	Internet hosts per 1,000 pop.	9.7

a 1998

BULGARIA

Area	110,994 sq km	Capital	Sofia
Arable as % of total land	39	Currency	Lev (BGL)

People

Population	7.9m	Life expectancy: men	67.1 yrs
Pop. per sq km	72	women	74.8 yrs
Av. ann. growth		Adult literacy	98.4%
in pop. 1995–2000	-1.12%	Fertility rate (per woman)	1.1
Pop. under 15	15.7%	Urban population	69.6%
Pop. over 65	16.1%		per 1,000 pop.
No. of men per 100 women	94.6	Crude birth rate	7.9
Human Development Index	77.2	Crude death rate	15.1

The economy

GDP	BGL25.5bn	GDP per head	$1,470
GDP	$12.0bn	GDP per head in purchasing	
Av. ann. growth in real		power parity (USA=100)	16.3
GDP 1990–2000	-2.6%	Economic freedom index	3.40

Origins of GDP		Components of GDP	
	% of total		% of total
Agriculture	14.5	Private consumption	79.9
Industry, of which:	27.8	Public consumption	10.0
manufacturing	...	Investment	16.6
Services	57.7	Exports	58.5
		Imports	-64.1

Structure of employment[a]

	% of total		% of labour force
Agriculture	27	Unemployed 2000	16.3
Industry	29	Av. ann. rate 1990–2000	14.3
Services	44		

Energy

	m TCE		
Total output	13.879	% output exported	17.0
Total consumption	26.843	% consumption imported	62.7
Consumption per head,			
kg coal equivalent	3,220		

Inflation and finance

Consumer price		av. ann change 1995–2000	
inflation 2001	7.4%	Narrow money (M1)	102%
Av. ann. inflation 1996–2001	75.7%	Broad money	73%
Money market rate 2001	5.56%		

Exchange rates

	end 2001		December 2001
BGL per $	2.22	Effective rates	1995 = 100
BGL per SDR	2.80	– Nominal	6.26
BGL per euro	1.99	– Real	128.43

Trade

Principal exports		Principal imports	
	$bn fob		*$bn fob*
Textiles	1.1	Mineral products & fuels	2.0
Base metals	1.0	Machinery & transport equip.	1.8
Minerals & fuels	0.8	Textiles	0.9
Chemicals	0.6	Chemicals	0.7
Machinery & transport equip.	0.5	Base metals	0.4
Total incl. others	**4.8**	Total incl. others	**6.0**

Main export destinations		Main origins of imports	
	% of total		*% of total*
Italy	14.2	Russia	24.4
Turkey	10.2	Germany	13.9
Germany	9.0	Italy	8.5
Greece	7.8	France	4.9
Serbia & Montenegro	7.8	Greece	4.9
EU15	51.0	EU15	44.1

Balance of payments, reserves and debt, $bn

Visible exports fob	4.8	Overall balance	0.1
Visible imports fob	-6.0	Change in reserves	0.2
Trade balance	-1.2	Level of reserves	
Invisibles inflows	2.5	end Dec.	3.6
Invisibles outflows	-2.3	No. months of import cover	5.2
Net transfers	0.3	Foreign debt	10.0
Current account balance	-0.7	– as % of GDP	80.0
– as % of GDP	-5.8	Debt service paid	1.2
Capital balance	0.9	Debt service ratio	18

Health and education

Health spending, % of GDP	4.1	Education spending, % of GDP	3.4
Doctors per 1,000 pop.	3.5	Enrolment, %: primary	101
Hospital beds per 1,000 pop.	8.6	secondary	87
Improved-water source access,		tertiary	43
% of pop.	100		

Society

No. of households	3.0m	Colour TVs per 100 households	61.8
Av. no. per household	2.7	Telephone lines per 100 pop.	35.9
Marriages per 1,000 pop.	4.0	Mobile telephone subscribers	
Divorces per 1,000 pop.	1.2	per 100 pop.	19.1
Cost of living, Dec. 2001		Computers per 100 pop.	4.4
New York = 100	...	Internet hosts per 1,000 pop.	3.0

a 1999

CAMEROON

Area	475,442 sq km	Capital	Yaoundé
Arable as % of total land	13	Currency	CFA franc (CFAfr)

People

Population	14.7m	Life expectancy: men	49.3 yrs
Pop. per sq km	31	women	50.6 yrs
Av. ann. growth		Adult literacy	75.8%
in pop. 1995–2000	2.28%	Fertility rate (per woman)	4.7
Pop. under 15	43.1%	Urban population	48.9%
Pop. over 65	3.7%		per 1,000 pop.
No. of men per 100 women	98.9	Crude birth rate	36.3
Human Development Index	50.6	Crude death rate	14.6

The economy

GDP[a]	CFAfr5,828bn	GDP per head	$600
GDP	$8.9bn	GDP per head in purchasing	
Av. ann. growth in real		power parity (USA=100)	4.7
GDP 1990–2000	0.7%	Economic freedom index	3.25

Origins of GDP		**Components of GDP**	
	% of total		% of total
Agriculture	43.6	Private consumption	71.5
Industry, of which:	22.8	Public consumption	14.0
manufacturing	...	Investment	14.5
Services	33.6	Exports	40.8
		Imports	-40.7

Structure of employment[b]

	% of total		% of labour force
Agriculture	70	Unemployed 1999	...
Industry	9	Av. ann. rate 1990–99	...
Services	21		

Energy

	m TCE		
Total output	8.768	% output exported	88.1
Total consumption	1.979	% consumption imported	7.3
Consumption per head,			
kg coal equivalent	138		

Inflation and finance

Consumer price		*av. ann. change 1995–2000*	
inflation 2000	1.2%	Narrow money (M1)	14.6%
Av. ann. inflation 1996–2000	1.9%	Broad money	9.2%
Deposit rate, 2001	5.00%		

Exchange rates

	end 2001		December 2001
CFAfr per $	744.31	Effective rates	1995 = 100
CFAfr per SDR	935.39	– nominal	97.2
CFAfr per euro	656.0	– real	...

Trade

Principal exports[a]	$bn fob	Principal imports[a]	$bn fob
Crude oil	0.9	Manufactures	1.3
Timber & cork	0.4	Primary products	0.1
Cocoa	0.1		
Total incl. others	**2.0**	Total incl. others	**1.5**

Main export destinations[d]	% of total	Main origins of imports[d]	% of total
Italy	28.7	France	35.6
France	12.6	Nigeria	14.4
Spain	10.6	Italy	4.6

Balance of payments[a], reserves and debt, $bn

Visible exports fob	2.0	Overall balance	-0.4
Visible imports fob	-1.4	Change in reserves	0.2
Trade balance	0.6	Level of reserves	
Invisibles inflows	...	end Dec.	0.2
Invisibles outflows, net	-0.5	No. months of import cover	1.6
Net transfers	0.1	Foreign debt	7.3
Current account balance	-0.2	– as % of GDP	70
– as % of GDP	-1.7	Debt service paid	0.6
Capital balance	-0.1	Debt service ratio	23

Health and education

Health spending, % of GDP	5.0	Education spending, % of GDP	2.6
Doctors per 1,000 pop.	0.1	Enrolment, %: primary	90
Hospital beds per 1,000 pop.	2.6	secondary	20
Improved-water source access,		tertiary	5
% of pop.	62		

Society

No. of households	4.0m	Colour TVs per 100 households	3.2
Av. no. per household	3.7	Telephone lines per 100 pop.	0.7
Marriages per 1,000 pop.	...	Mobile telephone subscribers	
Divorces per 1,000 pop.	...	per 100 pop.	2.0
Cost of living, Dec. 2001		Computers per 100 pop.	0.4
New York = 100	65	Internet hosts per 1,000 pop.	...

a Fiscal year ending June 30 2000.
b 1990
c 1995
d Estimate.

CANADA

Area[a]	9,970,610 sq km	Capital	Ottawa
Arable as % of total land	5	Currency	Canadian dollar (C$)

People

Population	30.8m	Life expectancy: men	76.2 yrs
Pop. per sq km	3	women	81.8 yrs
Av. ann. growth		Adult literacy	99.0%
in pop. 1995–2000	0.93%	Fertility rate (per woman)	1.58
Pop. under 15	19.1%	Urban population	77.1%
Pop. over 65	12.6%		per 1,000 pop.
No. of men per 100 women	98.0	Crude birth rate	10.9
Human Development Index	93.6	Crude death rate	7.7

The economy

GDP	C$1,022bn	GDP per head	$22,370
GDP	$688bn	GDP per head in purchasing	
Av. ann. growth in real		power parity (USA=100)	79.7
GDP 1990–2000	2.5%	Economic freedom index	2.00

Origins of GDP		Components of GDP	
	% of total		% of total
Agriculture	2.5	Private consumption	56.2
Industry, of which:	31.0	Public consumption	18.3
manufacturing & mining	22.1	Investment	20.5
Services	66.5	Exports	45.4
		Imports	-40.4

Structure of employment

	% of total		% of labour force
Agriculture	3	Unemployed 2000	6.8
Industry	23	Av. ann. rate 1990–2000	9.3
Services	74		

Energy

	m TCE		
Total output	515.584	% output exported	51.2
Total consumption	339.682	% consumption imported	24.5
Consumption per head,			
kg coal equivalent	11,114		

Inflation and finance

Consumer price		av. ann. increase 1995–2000	
inflation 2001	2.6%	Narrow money (M1)	10.3%
Av. ann. inflation 1996–2001	1.9%	Broad money	6.9%
Money market rate, 2001	2.24%		

Exchange rates

	end 2001		December 2001
C$ per $	1.59	Effective rates	1995 = 100
C$ per SDR	2.00	– nominal	92.0
C$ per euro	1.42	– real	93.9

Trade

Principal exports		Principal imports	
	$bn fob		*$bn fob*
Machinery & industrial		Machinery & industrial	
equipment	72.0	equipment	82.6
Motor vehicles & parts	65.6	Motor vehicles & parts	52.1
Industrial supplies	44.4	Industrial supplies	47.5
Energy products	35.6	Consumer goods	27.0
Forest products	28.1	Agric. products	12.5
Agricultural products	18.5	Energy products	12.1
Total incl. others	**284.6**	Total incl. others	**244.6**

Main export destinations		Main origins of imports	
	% of total		*% of total*
United States	85.1	United States	73.7
Japan	2.4	United Kingdom	3.3
United Kingdom	1.6	Japan	3.2
EU15 (excl. UK)	3.6	EU15 (excl. UK)	5.8

Balance of payments, reserves and aid, $bn

Visible exports fob	284.4	Capital balance	-6.5
Visible imports fob	-244.6	Overall balance	3.7
Trade balance	39.8	Change in reserves	3.6
Invisibles inflows	65.7	Level of reserves	
Invisibles outflows	-88.5	end Dec.	32.2
Net transfers	1.0	No. months of import cover	1.2
Current account balance	18.0	Aid given	1.74
– as % of GDP	2.6	– as % of GDP	0.25

Health and education

Health spending, % of GDP	9.3	Education spending, % of GDP	5.6
Doctors per 1,000 pop.	2.1	Enrolment, %: primary	97
Hospital beds per 1,000 pop.	4.1	secondary	105
Improved-water source access,		tertiary	58
% of pop.	100		

Society

No. of households	11.9m	Colour TVs per 100 households	98.7
Av. no. per household	2.5	Telephone lines per 100 pop.	65.5
Marriages per 1,000 pop.	4.8	Mobile telephone subscribers	
Divorces per 1,000 pop.	2.2	per 100 pop.	32.0
Cost of living, Dec. 2001		Computers per 100 pop.	39.0
New York = 100	73	Internet hosts per 1,000 pop.	93.8

a Including freshwater.

CHILE

Area	756,945 sq km	Capital	Santiago
Arable as % of total land	3	Currency	Chilean peso (Ps)

People

Population	15.2m	Life expectancy: men		73 yrs
Pop. per sq km	20		women	79 yrs
Av. ann. growth		Adult literacy		95.8%
in pop. 1995–2000	1.36%	Fertility rate (per woman)		2.35
Pop. under 15	28.5%	Urban population		84.0%
Pop. over 65	7.2%			per 1,000 pop.
No. of men per 100 women	98.1	Crude birth rate		18.2
Human Development Index	82.5	Crude death rate		5.7

The economy

GDP	37,775bn pesos	GDP per head	$4,640
GDP	$70.5bn	GDP per head in purchasing	
Av. ann. growth in real		power parity (USA=100)	26.7
GDP 1990–2000	6.3%	Economic freedom index	1.85

Origins of GDP		**Components of GDP**	
	% of total		% of total
Agriculture	9.1	Private consumption	67.1
Industry, of which:	37.8	Public consumption	7.8
manufacturing	17.3	Investment	29.8
Services	53.1	Exports	43.0
		Imports	-47.7

Structure of employment[a]

	% of total		% of labour force
Agriculture	14	Unemployed 1999	9.9
Industry	26	Av. ann. rate 1990–99	5.8
Services	60		

Energy

	m TCE		
Total output	6.361	% output exported	3.2
Total consumption	28.675	% consumption imported	82.7
Consumption per head,			
kg coal equivalent	1,934		

Inflation and finance

		av. ann. increase 1995–2000	
Consumer price			
inflation 2001	3.6%	Narrow money (M1)	11.0%
Av. ann. inflation 1996–2001	4.4%	Broad money	13.2%
Money market rate, 2001	681%		

Exchange rates

	end 2001		December 2001
Ps per $	656.2	Effective rates	1995 = 100
Ps per SDR	824.7	– nominal	80.4
Ps per Ecu	587.6	– real	93.0

Trade

Principal exports		Principal imports	
	$bn fob		$bn cif
Mining	8.4	Intermediate goods	11.0
Industrial goods	8.2	Capital goods	3.7
Copper	7.3	Consumer goods	3.4
Agricultural goods	1.6		
Total incl. others	**18.2**	Total incl. others	**18.1**

Main export destinations		Main origins of imports	
	% of total		% of total
United States	17.4	United States	18.5
Japan	13.8	Argentina	15.9
United Kingdom	5.8	Brazil	7.4
China	5.3	China	5.5
Brazil	5.2	Japan	3.9

Balance of payments, reserves and debt, $bn

Visible exports fob	18.2	Overall balance	0.2
Visible imports fob	-16.7	Change in reserves	-0.0
Trade balance	1.4	Level of reserves	
Invisibles inflows	5.5	end Dec.	14.7
Invisibles outflows	-8.5	No. months of import cover	7.0
Net transfers	0.5	Foreign debt	37.0
Current account balance	-1.0	– as % of GDP	51
– as % of GDP	-1.4	Debt service paid	6.2
Capital balance	1.2	Debt service ratio	29

Health and education

Health spending, % of GDP	5.9	Education spending, % of GDP	3.7
Doctors per 1,000 pop.	1.1	Enrolment, %: primary	106
Hospital beds per 1,000 pop.	2.7	secondary	85
Improved-water source access,		tertiary	34
% of pop.	94		

Society

No. of households	3.9m	Colour TVs per 100 households	59.3
Av. no. per household	3.8	Telephone lines per 100 pop.	23.9
Marriages per 1,000 pop.	5.1	Mobile telephone subscribers	
Divorces per 1,000 pop.	0.5	per 100 pop.	34.0
Cost of living, Dec. 2001		Computers per 100 pop.	8.4
New York = 100	57	Internet hosts per 1,000 pop.	8.1

a 1998

CHINA

Area	9,560,900 sq km	Capital	Beijing
Arable as % of total land	13	Currency	Yuan

People

Population	1,275.1m	Life expectancy: men	69.1 yrs
Pop. per sq km	133	women	73.5 yrs
Av. ann. growth		Adult literacy	84.1%
in pop. 1995–2000	0.90%	Fertility rate (per woman)	1.8
Pop. under 15	24.8%	Urban population	32.1%
Pop. over 65	6.9%		per 1,000 pop.
No. of men per 100 women	105.9	Crude birth rate	14.3
Human Development Index	71.8	Crude death rate	7.0

The economy

GDP	Yuan8,940bn	GDP per head	$860
GDP	$1,080bn	GDP per head in purchasing	
Av. ann. growth in real		power parity (USA=100)	11.5
GDP 1990–2000	9.6%	Economic freedom index	3.55

Origins of GDP		**Components of GDP**	
	% of total		% of total
Agriculture	16.3	Private consumption	48.0
Industry, of which:	51.6	Public consumption	13.1
manufacturing	...	Investment	36.5
Services	32.1	Exports	25.4
		Imports	-22.5

Structure of employment[a]

	% of total		% of labour force
Agriculture	65	Unemployed 2000	3.1
Industry	22	Av. ann. rate 1990–2000	2.8
Services	13		

Energy

	m TCE		
Total output	1,187.280	% output exported	5.8
Total consumption	1,139.226	% consumption imported	6.9
Consumption per head,			
kg coal equivalent	907		

Inflation and finance

		av. ann. increase 1995–2000	
Consumer price			
inflation 2001	0.7%	Narrow money (M1)	18.8%
Av. ann. inflation 1996–2001	0.3%	Broad money	17.5%
Deposit rate, 2001	2.25%		

Exchange rates

	end 2001		December 2001
Yuan per $	8.28	Effective rates	1995 = 100
Yuan per SDR	10.40	– nominal	124.6
Yuan per euro	7.41	– real	111.8

Trade

Principal exports		Principal imports	
	$bn fob		*$bn cif*
Machinery & transport		Machinery & transport	
equipment	82.6	equipment	91.6
Textiles & clothing	50.0	Chemicals	32.0
Chemicals	17.6	Fuels	20.7
Footwear & accessories	9.9	Textiles	16.1
Energy	7.9	Iron & steel	11.3
Total incl. others	**249.2**	Total incl. others	**225.1**

Main export destinations		Main origins of imports	
	% of total		*% of total*
United States	20.9	Japan	18.4
Hong Kong	17.9	Taiwan	11.3
Japan	16.7	South Korea	10.3
South Korea	4.5	United States	9.9
EU15	15.3	EU15	13.7

Balance of payments, reserves and debt, $bn

Visible exports fob	249.1	Overall balance	10.7
Visible imports fob	-214.7	Change in reserves	10.3
Trade balance	34.5	Level of reserves	
Invisibles inflows	43.0	end Dec.	171.8
Invisibles outflows	-63.2	No. months of import cover	7.4
Net transfers	6.3	Foreign debt	149.8
Current account balance	20.5	– as % of GDP	13
– as % of GDP	1.9	Debt service paid	21.7
Capital balance	1.9	Debt service ratio	9

Health and education

Health spending, % of GDP	5.1	Education spending, % of GDP[b]	2.3
Doctors per 1,000 pop.	1.7	Enrolment, %: primary	107
Hospital beds per 1,000 pop.	2.4	secondary	62
Improved-water source access,		tertiary	6
% of pop.	75		

Society

No. of households	351.4m	Colour TVs per 100 households	44.6
Av. no. per household	3.6	Telephone lines per 100 pop.	13.8
Marriages per 1,000 pop.	6.6	Mobile telephone subscribers	
Divorces per 1,000 pop.	0.9	per 100 pop.	11.2
Cost of living, Dec. 2001		Computers per 100 pop.	1.9
New York = 100	96	Internet hosts per 1,000 pop.	0.1

Note: Data excludes Special Administrative Regions, ie Hong Kong and Macau.
a 1998
b 1997

COLOMBIA

Area	1,141,748 sq km	Capital	Bogota
Arable as % of total land	2	Currency	Colombian peso (peso)

People

Population	42.1m	Life expectancy:	men	69.2 yrs
Pop. per sq km	37		women	75.3 yrs
Av. ann. growth		Adult literacy		91.7%
in pop. 1995–2000	1.77%	Fertility rate (per woman)		2.62
Pop. under 15	32.8%	Urban population		73.9%
Pop. over 65	4.7%			per 1,000 pop.
No. of men per 100 women	97.7	Crude birth rate		22.3
Human Development Index	76.5	Crude death rate		6.4

The economy

GDP	169,687bn pesos	GDP per head	$1,920
GDP	$81.3bn	GDP per head in purchasing	
Av. ann. growth in real		power parity (USA=100)	17.8
GDP 1990–2000	2.8%	Economic freedom index	2.85

Origins of GDP[a]		Components of GDP	
	% of total		% of total
Agriculture	12.1	Private consumption	64.4
Industry, of which:	18.7	Public consumption	22.8
manufacturing	16.6	Investment	13.1
Services	69.2	Exports	21.1
		Imports	-21.3

Structure of employment[ab]

	% of total		% of labour force
Agriculture	1	Unemployed 1999	20.1
Industry	24	Av. ann. rate 1990–99	11.3
Services	75		

Energy

	m TCE		
Total output	96.227	% output exported	64.6
Total consumption	30.985	% consumption imported	6.0
Consumption per head,			
kg coal equivalent	759		

Inflation and finance

Consumer price		av. ann. increase 1995–2000	
inflation 2001	8.7%	Narrow money (M1)	16.7%
Av. ann. inflation 1996–2001	13.6%	Broad money	14.3%
Money market rate, 2001	10.4%		

Exchange rates

	end 2001		December 2001
Peso per $	2,301	Effective rates	1995 = 100
Peso per SDR	2,892	– nominal	53.4
Peso per euro	2,061	– real	104.3

Trade

Principal exports		Principal imports	
	$bn fob		*$bn cif*
Oil	4.6	Intermediate goods &	
Coffee	1.1	raw materials	5.9
Coal	0.9	Capital goods	3.4
Nickel	0.2	Consumer goods	2.2
Total incl. others	**13.0**	Total	**11.5**

Main export destinations		Main origins of imports	
	% of total		*% of total*
United States	50.6	United States	34.0
Venezuela	9.9	Venezuela	8.2
Ecuador	3.5	Mexico	4.7
Germany	3.3	Japan	4.6

Balance of payments, reserves and debt, $bn

Visible exports fob	13.6	Overall balance	0.9
Visible imports fob	-11.1	Change in reserves	0.9
Trade balance	2.5	Level of reserves	
Invisibles inflows	2.9	end Dec.	9.0
Invisibles outflows	-6.7	No. months of import cover	6.1
Net transfers	1.6	Foreign debt	34.1
Current account balance	0.4	– as % of GDP	39.0
– as % of GDP	0.4	Debt service paid	5.2
Capital balance	0.6	Debt service ratio	32

Health and education

Health spending, % of GDP	9.4	Education spending, % of GDP[c]	4.1
Doctors per 1,000 pop.	1.2	Enrolment, %: primary	112
Hospital beds per 1,000 pop.	1.5	secondary	53
Improved-water source access,		tertiary[c]	17
% of pop.	91		

Society

No. of households	9.1m	Colour TVs per 100 households	84.8
Av. no. per household	3.9	Telephone lines per 100 pop.	17.1
Marriages per 1,000 pop.	3.3	Mobile telephone subscribers	
Divorces per 1,000 pop.	0.2	per 100 pop.	7.4
Cost of living, Dec. 2001		Computers per 100 pop.	4.2
New York = 100	60	Internet hosts per 1,000 pop.	1.4

a 1999
b Main cities.
c 1997

CÔTE D'IVOIRE

Area	322,463 sq km	Capital	Abidjan/Yamoussoukro
Arable as % of total land	9	Currency	CFA franc (CFAfr)

People

Population	16.0m	Life expectancy: men		47.7 yrs
Pop. per sq km	50		women	48.1 yrs
Av. ann. growth		Adult literacy		46.8%
in pop. 1995–2000	2.14%	Fertility rate (per woman)		4.64
Pop. under 15	42.1%	Urban population		46.4%
Pop. over 65	3.1%			per 1,000 pop.
No. of men per 100 women	105	Crude birth rate		35.3
Human Development Index	42.6	Crude death rate		15.3

The economy

GDP	CFAfr6,671bn	GDP per head	$590
GDP	$9.4bn	GDP per head in purchasing	
Av. ann. growth in real		power parity (USA=100)	4.4
GDP 1990–2000	2.3%	Economic freedom index	2.90

Origins of GDP		**Components of GDP**	
	% of total		% of total
Agriculture	33	Private consumption	64.3
Industry, of which:	24	Public consumption	12.5
manufacturing	...	Investment	11.5
Services	43	Exports	45.8
		Imports	-34.1

Structure of employment[a]

	% of total		% of labour force
Agriculture	60	Unemployed 2000	...
Industry	10	Av. ann. rate 1990–2000	...
Services	30		

Energy

	m TCE		
Total output	2.040	% output exported	20.0
Total consumption	3.394	% consumption imported	143.3
Consumption per head,			
kg coal equivalent	237		

Inflation and finance

Consumer price		av. ann. change 1995–2000	
inflation 2001	4.3%	Narrow money (M1)	4.1%
Av. ann. inflation 1996–2001	3.5%	Broad money	2.8%
Money market rate, 2001	4.95%		

Exchange rates

	end 2001		December 2001
CFAfr per $	744.3	Effective rates	1995 = 100
CFAfr per SDR	935.4	– nominal	96.5
CFAfr per euro	656.0	– real	...

Trade

Principal exports		Principal imports	
	$bn fob		$bn cif
Cocoa beans & products	1.0	Fuel & lubricants	0.8
Petroleum products	0.7	Capital goods	0.4
Coffee & products	0.3	Food products	0.4
Timber	0.3		
Total incl. others	**4.0**	Total incl. others	**2.2**

Main export destinations		Main origins of imports	
	% of total		% of total
France	11.4	Nigeria	19.8
Netherlands	7.5	France	15.1
United States	6.4	Belgium-Luxembourg	3.0
Mali	4.4	Germany	2.7
Italy	3.7	Italy	2.7

Balance of payments, reserves and debt, $bn

Visible exports fob	4.0	Overall balance	-0.6
Visible imports fob	-2.2	Change in reserves	0.0
Trade balance	1.8	Level of reserves	
Invisibles inflows	0.6	end Dec.	0.7
Invisibles outflows	-2.6	No. months of import cover	1.9ᵃ
Net transfers	-0.4	Foreign debt	12.1
Current account balance	-0.0	– as % of GDP	117
– as % of GDP	-0.1	Debt service paid	1.0
Capital balance	-0.7	Debt service ratio	20

Health and education

Health spending, % of GDP	3.7	Education spending, % of GDP	4.2
Doctors per 1,000 pop.	0.1	Enrolment, %: primary	78
Hospital beds per 1,000 pop.	0.8	secondary	23
Improved-water source access,		tertiary	7
% of pop.	77		

Society

No. of households	3.3m	Colour TVs per 100 households	38.7
Av. no. per household	4.5	Telephone lines per 100 pop.	1.8
Marriages per 1,000 pop.	...	Mobile telephone subscribers	
Divorces per 1,000 pop.	...	per 100 pop.	4.5
Cost of living, Dec. 2001		Computers per 100 pop.	0.6
New York = 100	78	Internet hosts per 1,000 pop.	0.1

a 1990

CZECH REPUBLIC

Area	78,864 sq km	Capital	Prague
Arable as % of total land	40	Currency	Koruna (Kc)

People

Population	10.3m	Life expectancy: men		72.1 yrs
Pop. per sq km	130	women		78.7 yrs
Av. ann. growth		Adult literacy		99.0%
in pop. 1995–2000	-0.11	Fertility rate (per woman)		1.16
Pop. under 15	16.4%	Urban population		74.7%
Pop. over 65	13.8%			per 1,000 pop.
No. of men per 100 women	94.9	Crude birth rate		8.8
Human Development Index	84.4	Crude death rate		10.8

The economy

GDP	Kcs1,960bn	GDP per head	$4,340
GDP	$50.8bn	GDP per head in purchasing	
Av. ann. growth in real		power parity (USA=100)	40.4
GDP 1991–2000	0.0%	Economic freedom index	2.40

Origins of GDP

	% of total
Agriculture	5.2
Industry, of which:	36.6
manufacturing	...
Services	58.2

Components of GDP

	% of total
Private consumption	54.4
Public consumption	19.6
Investment	29.7
Exports	71.4
Imports	-75.2

Structure of employment[a]

	% of total		% of labour force
Agriculture	5	Unemployed 2000	8.8
Industry	40	Av. ann. rate 1990–2000	4.8
Services	55		

Energy

	m TCE		
Total output	41.101	% output exported	27.5
Total consumption	55.472	% consumption imported	50.5
Consumption per head, kg coal equivalent	5,395		

Inflation and finance

Consumer price		av. ann. increase 1995–2000	
inflation 2001	4.7%	Narrow money (M1)	3.0%
Av. ann. inflation 1996–2001	5.9%	Broad money	5.9%
Refinancing rate, 2001	5.75%		

Exchange rates

	end 2001		December 2001
Kc per $	36.26	Effective rates	1995 = 100
Kc per SDR	45.57	– nominal	109.4
Kc per euro	32.47	– real	126.7

Trade

Principal exports		Principal imports	
	$bn fob		*$bn cif*
Machinery & transport		Machinery & transport	
equipment	12.9	equipment	12.9
Semi-manufactures	7.4	Semi-manufactures	6.7
Chemicals	2.1	Raw materials & fuels	4.1
Raw materials & fuels	1.9	Chemicals	3.6
Total incl. others	**29.0**	Total incl. others	**32.2**

Main export destinations		Main origins of imports	
	% of total		*% of total*
Germany	40.4	Germany	26.7
Slovakia	7.7	Russia	6.4
Austria	6.0	Slovakia	6.0
Poland	5.4	Italy	5.2
United Kingdom	4.3	Austria	4.9
EU15	68.5	EU15	62.0

Balance of payments, reserves and debt, $bn

Visible exports fob	29.0	Overall balance	0.8
Visible imports fob	-32.1	Change in reserves	0.2
Trade balance	-3.1	Level of reserves	
Invisibles inflows	8.5	end Dec.	13.1
Invisibles outflows	-8.0	No. months of import cover	3.9
Net transfers	0.3	Foreign debt	21.3
Current account balance	-2.2	– as % of GDP	40
– as % of GDP	-4.4	Debt service paid	4.8
Capital balance	3.4	Debt service ratio	13

Health and education

Health spending, % of GDP	7.2	Education spending, % of GDP	4.2
Doctors per 1,000 pop.	3.0	Enrolment, %: primary	104
Hospital beds per 1,000 pop.	8.7	secondary	82
Improved-water source access,		tertiary	26
% of pop.	...		

Society

No. of households	3.7m	Colour TVs per 100 households	87.1
Av. no. per household	2.8	Telephone lines per 100 pop.	37.4
Marriages per 1,000 pop.	4.3	Mobile telephone subscribers	
Divorces per 1,000 pop.	3.1	per 100 pop.	65.9
Cost of living, Dec. 2001		Computers per 100 pop.	12.1
New York = 100	57	Internet hosts per 1,000 pop.	20.8

a 1999

DENMARK

Area	43,075 sq km	Capital	Copenhagen
Arable as % of total land	54	Currency	Danish krone (DKr)

People

Population	5.3m	Life expectancy: men		74.2 yrs
Pop. per sq km	124	women		79.1 yrs
Av. ann. growth		Adult literacy		99.0%
in pop. 1995–2000	0.3	Fertility rate (per woman)		1.65
Pop. under 15	18.3%	Urban population		85.3%
Pop. over 65	15.0%			per 1,000 pop.
No. of men per 100 women	97.8	Crude birth rate		11.0
Human Development Index	92.1	Crude death rate		11.3

The economy

GDP	DKr1,312bn	GDP per head	$30,420
GDP	$162bn	GDP per head in purchasing	
Av. ann. growth in real		power parity (USA=100)	79.9
GDP 1990–2000	2.2%	Economic freedom index	1.90

Origins of GDP		Components of GDP	
	% of total		% of total
Agriculture	2.9	Private consumption	47.7
Industry, of which:	22.7	Public consumption	24.8
manufacturing	16.8	Investment	21.6
Services	74.4	Exports	43.0
		Imports	-37.1

Structure of employment[a]

	% of total		% of labour force
Agriculture	3	Unemployed 2000	5.4
Industry	27	Av. ann. rate 1990–2000	7.3
Services	70		

Energy

	m TCE		
Total output	26.163	% output exported	81.9
Total consumption	23.879	% consumption imported	89.9
Consumption per head,			
kg coal equivalent	4,531		

Inflation and finance

Consumer price		av. ann. increase 1995–2000	
inflation 2001	2.3%	Narrow money (M1)	5.9
Av. ann. inflation 1996–2001	2.3%	Broad money	4.3
Discount rate, 2001	3.25%		

Exchange rates

	end 2001		July 2001
DKr per $	8.41	Effective rates	1995 = 100
DKr per SDR	10.57	– nominal	93.4
DKr per euro	7.53	– real	94.3

Trade

Principal exports		Principal imports	
	$bn fob		*$bn cif*
Manufactured goods	37.0	Intermediate goods	19.5
Agric. products	5.2	Consumer goods	12.3
Energy & products	4.0	Capital goods	6.3
Ships	0.5	Transport equipment	3.4
Total incl. others	**50.9**	Total incl. others	**43.2**

Main export destinations		Main origins of imports	
	% of total		*% of total*
Germany	19.1	Germany	21.1
Sweden	12.9	Sweden	12.3
United Kingdom	9.8	United Kingdom	8.6
United States	5.9	Netherlands	7.5
Norway	5.5	France	5.2
Netherlands	5.0	Italy	4.4
EU15	65.9	EU15	69.7

Balance of payments, reserves and aid, $bn

Visible exports fob	50.7	Capital balance	-5.6
Visible imports fob	-43.9	Overall balance	-5.6
Trade balance	6.8	Change in reserves	-7.2
Invisibles inflows	32.2	Level of reserves	
Invisibles outflows	-33.3	end Dec.	15.7
Net transfers	-3.2	No. months of import cover	2.4
Current account balance	2.5	Aid given	1.66
– as % of GDP	1.5	– as % of GDP	1.04

Health and education

Health spending, % of GDP	8.4	Education spending, % of GDP	8.2
Doctors per 1,000 pop.	3.4	Enrolment, %: primary	103
Hospital beds per 1,000 pop.	4.5	secondary	126
Improved-water source access,		tertiary	55
% of pop.	100		

Society

No. of households	2.5m	Colour TVs per 100 households	92.1
Av. no. per household	2.1	Telephone lines per 100 pop.	72.3
Marriages per 1,000 pop.	9.3	Mobile telephone subscribers	
Divorces per 1,000 pop.	2.5	per 100 pop.	73.7
Cost of living, Dec. 2001		Computers per 100 pop.	43.2
New York = 100	91	Internet hosts per 1,000 pop.	133.4

a 1998

EGYPT

Area	1,000,250 sq km	Capital	Cairo
Arable as % of total land	3	Currency	Egyptian pound (£E)

People

Population	67.9m	Life expectancy: men	66.7 yrs
Pop. per sq km	68	women	69.9 yrs
Av. ann. growth		Adult literacy	55.3%
in pop. 1995–2000	1.82%	Fertility rate (per woman)	2.88
Pop. under 15	35.4%	Urban population	45.2%
Pop. over 65	4.1%		per 1,000 pop.
No. of men per 100 women	102.9	Crude birth rate	23.3
Human Development Index	63.5	Crude death rate	6.1

The economy

GDP	£E336bn	GDP per head	$1,540
GDP	$98.7bn	GDP per head in purchasing	
Av. ann. growth in real		power parity (USA=100)	10.8
GDP 1990–2000	4.5%	Economic freedom index	3.55

Origins of GDP[a]

	% of total
Agriculture	11.0
Industry, of which:	27.8
manufacturing	...
Services	61.2

Components of GDP[a]

	% of total
Private consumption	72.0
Public consumption	9.7
Investment	24.9
Exports	18.3
Imports	-24.9

Structure of employment[b]

	% of total		% of labour force
Agriculture	30	Unemployed 1998	8.2
Industry	22	Av. ann. rate 1990–98	9.6
Services	48		

Energy

	m TCE		
Total output	79.600	% output exported	17.3
Total consumption	50.565	% consumption imported	6.2
Consumption per head,			
kg coal equivalent	766		

Inflation and finance

Consumer price		*av. ann. increase 1995–2000*	
inflation 2001	2.3%	Narrow money (M1)	8.4%
Av. ann. inflation 1996–2001	3.4%	Broad money	8.7%
Treasury bill rate, 2001	9.1%		

Exchange rates

	end 2001		December 2001
£E per $	4.49	Effective rates	1995 = 100
£E per SDR	5.64	– nominal	...
£E per euro	4.02	– real	...

Trade

Principal exports[a]

	$bn fob
Petroleum & products	2.6
Cotton yarn & textiles	0.4
Engineering & metallurgical goods	0.2
Raw cotton	0.2
Other agricultural products	0.1
Total incl. others	**7.1**

Principal imports[a]

	$bn fob
Investment goods	5.6
Intermediate goods	4.2
Consumer goods	3.0
Raw materials	2.7
Fuels	1.1
Total incl. others	**17.6**

Main export destinations

	% of total
Italy	17.5
United States	14.9
Germany	4.2

Main origins of imports

	% of total
United States	17.9
Germany	7.7
Italy	7.5

Balance of payments, reserves and debt, $bn

Visible exports fob	7.1	Overall balance	-2.0
Visible imports fob	-15.4	Change in reserves	-1.4
Trade balance	-8.3	Level of reserves	
Invisibles inflows	11.7	end Dec.	13.8
Invisibles outflows	-8.5	No. months of import cover	6.9
Net transfers	4.2	Foreign debt	29.0
Current account balance	-1.0	– as % of GDP	25
– as % of GDP	-1.0	Debt service paid	1.8
Capital balance	-1.6	Debt service ratio	9

Health and education

Health spending, % of GDP	3.8	Education spending, % of GDP[c]	4.8
Doctors per 1,000 pop.	1.6	Enrolment, %: primary	100
Hospital beds per 1,000 pop.	2.1	secondary	81
Improved-water source access, % of pop.	95	tertiary	39

Society

No. of households	13.7m	Colour TVs per 100 households	45.7
Av. no. per household	4.5	Telephone lines per 100 pop.	10.3
Marriages per 1,000 pop.	10.1	Mobile telephone subscribers	
Divorces per 1,000 pop.	1.6	per 100 pop.	4.3
Cost of living, Dec. 2001		Computers per 100 pop.	1.6
New York = 100	68	Internet hosts per 1,000 pop.	0.1

a Year ending June 30, 2000.
b 1998
c 1997

EURO AREA[a]

Area	2,365,000 sq km	Capital	–
Arable as % of total land	26.6	Currency	Euro (€)

People

Population	302.8m	Life expectancy: men	75.2 yrs
Pop. per sq km	128	women	81.6 yrs
Av. ann. growth		Adult literacy	98.3%
in pop. 1995–2000	0.22%	Fertility rate (per woman)	1.5
Pop. under 15	16.1%	Urban population	77.2%
Pop. over 65	16.4%		per 1,000 pop.
No. of men per 100 women	95.9	Crude birth rate	10.3
Human Development Index	91.7	Crude death rate[b]	10.2

The economy

GDP	€5,454bn	GDP per head	$20,260
GDP	$5,920bn	GDP per head in purchasing	
Av. ann. growth in real		power parity (USA=100)	68.4
GDP 1990–99	1.7%	Economic freedom index	30

Origins of GDP[a]		Components of GDP[a]	
	% of total		% of total
Agriculture	2	Private consumption	57.0
Industry, of which:	28	Public consumption	19.9
manufacturing	...	Investment	22.1
Services	70	Exports	37.3
		Imports	-36.2

Structure of employment[b]

	% of total		% of labour force
Agriculture	4.8	Unemployed 2000	9.8
Industry	30.5	Av. ann. rate 1990–2000	10.7
Services	64.7		

Energy

	m TCE		
Total output	570.4	% output exported	...
Total consumption	1,491.6	% consumption imported	...
Consumption per head,			
kg coal equivalent	5,104		

Inflation and finance

Consumer price		av. ann. increase 1995–2000	
inflation 2001	2.6%	Narrow money (M1)	7.8%
Av. ann. inflation 1996–2001	1.8%	Broad money	4.5%
Interbank rate, 2001	4.26%		

Exchange rates

	end 2001		December 2001
€ per $	1.13	Effective rates	1995 = 100
€ per SDR	1.43	– nominal	80.4
		– real	74.9

Trade

Principal exports[c]		Principal imports[c]	
	$bn fob		*$bn fob*
Machinery & transport equip.	400.2	Machinery & transport equip.	357.9
Manufactures	230.9	Manufactures	254.8
Chemicals	119.6	Fuels & raw materials	180.3
Food, drink & tobacco	46.0	Chemicals	65.3
Fuels & raw materials	35.9	Food, drink & tobacco	50.6
Total incl. others	**2,207**	Total incl. others	**2,161**

Main export destinations[d]		Main origins of imports[d]	
	% of total		*% of total*
United States	24.8	United States	19.3
Switzerland	7.5	Japan	8.3
Japan	4.8	China	6.8
Poland	3.6	Switzerland	5.7
Turkey	3.2	Norway	4.4
China	2.7	Russia	4.4
Norway	2.7	Poland	1.7

Balance of payments, reserves and aid, $bn

Visible exports fob	908.2	Capital balance	81.9
Visible imports fob	-875.6	Overall balance	-16.1
Trade balance	32.5	Change in reserves	-21.8
Invisibles inflows	500	Level of reserves	
Invisibles outflows	-539.5	end Dec.	352.2
Net transfers	-47.9	No. months of import cover	3.0
Current account balance	-54.9	Aid given	19.31
– as % of GDP	-0.9	– as % of GDP	0.28

Health and education

Health spending, % of GDP	9.3	Education spending, % of GDP	4.81
Doctors per 1,000 pop.	3.7	Enrolment, %: primary	106
Hospital beds per 1,000 pop.	80	secondary	104
Improved-water source access,		tertiary	50
% of pop.	...		

Society

No. of households	150.9m	Colour TVs per 100 households	96.2
Av. no. per household	1.94	Telephone lines per 100 pop.	50.1
Marriages per 1,000 pop.	5.0	Mobile telephone subscribers	
Divorces per 1,000 pop.	1.7	per 100 pop.	64.1
Cost of living, Dec. 2001		Computers per 100 pop.	26.4
New York = 100	...	Internet hosts per 1,000 pop.	40.1

a Data refer to EU11; Greece joined on January 1, 2001. Where necessary, population-weighted averages have been calculated.
b 2001
c EU15 data including intra-EU trade.
d Extra-EU trade only.

FINLAND

Area	338,145 sq km	Capital	Helsinki
Arable as % of total land	7	Currency	Euro (€)

People

Population	5.2m	Life expectancy: men	74.4 yrs
Pop. per sq km	15	women	81.5 yrs
Av. ann. growth		Adult literacy	99.0%
in pop. 1995–2000	0.25%	Fertility rate (per woman)	1.55
Pop. under 15	18.0%	Urban population	67.3%
Pop. over 65	14.9%		per 1,000 pop.
No. of men per 100 women	95.2	Crude birth rate	9.7
Human Development Index	92.5	Crude death rate	9.8

The economy

GDP	Fmk785bn	GDP per head	$23,460
GDP	$122bn	GDP per head in purchasing	
Av. ann. growth in real		power parity (USA=100)	72.1
GDP 1990–2000	2.0%	Economic freedom index	1.95

Origins of GDP

	% of total
Agriculture	3.6
Industry, of which:	32.7
manufacturing & mining	26.6
Services	63.7

Components of GDP

	% of total
Private consumption	48.8
Public consumption	19.8
Investment	17.9
Exports	47.9
Imports	-34.3

Structure of employment

	% of total		% of labour force
Agriculture	6	Unemployed 2000	9.8
Industry	28	Av. ann. rate 1990–2000	11.7
Services	66		

Energy

	m TCE		
Total output	10.589	% output exported[a]	60.4
Total consumption	37.111	% consumption imported[a]	82.4
Consumption per head,			
kg coal equivalent	7,200		

Inflation and finance

Consumer price		av. ann. increase 1995–2000	
inflation 2001	2.5%	Euro area:	
Av. ann. inflation 1996–2001	1.9%	Narrow money (M1)	7.8%
Money market rate, 2001	4.26%	Broad money	4.5%

Exchange rates

	end 2001		December 2001
			1995 = 100
Euro per $	1.13	Effective rates	
Euro per SDR	1.43	– nominal	90.0
		– real	78.7

Trade

Principal exports		Principal imports	
	$bn fob		$bn cif
Electrical & optical equipment	14.1	Intermediate goods	13.8
Metals, machinery &		Capital goods	8.1
transport equipment	11.3	Consumer goods	7.8
Paper & products	9.9	Energy & products	6.1
Chemicals	3.2		
Total incl. others	**45.4**	Total incl. others	**33.8**

Main export destinations		Main origins of imports	
	% of total		% of total
Germany	12.5	Germany	14.2
Sweden	9.3	Sweden	10.3
United Kingdom	9.1	Russia	9.4
United States	7.4	United States	7.1
France	5.2	United Kingdom	6.4
Netherlands	4.4	Japan	5.3

Balance of payments, reserves and aid, $bn

Visible exports fob	45.7	Capital balance	-9.6
Visible imports fob	-32.0	Overall balance	0.4
Trade balance	13.7	Change in reserves	0.2
Invisibles inflows	13.2	Level of reserves	
Invisibles outflows	-17.4	end Dec.	8.9
Net transfers	0.6	No. months of import cover	2.2
Current account balance	8.9	Aid given	0.37
– as % of GDP	7.3	– as % of GDP	0.31

Health and education

Health spending, % of GDP	6.8	Education spending, % of GDP[b]	7.5
Doctors per 1,000 pop.	3.1	Enrolment, %: primary	99
Hospital beds per 1,000 pop.	7.5	secondary	121
Improved-water source access,		tertiary	83
% of pop.	100		

Society

No. of households	2.3m	Colour TVs per 100 households	98.1
Av. no. per household	2.2	Telephone lines per 100 pop.	54.8
Marriages per 1,000 pop.	4.9	Mobile telephone subscribers	
Divorces per 1,000 pop.	2.6	per 100 pop.	77.8
Cost of living, Dec. 2001		Computers per 100 pop.	42.4
New York = 100	84	Internet hosts per 1,000 pop.	181.7

a Energy trade data are distorted by transitory and oil refinery activities.
b 1997

FRANCE

Area	543,965 sq km	Capital	Paris
Arable as % of total land	33	Currency	Euro (€)

People

Population	59.2m	Life expectancy: men	75.2 yrs
Pop. per sq km	107	women	82.8 yrs
Av. ann. growth		Adult literacy	99.0%
in pop. 1995–2000	0.37%	Fertility rate (per woman)	1.80
Pop. under 15	18.7%	Urban population	75.0%
Pop. over 65	16.0%		per 1,000 pop.
No. of men per 100 women	95.1	Crude birth rate	12.3
Human Development Index	92.4	Crude death rate	9.4

The economy

GDP	FFr9,215bn	GDP per head	$21,980
GDP	$1,294bn	GDP per head in purchasing	
Av. ann. growth in real		power parity (USA=100)	71.6
GDP 1990–2000	1.8%	Economic freedom index	2.70

Origins of GDP		**Components of GDP**	
	% of total		% of total
Agriculture	3.3	Private consumption	54.7
Industry, of which:	25.7	Public consumption	23.3
manufacturing	...	Investment	20.5
Services	71.0	Exports	28.7
		Imports	-27.2

Structure of employment

	% of total		% of labour force
Agriculture	1	Unemployed 2000	10.0
Industry	25	Av. ann. rate 1990–2000	11.0
Services	74		

Energy

	m TCE		
Total output	165.031	% output exported	22.4
Total consumption	336.253	% consumption imported	67.5
Consumption per head,			
kg coal equivalent	5,727		

Inflation and finance

Consumer price		*av. ann. increase 1995–2000*	
inflation 2001	1.6%	Euro area:	
Av. ann. inflation 1996–2001	1.1%	Narrow money (M1)	7.8%
Interbank rate, 2001	4.26%	Broad money	4.5%

Exchange rates

	end 2001		December 2001
Euro per $	1.13	Effective rates	1995 = 100
Euro per SDR	1.43	– nominal	93.1
		– real	87.2

Trade

Principal exports		Principal imports	
	$bn fob		*$bn cif*
Intermediate goods	94.6	Intermediate goods	99.6
Capital equipment	75.8	Capital equipment	68.4
Consumer goods	39.9	Consumer goods	46.2
Motor vehicles & other		Motor vehicles & other	
transport equipment	39.5	transport equipment	30.9
Food & drink	25.6	Energy	30.8
Total incl. others	**295.3**	Total incl. others	**287.5**

Main export destinations		Main origins of imports	
	% of total		*% of total*
Germany	15.1	Germany	16.2
United Kingdom	9.8	Italy	8.8
Spain	9.7	United States	8.7
Italy	8.9	United Kingdom	8.0
United States	8.8	Belgium & Luxembourg	7.1
EU15	62.5	EU15	59.6

Balance of payments, reserves and aid, $bn

Visible exports fob	295.5	Capital balance	-28.9
Visible imports fob	-294.4	Overall balance	-2.4
Trade balance	1.1	Change in reserves	-4.2
Invisibles inflows	153.1	Level of reserves	
Invisibles outflows	-120.3	end Dec.	63.7
Net transfers	-13.5	No. months of import cover	1.8
Current account balance	20.4	Aid given[a]	4.10
– as % of GDP	1.6	– as % of GDP	0.32

Health and education

Health spending, % of GDP	9.3	Education spending, % of GDP	5.9
Doctors per 1,000 pop.	3.0	Enrolment, %: primary	105
Hospital beds per 1,000 pop.	8.5	secondary	111
Improved-water source access,		tertiary	51
% of pop.	...		

Society

No. of households	24.1m	Colour TVs per 100 households	95.9
Av. no. per household	2.5	Telephone lines per 100 pop.	57.4
Marriages per 1,000 pop.	4.9	Mobile telephone subscribers	
Divorces per 1,000 pop.	2.0	per 100 pop.	60.5
Cost of living, Dec. 2001		Computers per 100 pop.	33.7
New York = 100	93	Internet hosts per 1,000 pop.	28.2

a Including aid to French overseas territories.

GERMANY

Area	357,868 sq km	Capital	Berlin
Arable as % of total land	33	Currency	Euro (€)

People

Population	82.0m	Life expectancy: men	75.0 yrs
Pop. per sq km	230	women	81.1 yrs
Av. ann. growth		Adult literacy	99.0%
in pop. 1995–2000	0.09%	Fertility rate (per woman)	1.29
Pop. under 15	15.5%	Urban population	87.5%
Pop. over 65	16.4%		per 1,000 pop.
No. of men per 100 women	96.0	Crude birth rate	8.2
Human Development Index	92.1	Crude death rate	10.8

The economy

GDP	DM3,976bn	GDP per head	$22,800
GDP	$1,873bn	GDP per head in purchasing	
Av. ann. growth in real		power parity (USA=100)	73.1
GDP 1990–2000	1.8%	Economic freedom index	2.10

Origins of GDP		Components of GDP	
	% of total		% of total
Agriculture	1.2	Private consumption	58.2
Industry, of which:	30.1	Public consumption	18.8
manufacturing	...	Investment	22.5
Services	68.7	Exports	33.3
		Imports	-32.8

Structure of employment

	% of total		% of labour force
Agriculture	3	Unemployed 2000	8.1
Industry	35	Av. ann. rate 1991–2000	8.1
Services	63		

Energy

	m TCE		
Total output	182.295	% output exported	16.8
Total consumption	460.822	% consumption imported	72.0
Consumption per head,			
kg coal equivalent	5,626		

Inflation and finance

Consumer price		av. ann. increase 1995–2000	
inflation 2001	2.4%	Euro area:	
Av. ann. inflation 1996–2001	1.6%	Narrow money (M1)	7.8%
Money market rate, 2001	4.37%	Broad money	4.5%

Exchange rates

	end 2001		December 2001
Euro per $	1.13	Effective rates	1995 = 100
Euro per SDR	1.43	– nominal	88.2
		– real	83.1

Trade

Principal exports		Principal imports	
	$bn fob		*$bn fob*
Machinery	184.1	Machinery	143.2
Road vehicles	96.6	Chemicals	49.0
Chemicals	75.5	Fuels	42.5
Metals & manufactures	40.2	Road vehicles	41.7
Scientific instruments	22.8	Metals & manufactures	30.9
Total incl. others	**549.2**	Total incl. others	**491.9**

Main export destinations		Main origins of imports	
	% of total		*% of total*
France	11.4	France	9.6
United States	10.3	Netherlands	8.9
United Kingdom	8.3	United States	8.6
Italy	7.5	United Kingdom	6.9
Netherlands	6.5	Italy	6.7
Japan	2.2	Japan	4.9
EU15	56.5	EU15	52.1

Balance of payments, reserves and aid, $bn

Visible exports fob	549.2	Capital balance	27.1
Visible imports fob	-491.9	Overall balance	-5.2
Trade balance	57.3	Change in reserves	-5.9
Invisibles inflows	181.1	Level of reserves	
Invisibles outflows	232.2	end Dec.	87.5
Net transfers	-24.9	No. months of import cover	1.5
Current account balance	-18.7	Aid given	5.03
– as % of GDP	-1.0	– as % of GDP	0.27

Health and education

Health spending, % of GDP	10.5	Education spending, % of GDP	4.6
Doctors per 1,000 pop.	3.5	Enrolment, %: primary	105
Hospital beds per 1,000 pop.	9.3	secondary	98
Improved-water source access,		tertiary	46
% of pop.	...		

Society

No. of households	37.5m	Colour TVs per 100 households	97.0
Av. no. per household	2.2	Telephone lines per 100 pop.	63.5
Marriages per 1,000 pop.	5.4	Mobile telephone subscribers	
Divorces per 1,000 pop.	2.4	per 100 pop.	68.3
Cost of living, Dec. 2001		Computers per 100 pop.	33.6
New York = 100	78	Internet hosts per 1,000 pop.	32.7

GREECE

Area	131,957 sq km	Capital	Athens
Arable as % of total land	21	Currency	Euro (€)

People

Population	10.6m	Life expectancy: men	75.9 yrs
Pop. per sq km	80	women	81.2 yrs
Av. ann. growth		Adult literacy	97.2%
in pop. 1995–2000	0.30%	Fertility rate (per woman)	1.24
Pop. under 15	15.1%	Urban population	60.1%
Pop. over 65	17.6%		per 1,000 pop.
No. of men per 100 women	96.9	Crude birth rate	8.9
Human Development Index	88.1	Crude death rate	10.4

The economy

GDP	Dr41,161bn	GDP per head	$10,670
GDP	$113bn	GDP per head in purchasing	
Av. ann. growth in real		power parity (USA=100)	49.4
GDP 1990–2000	2.1%	Economic freedom index	2.80

Origins of GDP		**Components of GDP**	
	% of total		% of total
Agriculture	8.5	Private consumption	69.1
Industry, of which:	24.4	Public consumption	14.9
manufacturing & mining	13.4	Investment	23.0
Services	67.1	Exports	19.2
		Imports	-26.8

Structure of employment[a]

	% of total		% of labour force
Agriculture	18	Unemployed 1998	10.8
Industry	23	Av. ann. rate 1990–98	9.3
Services	59		

Energy

	m TCE		
Total output	12.466	% output exported[b]	26.4
Total consumption	37.736	% consumption imported[b]	91.8
Consumption per head,			
kg coal equivalent	3,560		

Inflation and finance

		av. ann. increase 1994–99	
Consumer price			
inflation 2001	3.4%	Narrow money (M1)	16.3%
Av. ann. inflation 1996–2001	3.9%	Broad money	11.9%
Treasury bill rate, 2001	4.10%		

Exchange rates

	end 2001		December 2001
		Effective rates	1995 = 100
Euro per $	1.13	– nominal	84.3
Euro per SDR	1.43	– real	101.8

Trade

Principal exports[c]		Principal imports[c]	
	$bn fob		*$bn cif*
Food & beverages	1.5	Machinery	5.1
Petroleum products	0.9	Transport equipment	4.2
Chemicals	0.8	Chemicals	3.3
Textiles	0.7	Fuels	1.4
Non-ferrous metals	0.7	Iron & steel	1.0
Total incl. others	**11.6**	Total incl. others	**26.1**

Main export destinations		Main origins of imports	
	% of total		*% of total*
Germany	12.3	Italy	13.5
Italy	9.2	Germany	13.4
United Kingdom	6.4	France	7.1
United States	5.5	Netherlands	6.2
Turkey	5.1	United Kingdom	5.2

Balance of payments, reserves and debt, $bn

Visible exports fob	10.2	Overall balance	2.6
Visible imports fob	-30.4	Change in reserves	-4.8
Trade balance	-20.2	Level of reserves	
Invisibles inflows	22.0	end Dec.	14.6
Invisibles outflows	-15.0	No. months of import cover	3.9
Net transfers	3.4	Aid given	0.23
Current account balance	-9.8	– as % of GDP	0.20
– as % of GDP	-8.7		
Capital balance	12.9		

Health and education

Health spending, % of GDP	8.4	Education spending, % of GDP[d]	3.1
Doctors per 1,000 pop.	4.1	Enrolment, %: primary	97
Hospital beds per 1,000 pop.	5.0	secondary	96
Improved-water source access,		tertiary	50
% of pop.	...		

Society

No. of households	3.5m	Colour TVs per 100 households	91.0
Av. no. per household	2.9	Telephone lines per 100 pop.	52.9
Marriages per 1,000 pop.	5.6	Mobile telephone subscribers	
Divorces per 1,000 pop.	0.9	per 100 pop.	75.1
Cost of living, Dec. 2001		Computers per 100 pop.	8.1
New York = 100	67	Internet hosts per 1,000 pop.	17.2

a 1998
b Energy trade figures are distorted by transitory and oil refining activities.
c 1999
d 1997

HONG KONG

Area	1,075 sq km	Capital	Victoria
Arable as % of total land	5	Currency	Hong Kong dollar (HK$)

People

Population	6.9m	Life expectancy: men	77.3 yrs
Pop. per sq km	6,564	women	82.8 yrs
Av. ann. growth		Adult literacy	93.6%
in pop. 1995–2000	1.99%	Fertility rate (per woman)	1.17
Pop. under 15	16.3%	Urban population	100.0%
Pop. over 65	10.6%		per 1,000 pop.
No. of men per 100 women	104	Crude birth rate	9.5
Human Development Index	88.0	Crude death rate	5.9

The economy

GDP	HK$1,267bn	GDP per head	$23,930
GDP	$163bn	GDP per head in purchasing	
Av. ann. growth in real		power parity (USA=100)	75.0
GDP 1990–2000	4.3%	Economic freedom index	1.35

Origins of GDP		Components of GDP	
	% of total		% of total
Agriculture	0.1	Private consumption	58.3
Industry, of which:	14.1	Public consumption	9.6
manufacturing	5.8	Investment	27.5
Services	85.8	Exports	149.9
		Imports	-145.2

Structure of employment

	% of total		% of labour force
Agriculture	0	Unemployed 2000	5.0
Industry	21	Av. ann. rate 1990–2000	3.0
Services	79		

Energy

	m TCE		
Total output	nil	% output exported	nil
Total consumption	17.2	% consumption imported	218.6
Consumption per head,			
kg coal equivalent	2,582		

Inflation and finance

Consumer price		av. ann. increase 1995–2000	
inflation 2001	-1.6%	Narrow money (M1)	4.1%
Av. ann. inflation 1996–2001	-0.2%	Broad money	10.0%
Money market rate, 2001	2.69%		

Exchange rates

	end 2001		December 2001
		Effective rates	1995 = 100
HK$ per $	7.80		
HK$ per SDR	9.80	– nominal	...
HK$ per euro	6.98	– real	...

Trade

Principal exports[a]		Principal imports	
	$bn fob		*$bn cif*
Clothing	9.9	Electrical machinery & appliances	37.1
Electrical machinery & apparatus	3.7	Telecommunications & sound equipment	20.7
Textiles	1.2	Office machinery	18.3
Specialised scientific equipment	1.0	Clothing	16.5
Office machinery	0.9		
Total incl. others	**23.2**	**Total incl. others**	**213.1**

Main export destinations[b]		Main origins of imports	
	% of total		*% of total*
China	34.5	China	43.1
United States	23.2	Japan	12.0
Japan	5.5	Taiwan	7.5
United Kingdom	4.0	United States	6.8

Balance of payments, reserves and debt, $bn

Visible exports fob	202.7	Overall balance	10.0
Visible imports cif	-210.9	Change in reserves	11.3
Trade balance	-8.2	Level of reserves	
Services inflows	94.8	end Dec.	107.6
Services outflows	-76.1	No. months of import cover	4.5
Net transfers	-1.7	Foreign debt	42.2
Current account balance	8.8	– as % of GDP	26.0
– as % of GDP	5.4	Debt service paid	5.6
Capital balance	2.6	Debt service ratio	1.9

Health and education

Health spending, % of GDP	5.0	Education spending, % of GDP[c]	2.9
Doctors per 1,000 pop.	1.3	Enrolment, %: primary[c]	94
Hospital beds per 1,000 pop.	...	secondary[c]	73
Improved-water source access, % of pop.	...	tertiary[c]	23

Society

No. of households	2.1m	Colour TVs per 100 households	99.2
Av. no. per household	3.3	Telephone lines per 100 pop.	58.1
Marriages per 1,000 pop.	4.2	Mobile telephone subscribers per 100 pop.	84.4
Divorces per 1,000 pop.	1.7		
Cost of living, Dec. 2001		Computers per 100 pop.	38.5
New York = 100	117	Internet hosts per 1,000 pop.	56.2

a Domestic.
b Including re-exports.
c 1997
Note: Hong Kong became a Special Administrative Region of China from July 1 1997.

HUNGARY

Area	93,030 sq km	Capital	Budapest
Arable as % of total land	52	Currency	Forint (Ft)

People

Population	10.0m	Life expectancy: men	67.8 yrs
Pop. per sq km	107	women	76.1 yrs
Av. ann. growth		Adult literacy	99.3%
in pop. 1995–2000	-0.49%	Fertility rate (per woman)	1.2
Pop. under 15	16.9%	Urban population	64.0%
Pop. over 65	14.6%		per 1,000 pop.
No. of men per 100 women	91.5	Crude birth rate	8.8
Human Development Index	82.9	Crude death rate	13.5

The economy

GDP	Ft12,877bn	GDP per head	$4,550
GDP	$45.6bn	GDP per head in purchasing	
Av. ann. growth in real		power parity (USA=100)	35.2
GDP 1990–2000	0.4%	Economic freedom index	2.40

Origins of GDP[a]

	% of total
Agriculture	5.0
Industry, of which:	33.5
manufacturing	...
Services	61.5

Components of GDP

	% of total
Private consumption	63.8
Public consumption	9.8
Investment	30.6
Exports	62.5
Imports	-66.7

Structure of employment

	% of total		% of labour force
Agriculture	7	Unemployed 2000	6.5
Industry	34	Av. ann. rate 1990–2000	8.4
Services	59		

Energy

	m TCE		
Total output	17.914	% output exported	11.8
Total consumption	35.628	% consumption imported	67.2
Consumption per head,			
kg coal equivalent	3,522		

Inflation and finance

Consumer price		av. ann. increase 1995–2000	
inflation 2001	9.1%	Narrow money (M1)	18.7%
Av. ann. inflation 1996–2001	12.3%	Broad money	17.1%
Treasury bill rate, 2001	10.8%		

Exchange rates

	end 2001		December 2001
Ft per $	279.0	Effective rates	1995 = 100
Ft per SDR	350.7	– nominal	67.0
Ft per euro	249.8	– real	125.6

Trade

Principal exports		Principal imports	
	$bn fob		*$bn cif*
Machinery & transport		Machinery & transport	
equipment	16.8	equipment	16.5
Other manufactures	8.2	Other manufactures	11.3
Food & beverages	1.9	Fuels	2.7
Raw materials	0.7	Food & food products	0.9
Total incl. others	**28.1**	Total incl. others	**32.1**

Main export destinations		Main origins of imports	
	% of total		*% of total*
Germany	37.2	Germany	25.5
Austria	8.7	Russia	8.1
Italy	5.9	Italy	7.5
Netherlands	5.4	Austria	7.4

Balance of payments, reserves and debt, $bn

Visible exports fob	25.4	Overall balance	1.1
Visible imports fob	-27.5	Change in reserves	0.2
Trade balance	-2.1	Level of reserves	
Invisibles inflows	7.2	end Dec.	11.2
Invisibles outflows	-7.0	No. months of import cover	3.9
Net transfers	0.4	Foreign debt	29.4
Current account balance	-1.5	– as % of GDP	62
– as % of GDP	-3.3	Debt service paid	7.9
Capital balance	2.6	Debt service ratio	27

Health and education

Health spending, % of GDP	6.8	Education spending, % of GDP	4.6
Doctors per 1,000 pop.	3.2	Enrolment, %: primary	103
Hospital beds per 1,000 pop.	8.3	secondary	98
Improved-water source access,		tertiary	34
% of pop.	99		

Society

No. of households	4.1m	Colour TVs per 100 households	87.9
Av. no. per household	2.4	Telephone lines per 100 pop.	37.4
Marriages per 1,000 pop.	4.6	Mobile telephone subscribers	
Divorces per 1,000 pop.	2.6	per 100 pop.	49.8
Cost of living, Dec. 2001		Computers per 100 pop.	10.0
New York = 100	50	Internet hosts per 1,000 pop.	21.1

a 1999

INDIA

Area	3,287,263 sq km	Capital	New Delhi
Arable as % of total land	54	Currency	Indian rupee (Rs)

People

Population	1,008.9m	Life expectancy: men	63.6 yrs
Pop. per sq km	307	women	64.9 yrs
Av. ann. growth		Adult literacy	57.2%
in pop. 1995–2000	1.69%	Fertility rate (per woman)	2.97
Pop. under 15	33.5%	Urban population	28.4%
Pop. over 65	5.0%		per 1,000 pop.
No. of men per 100 women	106	Crude birth rate	23.8
Human Development Index	97.1	Crude death rate	8.4

The economy

GDP	Rs20,880bn	GDP per head	$450
GDP	$457bn	GDP per head in purchasing	
Av. ann. growth in real		power parity (USA=100)	6.9
GDP 1990–2000	5.5%	Economic freedom index	3.55

Origins of GDP[a]		Components of GDP[a]	
	% of total		% of total
Agriculture	24.3	Private consumption	61.3
Industry, of which:	27.7	Public consumption	12.1
manufacturing	17.6	Investment	24.4
Services	48.0	Exports	13.8
		Imports	-12.5

Structure of employment[b]

	% of total		% of labour force
Agriculture	60	Unemployed 2000	...
Industry	18	Av. ann. rate 1990–2000	...
Services	22		

Energy

	m TCE		
Total output	356.567	% output exported	0.5
Total consumption	422.667	% consumption imported	23.9
Consumption per head,			
kg coal equivalent	430		

Inflation and finance

		av. ann. increase 1995–2000	
Consumer price			
inflation 2001	3.7%	Narrow money (M1)	13.2%
Av. ann. inflation 1996–2001	6.5%	Broad money	17.4%
Bank rate, 2000	6.50%		

Exchange rates

	end 2001		December 2001
			1995 = 100
Rs per $	48.18	Effective rates	
Rs per SDR	60.55	– nominal	...
Rs per euro	43.15	– real	...

Trade

Principal exports[c]

	$bn fob
Textiles	9.4
Gems & jewellery	7.6
Engineering goods	5.0
Chemicals	3.8
Total incl. others	**36.6**

Principal imports[c]

	$bn cif
Petroleum & products	10.5
Capital goods	5.4
Gems	5.4
Machine tools	3.0
Total incl. others	**44.6**

Main export destinations

	% of total
United States	22.8
Hong Kong	5.8
Japan	5.3
United Kingdom	5.3
Germany	4.6

Main origins of imports

	% of total
Belgium & Luxembourg	8.5
United States	8.0
United Kingdom	6.2
Japan	5.7
Saudi Arabia	4.6

Balance of payments, reserves and debt, $bn

Visible exports fob	43.1	Overall balance	6.1
Visible imports fob	-55.3	Change in reserves	5.1
Trade balance	-12.2	Level of reserves	
Invisibles inflows	20.6	end Dec.	41.1
Invisibles outflows	-26.1	No. months of import cover	6.1
Net transfers	13.5	Foreign debt	100.4
Current account balance	-4.2	– as % of GDP	16
– as % of GDP	-0.9	Debt service paid	9.9
Capital balance	9.6	Debt service ratio	15

Health and education

Health spending, % of GDP	5.4	Education spending, % of GDP[d]	3.2
Doctors per 1,000 pop.	0.4	Enrolment, %: primary	100
Hospital beds per 1,000 pop.	0.8	secondary	49
Improved-water source access,		tertiary[d]	7
% of pop.	88		

Society

No. of households	170.0m	Colour TVs per 100 households	29.6
Av. no. per household	5.4	Telephone lines per 100 pop.	3.4
Marriages per 1,000 pop.	...	Mobile telephone subscribers	
Divorces per 1,000 pop.	...	per 100 pop.	0.6
Cost of living, Dec. 2001		Computers per 100 pop.	0.6
New York = 100	39	Internet hosts per 1,000 pop.	0.1

a Year ending March 31, 2001.
b 1998
c Year ending March 31, 2000.
d 1997

INDONESIA

Area[a]	1,904,443 sq km	Capital	Jakarta
Arable as % of total land	10	Currency	Rupiah (Rp)

People

Population	212.1m	Life expectancy: men	65.3 yrs
Pop. per sq km	111	women	69.3 yrs
Av. ann. growth		Adult literacy	86.9%
in pop. 1995–2000	1.41%	Fertility rate (per woman)	2.27
Pop. under 15	30.8%	Urban population	40.0%
Pop. over 65	4.8%		per 1,000 pop.
No. of men per 100 women	101	Crude birth rate	20.0
Human Development Index	67.7	Crude death rate	7.1

The economy

GDP	Rp1,291trn	GDP per head	$730
GDP	$153bn	GDP per head in purchasing	
Av. ann. growth in real		power parity (USA=100)	8.3
GDP 1990–2000	4.6%	Economic freedom index	3.35

Origins of GDP

	% of total
Agriculture	16.6
Industry, of which:	43.1
manufacturing	26.2
Services	40.3

Components of GDP

	% of total
Private consumption	67.3
Public consumption	7.0
Investment	17.8
Exports	38.5
Imports	-30.7

Structure of employment[b]

	% of total		% of total
Agriculture	45	Unemployed 2000	6.1
Industry	16	Av. ann. rate 1996–2000	5.3
Services	39		

Energy

	m TCE		
Total output	300.972	% output exported	52.4
Total consumption	114.493	% consumption imported	22.5
Consumption per head,			
kg coal equivalent	555		

Inflation and finance

Consumer price		*av. ann. increase 1995–2000*	
inflation 2001	11.5%	Narrow money (M1)	27.2%
Av. ann. inflation 1996–2001	18.6%	Broad money	27.7%
Money market rate, 2001	15.03%		

Exchange rates

	end 2001		December 2001
Rp per $	10,400	Effective rates	1995 = 100
Rp per SDR	13,070	– nominal	...
Rp per euro	9,813	– real	...

Trade

Principal exports		Principal imports	
	$bn fob		*$bn cif*
Petroleum & products	7.7	Raw materials	25.9
Natural gas	6.6	Capital goods	4.5
Electrical appliances	6.4	Consumer goods	2.7
Garments	4.6		
Plywood	3.6		
Total incl. others	**61.5**	Total incl. others	**33.1**

Main export destinations		Main origins of imports	
	% of total		*% of total*
Japan	23.4	Japan	16.3
United States	13.8	Singapore	11.4
Singapore	10.7	United States	10.2
South Korea	7.0	South Korea	6.3
China	4.5	China	6.1
Malaysia	3.2	Australia	5.1

Balance of payments, reserves and debt, $bn

Visible exports fob	65.4	Overall balance	3.7
Visible imports fob	-40.4	Change in reserves	2.0
Trade balance	25.0	Level of reserves	
Invisibles inflows	7.7	end Dec.	29.4
Invisibles outflows	-26.5	No. months of import cover	5.3
Net transfers	1.8	Foreign debt	141.8
Current account balance	8.0	– as % of GDP	111
– as % of GDP	5.2	Debt service paid	18.8
Capital balance	-7.9	Debt service ratio	30

Health and education

Health spending, % of GDP	1.6	Education spending, % of GDP	1.4
Doctors per 1,000 pop.	0.2	Enrolment, %: primary[c]	113
Hospital beds per 1,000 pop.	0.7	secondary[c]	56
Improved-water source access,		tertiary[c]	11
% of pop.	76		

Society

No. of households	52.3m	Colour TVs per 100 households	45.6
Av. no. per household	4.2	Telephone lines per 100 pop.	3.7
Marriages per 1,000 pop.	6.7	Mobile telephone subscribers	
Divorces per 1,000 pop.	1.0	per 100 pop.	2.5
Cost of living, Dec. 2001		Computers per 100 pop.	1.1
New York = 100	65	Internet hosts per 1,000 pop.	0.2

a Excludes East Timor, 14,874 sq km.
b 1998
c 1997

IRAN

Area	1,648,000 sq km	Capital	Tehran
Arable as % of total land	11	Currency	Rial (IR)

People

Population	70.3m	Life expectancy: men	68.8 yrs
Pop. per sq km	43	women	70.8 yrs
Av. ann. growth		Adult literacy	76.3%
in pop. 1995–2000	1.69%	Fertility rate (per woman)	2.76
Pop. under 15	37.4%	Urban population	61.0%
Pop. over 65	3.4%		per 1,000 pop.
No. of men per 100 women	105	Crude birth rate	22.1
Human Development Index	71.4	Crude death rate	5.0

The economy

GDP	IR535trn	GDP per head	$1,650
GDP	$105bn	GDP per head in purchasing	
Av. ann. growth in real		power parity (USA=100)	17.3
GDP 1990–2000	4.7%	Economic freedom index	4.55

Origins of GDP[a]

	% of total
Agriculture	12.9
Industry, of which:	40.1
manufacturing	...
Services	47.0

Components of GDP[a]

	% of total
Private consumption	58.0
Public consumption	10.1
Investment	23.8
Net exports	8.1

Structure of employment[b]

	% of total		% of labour force
Agriculture	23	Unemployed 2000	...
Industry	31	Av. ann. rate 1990–2000	...
Services	45		

Energy

	m TCE		
Total output	334.728	% output exported	50.2
Total consumption	142.976	% consumption imported	3.3
Consumption per head, kg coal equivalent	2,174		

Inflation and finance

		av. ann. increase 1995–2000	
Consumer price inflation 2001	11.3%	Narrow money (M1)	24.4%
Av. ann. inflation 1996–2001	16.6%	Broad money	24.0%

Exchange rates

	end 2001		December 2001
			1995 = 100
IR per $	1,751	Effective rates	
IR per SDR	2,200	– nominal	170.8
IR per euro	1,568	– real	367.0

Trade

Principal exports[c]		Principal imports[d]	
	$bn fob		*$bn cif*
Oil & gas	16.3	Transport, machinery & tools	6.3
Industrial goods	1.8	Chemicals & pharmaceuticals	1.8
Agricultural goods	1.5	Food & animals	1.6
Total incl. others	**19.7**	**Total incl. others**	**14.3**

Main export destinations		Main origins of imports	
	% of total		*% of total*
Japan	17.7	Germany	9.8
Italy	7.9	Japan	9.4
France	7.5	Italy	6.2
United Arab Emirates	7.5	United Arab Emirates	6.2
China	5.9	China	4.9

Balance of payments[a], reserves and debt, $bn

Visible exports fob	28.3	Overall balance	1.1
Visible imports fob	-15.2	Change in reserves	...
Trade balance	13.1	Level of reserves	
Invisibles inflows	1.8	end Dec.	...
Invisibles outflows	-2.9	No. months of import cover	...
Net transfers	0.5	Foreign debt	8.0
Current account balance	12.6	– as % of GDP	7.0
– as % of GDP	12.1	Debt service paid	3.4
Capital balance	-10.2	Debt service ratio	15

Health and education

Health spending, % of GDP	4.2	Education spending, % of GDP	4.6
Doctors per 1,000 pop.	0.9	Enrolment, %: primary[e]	98
Hospital beds per 1,000 pop.	1.6	secondary[e]	77
Improved-water source access,		tertiary[e]	18
% of pop.	95		

Society

No. of households	12.6m	Colour TVs per 100 households	15.7
Av. no. per household	5.3	Telephone lines per 100 pop.	15.5
Marriages per 1,000 pop.	7.8	Mobile telephone subscribers	
Divorces per 1,000 pop.	0.7	per 100 pop.	2.3
Cost of living, Dec. 2001		Computers per 100 pop.	7.0
New York = 100	28	Internet hosts per 1,000 pop.	...

a Iranian year ending March 20, 2001.
b 1996
c 1999
d 1998
e 1997

IRELAND

Area	70,282 sq km	Capital	Dublin
Arable as % of total land	16	Currency	Euro (€)

People

Population	3.8m	Life expectancy: men	74.4 yrs
Pop. per sq km	54	women	79.6 yrs
Av. ann. growth		Adult literacy	99.0%
in pop. 1995–2000	1.05%	Fertility rate (per woman)	2.02
Pop. under 15	21.6%	Urban population	59.0%
Pop. over 65	11.3%		per 1,000 pop.
No. of men per 100 women	98.6	Crude birth rate	15.3
Human Development Index	91.6	Crude death rate	8.2

The economy

GDP	I£80.2bn	GDP per head	$24,740
GDP	$93.9bn	GDP per head in purchasing	
Av. ann. growth in real		power parity (USA=100)	74.8
GDP 1990–2000	7.2%	Economic freedom index	1.80

Origins of GDP		Components of GDP	
	% of total		% of total
Agriculture	5.2	Private consumption	49.0
Industry, of which:	45.1	Public consumption	12.2
manufacturing	...	Investment	23.9
Services	49.7	Exports	94.9
		Imports	-80.7

Structure of employment

	% of total		% of labour force
Agriculture	8	Unemployed 2000	4.7
Industry	29	Av. ann. rate 1990–2000	11.5
Services	63		

Energy

	m TCE		
Total output	3.555	% output exported	45.7
Total consumption	18.271	% consumption imported	93.9
Consumption per head,			
kg coal equivalent	4,964		

Inflation and finance

		av. ann. increase 1995–2000	
Consumer price			
inflation 2001	4.1%	Euro area:	
Av. ann. inflation 1996–2001	3.0%	Narrow money (M1)	7.8%
Money market rate, 2001	3.31%	Broad money	4.5%

Exchange rates

	end 2001		December 2001
		Effective rates	1995 = 100
Euro per $	1.13	– nominal	89.8
Euro per SDR	1.43	– real	...

Trade

Principal exports		Principal imports	
	$bn fob		*$bn cif*
Machinery & transport equipment	34.4	Machinery & transport equipment	27.0
Chemicals	25.8	Chemicals	6.2
Foodstuffs & tobacco	6.3	Foodstuffs & tobacco	3.0
Scientific instruments, etc	2.8	Fuels	2.1
Total incl. others	**76.3**	Total incl. others	**50.6**

Main export destinations		Main origins of imports	
	% of total		*% of total*
United Kingdom	19.8	United Kingdom	33.4
United States	17.1	United States	16.2
Germany	11.3	Germany	5.9
France	7.7	France	4.5
Netherlands	5.6	Japan	4.0
Belgium & Luxembourg	4.8	Netherlands	3.5
EU15	62.8	EU15	61.4

Balance of payments, reserves and aid, $bn

Visible exports fob	73.4	Capital balance	10.0
Visible imports fob	-48.0	Overall balance	0.1
Trade balance	25.4	Change in reserves	0.1
Invisibles inflows	46.8	Level of reserves	
Invisibles outflows	-73.7	end Dec.	5.4
Net transfers	0.9	No. months of import cover	0.5
Current account balance	-0.6	Aid given	0.23
– as % of GDP	-0.6	– as % of GDP	0.25

Health and education

Health spending, % of GDP	6.8	Education spending, % of GDP	4.5
Doctors per 1,000 pop.	2.3	Enrolment, %: primary	141
Hospital beds per 1,000 pop.	3.7	secondary	109
Improved-water source access, % of pop.	...	tertiary	45

Society

No. of households	1.2m	Colour TVs per 100 households	99.2
Av. no. per household	3.2	Telephone lines per 100 pop.	48.5
Marriages per 1,000 pop.	2.1	Mobile telephone subscribers	
Divorces per 1,000 pop.	...	per 100 pop.	72.9
Cost of living, Dec. 2001		Computers per 100 pop.	39.1
New York = 100	76	Internet hosts per 1,000 pop.	25.1

ISRAEL

Area	20,770 sq km	Capital	Jerusalem
Arable as % of total land	17	Currency	New Shekel (NIS)

People

Population	6.0m	Life expectancy:	men	77.1 yrs
Pop. per sq km	273		women	81.0 yrs
Av. ann. growth		Adult literacy		94.4%
in pop. 1995–2000	2.43%	Fertility rate (per woman)		2.7
Pop. under 15	28.3%	Urban population		91.2%
Pop. over 65	9.9%			per 1,000 pop.
No. of men per 100 women	97	Crude birth rate		19.8
Human Development Index	89.3	Crude death rate		6.0

The economy

GDP	NIS450bn	GDP per head	$17,710
GDP	$110bn	GDP per head in purchasing	
Av. ann. growth in real		power parity (USA=100)	56.7
GDP 1990–2000	5.3%	Economic freedom index	2.65

Origins of GDP[a]		Components of GDP	
	% of total		% of total
Agriculture	3.9	Private consumption	59.1
Industry, of which:	36.6	Public consumption	28.8
manufacturing	...	Investment	19.1
Services	59.5	Exports	40.0
		Imports	-47.0

Structure of employment[a]

	% of total		% of labour force
Agriculture	2	Unemployed 2000	8.3
Industry	25	Av. ann. rate 1990–2000	8.7
Services	73		

Energy

	m TCE		
Total output	0.159	% output exported[b]	...
Total consumption	24.187	% consumption imported[b]	124.1
Consumption per head,			
kg coal equivalent	4,042		

Inflation and finance

Consumer price		av. ann. increase 1995–2000	
inflation 2001	1.1%	Narrow money (M1)	13.2%
Av. ann. inflation 1996–2001	4.3%	Broad money	16.5%
Deposit rate, 2001	5.5%		

Exchange rates

	end 2001		December 2001
NIS per $	4.42	Effective rates	1995 = 100
NIS per SDR	5.55	– nominal	91.69
NIS per euro	3.96	– real	112.35

Trade

Principal exports		Principal imports	
	$bn fob		*$bn fob*
Manufactures	20.8	Raw materials	14.7
Diamonds	6.8	Diamonds	6.4
Agricultural goods	0.7	Investment goods	5.9
		Consumer goods	4.5
		Fuel	3.5
Total incl. others	**28.3**	Total incl. others	**35.2**

Main export destinations		Main origins of imports	
	% of total		*% of total*
United States	37.4	United States	17.8
Belgium & Luxembourg	6.0	Belgium & Luxembourg	10.0
Germany	4.8	United Kingdom	7.6
United Kingdom	4.3	Germany	7.5
Hong Kong	4.4	Switzerland	5.4
Netherlands	2.8	Italy	4.8

Balance of payments, reserves and debt, $bn

Visible exports fob	30.8	Overall balance	-1.1
Visible imports fob	-34.2	Change in reserves	0.7
Trade balance	-3.4	Level of reserves	
Invisibles inflows	18.6	end Dec.	23.3
Invisibles outflows	-23.3	No. months of import cover	4.9
Net transfers	6.6	Foreign debt	42.9
Current account balance	-1.4	– as % of GDP	38.1
– as % of GDP	-1.3	Debt service	10.6
Capital balance	1.9	Debt service ratio	20.3

Health and education

Health spending, % of GDP	9.5	Education spending, % of GDP	7.7
Doctors per 1,000 pop.	3.9	Enrolment, %: primary	107
Hospital beds per 1,000 pop.	6.0	secondary	89
Improved-water source access, % of pop.	...	tertiary	49

Society

No. of households	1.7m	Colour TVs per 100 households	95.1
Av. no. per household	4.5	Telephone lines per 100 pop.	47.6
Marriages per 1,000 pop.	4.6	Mobile telephone subscribers	
Divorces per 1,000 pop.	2.0	per 100 pop.	80.8
Cost of living, Dec. 2001		Computers per 100 pop.	24.6
New York = 100	93	Internet hosts per 1,000 pop.	37.2

a 1999
b Energy trade data are distorted by transitory and oil refining activities.

ITALY

Area	301,245 sq km	Capital	Rome
Arable as % of total land	29	Currency	Euro (€)

People

Population	57.5m	Life expectancy:	men	75.5 yrs
Pop. per sq km	191		women	81.9 yrs
Av. ann. growth		Adult literacy		98.4%
in pop. 1995–2000	0.08%	Fertility rate (per woman)		1.2
Pop. under 15	14.3%	Urban population		67.0%
Pop. over 65	18.1%			per 1,000 pop.
No. of men per 100 women	94.3	Crude birth rate		8.6
Human Development Index	90.9	Crude death rate		10.9

The economy

GDP	L2,257trn	GDP per head	$18,620
GDP	$1,074bn	GDP per head in purchasing	
Av. ann. growth in real		power parity (USA=100)	68.8
GDP 1990–2000	1.6%	Economic freedom index	2.35

Origins of GDP

	% of total
Agriculture	2.8
Industry, of which:	31.9
manufacturing	...
Services	65.3

Components of GDP

	% of total
Private consumption	60.0
Public consumption	18.5
Investment	20.4
Exports	28.4
Imports	-27.2

Structure of employment

	% of total		% of labour force
Agriculture	5	Unemployed 2000	10.8
Industry	33	Av. ann. rate 1990–2000	11.2
Services	62		

Energy

	m TCE		
Total output	43.454	% output exported	69.9
Total consumption	238.864	% consumption imported	97.9
Consumption per head,			
kg coal equivalent	4,162		

Inflation and finance

Consumer price		av. ann. increase 1995–2000	
inflation 2001	2.7%	Euro area:	
Av. ann. inflation 1996–2001	2.2%	Narrow money (M1)	7.8%
Money market rate, 2001	4.26%	Broad money	4.5%

Exchange rates

	end 2001		December 2001
		Effective rates	1995 = 100
Euro per $	1.13		
Euro per SDR	1.43	– nominal	104.7
		– real	111.0

Trade

Principal exports		Principal imports	
	$bn fob		*$bn cif*
Engineering products	84.7	Engineering products	77.5
Textiles & clothing	36.6	Transport equipment	32.2
Transport equipment	27.6	Chemicals	30.5
Chemicals	22.1	Energy products	25.3
Food, drink & tobacco	11.9	Textiles & clothing	16.7
		Food, drink & tobacco	15.6
Total incl. others	**238.3**	Total incl. others	**236.6**

Main export destinations		Main origins of imports	
	% of total		*% of total*
Germany	15.1	Germany	17.5
France	12.6	France	11.4
United States	10.4	Netherlands	5.9
United Kingdom	6.9	United Kingdom	5.4
Spain	6.2	United States	5.3
EU15	54.9	EU15	56.3

Balance of payments, reserves and aid, $bn

Visible exports fob	238.7	Capital balance	10.4
Visible imports fob	-228.0	Overall balance	3.2
Trade balance	10.7	Change in reserves	1.9
Invisibles inflows	94.8	Level of reserves	
Invisibles outflows	-106.8	end Dec.	47.2
Net transfers	-4.3	No. months of import cover	1.7
Current account balance	-5.7	Aid given	1.38
– as % of GDP	-0.5	– as % of GDP	0.13

Health and education

Health spending, % of GDP	8.2	Education spending, % of GDP	4.7
Doctors per 1,000 pop.	5.9	Enrolment, %: primary	102
Hospital beds per 1,000 pop.	5.5	secondary	95
Improved-water source access,		tertiary	47
% of pop.	...		

Society

No. of households	22.0m	Colour TVs per 100 households	94.9
Av. no. per household	2.6	Telephone lines per 100 pop.	47.1
Marriages per 1,000 pop.	4.6	Mobile telephone subscribers	
Divorces per 1,000 pop.	0.8	per 100 pop.	83.9
Cost of living, Dec. 2001		Computers per 100 pop.	19.5
New York = 100	70	Internet hosts per 1,000 pop.	39.7

JAPAN

Area	377,727 sq km	Capital	Tokyo
Arable as % of total land	12	Currency	Yen (¥)

People

Population	127.1m	Life expectancy:	men	77.8 yrs
Pop. per sq km	336		women	85.0 yrs
Av. ann. growth		Adult literacy		99.0%
in pop. 1995–2000	0.26%	Fertility rate (per woman)		1.33
Pop. under 15	14.7%	Urban population		78.8%
Pop. over 65	17.2%			per 1,000 pop.
No. of men per 100 women	96.1	Crude birth rate		9.2
Human Development Index	92.8	Crude death rate		8.3

The economy

GDP	¥522trn	GDP per head	$38,160
GDP	$4,842bn	GDP per head in purchasing	
Av. ann. growth in real		power parity (USA=100)	79.4
GDP 1990–2000	1.8%	Economic freedom index	2.45

Origins of GDP		Components of GDP	
	% of total		% of total
Agriculture	1.4	Private consumption	55.9
Industry, of which:	31.8	Public consumption	16.7
manufacturing	21.6	Investment	26.0
Services	66.8	Exports	10.8
		Imports	-9.3

Structure of employment

	% of total		% of labour force
Agriculture	5	Unemployed 2000	4.8
Industry	31	Av. ann. rate 1990–2000	3.2
Services	64		

Energy

	m TCE		
Total output	147.790	% output exported[a]	7.2
Total consumption	659.660	% consumption imported[a]	83.9
Consumption per head,			
kg coal equivalent	5,224		

Inflation and finance

		av. ann. increase 1995–2000	
Consumer price			
inflation 2001	-0.7%	Narrow money (M1)	7.6%
Av. ann. inflation 1996–2001	0.1%	Broad money	2.8%
Money market rate, 2001	0.06%		

Exchange rates

	end 2001		December 2001
¥ per $	131.8	Effective rates	1995 = 100
¥ per SDR	165.6	– nominal	85.8
¥ per euro	118.0	– real	78.2

Trade

Principal exports		Principal imports	
	$bn fob		*$bn cif*
Electrical machinery	126.8	Machinery & equipment	119.8
Non-electrical machinery	102.9	Mineral fuels	77.1
Transport equipment	100.4	Food	46.0
Chemicals	35.3	Chemicals	26.5
Metals	26.5	Raw materials	24.5
Total incl. others	**479.2**	Total incl. others	**379.8**

Main export destinations		Main origins of imports	
	% of total		*% of total*
United States	29.7	United States	19.0
Taiwan	7.5	China	14.5
South Korea	6.4	South Korea	5.4
China	6.3	Taiwan	4.7
Hong Kong	5.7	Indonesia	4.3

Balance of payments, reserves and aid, $bn

Visible exports fob	459.5	Capital balance	-84.8
Visible imports fob	-342.8	Overall balance	49.0
Trade balance	116.7	Change in reserves	67.7
Invisibles inflows	276.2	Level of reserves	
Invisibles outflows	-266.2	end Dec.	361.6
Net transfers	-9.8	No. months of import cover	7.1
Current account balance	116.9	Aid given	13.51
– as % of GDP	2.4	– as % of GDP	0.29

Health and education

Health spending, % of GDP	7.2	Education spending, % of GDP	3.5
Doctors per 1,000 pop.	1.9	Enrolment, %: primary	102
Hospital beds per 1,000 pop.	16.4	secondary	102
Improved-water source access,		tertiary	44
% of pop.	97		

Society

No. of households	47.0m	Colour TVs per 100 households	99.1
Av. no. per household	2.7	Telephone lines per 100 pop.	54.7
Marriages per 1,000 pop.	6.1	Mobile telephone subscribers	
Divorces per 1,000 pop.	1.8	per 100 pop.	57.2
Cost of living, Dec. 2001		Computers per 100 pop.	34.9
New York = 100	137	Internet hosts per 1,000 pop.	56.0

a Energy trade data are distorted by transitory and oil refining activities.

KENYA

Area	582,646 sq km	Capital	Nairobi
Arable as % of total land	7	Currency	Kenyan shilling (KSh)

People

Population	30.7m	Life expectancy: men	48.7 yrs
Pop. per sq km	53	women	49.9 yrs
Av. ann. growth		Adult literacy	82.4%
in pop. 1995–2000	2.32%	Fertility rate (per woman)	4.15%
Pop. under 15	43.5%	Urban population	32.0%
Pop. over 65	2.8%		per 1,000 pop.
No. of men per 100 women	99	Crude birth rate	34.1
Human Development Index	51.4	Crude death rate	13.7

The economy

GDP	KSh789bn	GDP per head	$340
GDP	$10.4bn	GDP per head in purchasing	
Av. ann. growth in real		power parity (USA=100)	3.0
GDP 1990–2000	1.9%	Economic freedom index	3.20

Origins of GDP		Components of GDP	
	% of total		% of total
Agriculture	24.0	Private consumption	70.7
Industry, of which:	...	Public consumption	17.6
manufacturing	13.1	Investment	16.8
Other	62.9	Exports	25.0
		Imports	-30.1

Structure of employment[a]

	% of total		% of labour force
Agriculture	19	Unemployed 1994	21.3
Industry	20	Av. ann. rate 1990–2000	...
Services	61		

Energy

	m TCE		
Total output	1.079	% output exported[b]	86.9
Total consumption	4.511	% consumption imported[b]	115.5
Consumption per head,			
kg coal equivalent	156		

Inflation and finance

Consumer price		av. ann. increase 1995–2000	
inflation 2001	0.8%	Narrow money (M1)	11.4%
Av. ann. inflation 1996–2001	5.3%	Broad money	11.1%
Treasury bill rate, 2001	12.59%		

Exchange rates

	end 2001		December 2001
KSh per $	78.6	Effective rates	1995 = 100
KSh per SDR	98.8	– nominal	...
KSh per euro	70.4	– real	...

Trade

Principal exports[c]

	$m fob
Tea	461
Horticultural products	278
Coffee	154
Petroleum products	124
Total incl. others[d]	**1,735**

Principal imports[c]

	$m cif
Crude petroleum	551
Industrial machinery	518
Refined petroleum products	286
Motor vehicles & chassis	127
Total incl. others[d]	**3,106**

Main export destinations

	% of total
United Kingdom	13.5
Tanzania	12.5
Uganda	12.0
Germany	5.5

Main origins of imports

	% of total
United Kingdom	12.0
United Arab Emirates	9.8
Japan	6.5
India	4.4

Balance of payments, reserves and debt, $bn

Visible exports fob	1.8	Overall balance	-0.0
Visible imports fob	-3.0	Change in reserves	0.1
Trade balance	-1.3	Level of reserves	
Invisibles inflows	1.0	end Dec.	0.9
Invisibles outflows	-0.9	No. months of import cover	2.7
Net transfers	0.9	Foreign debt	6.3
Current account balance	-0.2	– as % of GDP	44
– as % of GDP	-2.3	Debt service paid	0.5
Capital balance	0.2	Debt service ratio	17

Health and education

Health spending, % of GDP	7.8	Education spending, % of GDP	6.6
Doctors per 1,000 pop.	0.1	Enrolment, %: primary	92
Hospital beds per 1,000 pop.	1.6	secondary	31
Improved-water source access,		tertiary	1
% of pop.	49		

Society

No. of households	6.7m	Colour TVs per 100 households	2.1
Av. no. per household	4.4	Telephone lines per 100 pop.	1.0
Marriages per 1,000 pop.	...	Mobile telephone subscribers	
Divorces per 1,000 pop.	...	per 100 pop.	1.6
Cost of living, Dec. 2001		Computers per 100 pop.	0.6
New York = 100	60	Internet hosts per 1,000 pop.	0.1

a 1999
b Energy trade data are distorted by transitory and oil refining activities.
c Provisional estimates.
d Actual.

MALAYSIA

Area	332,665 sq km	Capital	Kuala Lumpur
Arable as % of total land	6	Currency	Malaysian dollar/ringgit (M$)

People

Population	22.2m	Life expectancy: men	70.6 yrs
Pop. per sq km	67	women	75.5 yrs
Av. ann. growth		Adult literacy	87.5%
in pop. 1995–2000	2.09%	Fertility rate (per woman)	2.9
Pop. under 15	34.1%	Urban population	57.4%
Pop. over 65	4.1%		per 1,000 pop.
No. of men per 100 women	102.8	Crude birth rate	22.3
Human Development Index	77.4	Crude death rate	4.7

The economy

GDP	M$341bn	GDP per head	$3,850
GDP	$89.7bn	GDP per head in purchasing	
Av. ann. growth in real		power parity (USA=100)	24.4
GDP 1990–2000	7.2%	Economic freedom index	3.10

Origins of GDP

Components of GDP

	% of total		% of total
Agriculture	7.7	Private consumption	42.5
Industry, of which:	38.1	Public consumption	10.7
manufacturing	29.6	Investment	27.0
Services	54.2	Exports	125.7
		Imports	-105.8

Structure of employment[a]

	% of total		% of labour force
Agriculture	18	Unemployed 2000	3.3
Industry	32	Av. ann. rate 1990–2000	3.2
Services	50		

Energy

	m TCE		
Total output	103.030	% output exported	54.9
Total consumption	55.551	% consumption imported	29.6
Consumption per head,			
kg coal equivalent	2,595		

Inflation and finance

		av. ann. increase 1995–2000	
Consumer price			
inflation 2001	1.4%	Narrow money (M1)	4.8%
Av. ann. inflation 1996–2001	2.7%	Broad money	13.1%
Money market rate, 2001	2.79%		

Exchange rates

	end 2001		December 2001
M$ per $	3.80	Effective rates	1995 = 100
M$ per SDR	4.78	– nominal	85.7
M$ per euro	3.40	– real	93.1

Trade

Principal exports		Principal imports	
	$bn fob		*$bn cif*
Electronics & electrical machinery	60.6	Machinery & transport equip.	51.4
Petroleum & LNG	6.7	Manufacturing supplies	8.7
Chemicals & products	3.9	Chemicals	5.9
Textiles, clothing & footwear	2.7	Misc. manufactured articles	4.7
Palm oil	2.6	Mineral fuels & lubricants	3.9
		Food	3.0
Total incl. others	**98.2**	Total incl. others	**82.2**

Main export destinations		Main origins of imports	
	% of total		*% of total*
United States	20.5	Japan	21.1
Singapore	18.4	United States	16.6
Japan	13.1	Singapore	14.3
Hong Kong	4.5	Taiwan	5.6
Taiwan	3.8	South Korea	4.5
EU15	13.7	EU15	10.8

Balance of payments, reserves and debt, $bn

Visible exports fob	98.4	Overall balance	-1.0
Visible imports fob	-77.6	Change in reserves	-1.1
Trade balance	20.9	Level of reserves	
Invisibles inflows	15.9	end Dec.	29.8
Invisibles outflows	-26.3	No. months of import cover	3.4
Net transfers	-2.0	Foreign debt	41.8
Current account balance	8.4	as % of GDP	57.0
– as % of GDP	9.4	Debt service paid	6.0
Capital balance	-6.3	Debt service ratio	6.0

Health and education

Health spending, % of GDP	2.5	Education spending, % of GDP[b]	4.9
Doctors per 1,000 pop.	0.7	Enrolment, %: primary	99
Hospital beds per 1,000 pop.	2.0	secondary	98
Improved-water source access, % of pop.	…	tertiary[b]	11

Society

No. of households	4.9m	Colour TVs per 100 households	90.3
Av. no. per household	4.6	Telephone lines per 100 pop.	19.9
Marriages per 1,000 pop.	3.1	Mobile telephone subscribers	
Divorces per 1,000 pop.	…	per 100 pop.	30.0
Cost of living, Dec. 2001		Computers per 100 pop.	12.6
New York = 100	60	Internet hosts per 1,000 pop.	3.3

a 1999
b 1997

MEXICO

Area	1,972,545 sq km	Capital	Mexico city
Arable as % of total land	13	Currency	Mexican peso (PS)

People

Population	98.9m	Life expectancy: men		70.4 yrs
Pop. per sq km	50		women	76.4 yrs
Av. ann. growth		Adult literacy		91.4%
in pop. 1995–2000	1.63%	Fertility rate (per woman)		2.49
Pop. under 15	33.1%	Urban population		74.4%
Pop. over 65	4.7%			per 1,000 pop.
No. of men per 100 women	98.0	Crude birth rate		22.2
Human Development Index	79.0	Crude death rate		5.1

The economy

GDP	5,432bn pesos	GDP per head	$5,860
GDP	$575bn	GDP per head in purchasing	
Av. ann. growth in real		power parity (USA=100)	25.8
GDP 1990–2000	3.6%	Economic freedom index	2.90

Origins of GDP		**Components of GDP**	
	% of total		% of total
Agriculture	4.4	Private consumption	67.5
Industry, of which:	28.4	Public consumption	11.0
manufacturing & mining	23.4	Investment	23.3
Services	67.3	Exports	31.4
		Imports	-33.2

Structure of employment[a]

	% of total		% of labour force
Agriculture	21	Unemployed 1999	2.0
Industry	25	Av. ann. rate 1991–99	3.5
Services	54		

Energy

	m TCE		
Total output	314.821	% output exported	43.5
Total consumption	187.648	% consumption imported	13.1
Consumption per head,			
kg coal equivalent	1,958		

Inflation and finance

Consumer price		av. ann. increase 1995–2000	
inflation 2001	6.3%	Narrow money (M1)	26.9%
Av. ann. inflation 1996–2001	13.7%	Broad money	24.7%
Money market rate, 2001	12.89%		

Exchange rates

	end 2001		December 2001
			1995 = 100
PS per $	9.14	Effective rates	
PS per SDR	11.49	– nominal	...
PS per euro	8.18	– real	...

Trade

Principal exports		Principal imports	
	$bn fob		*$bn fob*
Manufactured products	146.5	Intermediate goods	133.6
Crude oil & products	16.4	Capital goods	24.1
Agricultural products	3.6	Consumer goods	16.7
Total incl. others	**166.5**	Total	**174.5**

Main export destinations		Main origins of imports	
	% of total		*% of total*
United States	88.7	United States	80.4
Canada	2.0	Japan	4.1
Japan	0.6	Germany	3.6
EU15	3.4	Canada	2.5

Balance of payments, reserves and debt, $bn

Visible exports fob	166.5	Overall balance	7.2
Visible imports fob	-174.5	Change in reserves	3.7
Trade balance	-8.0	Level of reserves	
Invisibles inflows	19.8	end Dec.	35.6
Invisibles outflows	-37.0	No. months of import cover	2.0
Net transfers	7.0	Foreign debt	150.3
Current account balance	-18.2	– as % of GDP	33
– as % of gdp	-3.2	Debt service paid	58.3
Capital balance	22.3	Debt service ratio	36

Health and education

Health spending, % of GDP	5.3	Education spending, % of GDP[b]	4.9
Doctors per 1,000 pop.	1.7	Enrolment, %: primary	114
Hospital beds per 1,000 pop.	1.1	secondary	71
Improved-water source access,		tertiary	18
% of pop.	86		

Society

No. of households	22.6m	Colour TVs per 100 households	88.7
Av. no. per household	4.3	Telephone lines per 100 pop.	13.5
Marriages per 1,000 pop.	6.9	Mobile telephone subscribers	
Divorces per 1,000 pop.	0.5	per 100 pop.	20.1
Cost of living, Dec. 2001		Computers per 100 pop.	6.7
New York = 100	90	Internet hosts per 1,000 pop.	9.3

a 1999
b 1997

MOROCCO

Area	446,550 sq km	Capital	Rabat
Arable as % of total land	19	Currency	Dirham (Dh)

People

Population	29.9m	Life expectancy: men	66.8 yrs
Pop. per sq km	67	women	70.5 yrs
Av. ann. growth		Adult literacy	48.9%
in pop. 1995–2000	1.87%	Fertility rate (per woman)	3.03
Pop. under 15	34.7%	Urban population	55.0%
Pop. over 65	4.1%		per 1,000 pop.
No. of men per 100 women	100.2	Crude birth rate	24.8
Human Development Index	59.6	Crude death rate	6.0

The economy

GDP	Dh354bn	GDP per head	$1,160
GDP	$33.3bn	GDP per head in purchasing	
Av. ann. growth in real		power parity (USA=100)	10.1
GDP 1990–2000	2.4%	Economic freedom index	3.05

Origins of GDP		**Components of GDP**	
	% of total		% of total
Agriculture	15.2	Private consumption	61.5
Industry, of which:	38.4	Public consumption	19.4
manufacturing	20.8	Investment	25.2
Services	46.4	Exports	26.5
		Imports	-32.6

Structure of employment[a]

	% of total		% of labour force
Agriculture	6	Unemployed 1999	22.0
Industry	33	Av. ann. rate 1990–99	18.2
Services	61		

Energy

	m TCE		
Total output	0.552	% output exported	nil
Total consumption	12.402	% consumption imported	105.7
Consumption per head,			
kg coal equivalent	453		

Inflation and finance

Consumer price		av. ann. increase 1995–2000	
inflation 2001	0.6%	Narrow money (M1)	9.8%
Av. ann. inflation 1996–2001	1.4%	Broad money	9.4%
Money market rate, 2001	4.44%		

Exchange rates

	end 2001		December 2001
Dh per $	11.56	Effective rates	1995 = 100
Dh per SDR	14.53	– nominal	104.9
Dh per euro	10.35	– real	103.1

Trade

Principal exports		Principal imports	
	$bn fob		*$bn cif*
Consumer goods	2.8	Consumer goods	2.7
Semi-finished goods	1.6	Machinery & equipment	2.3
Food, drink & tobacco	1.5	Semi-finished goods	2.2
Minerals	0.6	Energy & lubricants	2.0
Energy & lubricants	0.3	Food, drink & tobacco	1.3
Total incl. others	**7.4**	Total incl. others	**11.5**

Main export destinations		Main origins of imports	
	% of total		*% of total*
France	25.9	France	25.3
Spain	9.6	Spain	10.8
United Kingdom	7.9	Italy	5.9
Italy	5.6	Germany	5.8

Balance of payments, reserves and debt, $bn

Visible exports fob	7.4	Overall balance	-1.1
Visible imports fob	-10.7	Change in reserves	-0.9
Trade balance	-3.2	Level of reserves	
Invisibles inflows	3.3	end Dec.	5.0
Invisibles outflows	-3.0	No. months of import cover	4.4
Net transfers	2.5	Foreign debt	17.9
Current account balance	-0.5	– as % of GDP	47
– as % of GDP	-1.5	Debt service paid	3.3
Capital balance	-0.7	Debt service ratio	26

Health and education

Health spending, % of GDP	4.4	Education spending, % of GDP[b]	5.0
Doctors per 1,000 pop.	0.5	Enrolment, %: primary	97
Hospital beds per 1,000 pop.	1.0	secondary	40
Improved-water source access,		tertiary	9
% of pop.	82		

Society

No. of households	5.3m	Colour TVs per 100 households	42.5
Av. no. per household	5.3	Telephone lines per 100 pop.	3.9
Marriages per 1,000 pop.	...	Mobile telephone subscribers	
Divorces per 1,000 pop.	...	per 100 pop.	15.7
Cost of living, Dec. 2001		Computers per 100 pop.	1.3
New York = 100	60	Internet hosts per 1,000 pop.	...

a 1999
b 1997

NETHERLANDS

Area[a]	41,526 sq km	Capital	Amsterdam
Arable as % of total land	27	Currency	Euro (€)

People

Population	15.9m	Life expectancy: men	75.6 yrs
Pop. per sq km	388	women	81.0 yrs
Av. ann. growth		Adult literacy	99.0%
in pop. 1995–2000	0.52%	Fertility rate (per woman)	1.5
Pop. under 15	18.3%	Urban population	89.4%
Pop. over 65	13.6%		per 1,000 pop.
No. of men per 100 women	98.1	Crude birth rate	10.6
Human Development Index	93.1	Crude death rate	9.0

The economy

GDP	Fl873bn	GDP per head	$22,910
GDP	$365bn	GDP per head in purchasing	
Av. ann. growth in real		power parity (USA=100)	75.8
GDP 1990–2000	2.9%	Economic freedom index	1.80

Origins of GDP		Components of GDP	
	% of total		% of total
Agriculture	2.8	Private consumption	49.8
Industry, of which:	26.4	Public consumption	22.7
manufacturing	...	Investment	22.3
Services	70.8	Exports	67.1
		Imports	-61.9

Structure of employment

	% of total		% of labour force
Agriculture	3	Unemployed 1999	3.6
Industry	22	Av. ann. rate 1990–99	6.0
Services	75		

Energy

	m TCE		
Total output	96.719	% output exported[b]	125.9
Total consumption	119.048	% consumption imported[b]	130.3
Consumption per head,			
kg coal equivalent	7,593		

Inflation and finance

Consumer price		av. ann. increase 1995–2000	
inflation 2001	4.5%	Euro area:	
Av. ann. inflation 1996–2001	2.7%	Narrow money (M1)	7.8%
Interbank rate, 2001	4.26%	Broad money	4.5%

Exchange rates

	end 2001		December 2001
Euro per $	1.13	Effective rates	1995 = 100
Euro per SDR	1.43	– nominal	89.7
		– real	93.9

Trade

Principal exports		Principal imports	
	$bn fob		*$bn cif*
Machinery & transport equipment	71.2	Machinery & transport equipment	78.5
Food, drink & tobacco	33.7	Chemicals	22.3
Chemicals	31.1	Fuels	20.5
Fuels	18.6	Food, drink & tobacco	17.7
		Clothing	7.4
Total incl. others	**213.3**	Total incl. others	**198.8**

Main export destinations		Main origins of imports	
	% of total		*% of total*
Germany	25.8	Germany	18.0
Belgium	11.8	United States	10.2
United Kingdom	10.8	Belgium	9.4
France	10.5	United Kingdom	9.3
Italy	5.9	France	5.8
EU15	77.3	EU15	55.1

Balance of payments, reserves and aid, $bn

Visible exports fob	208.1	Capital balance	1.3
Visible imports fob	-186.9	Overall balance	0.2
Trade balance	21.3	Change in reserves	-1.6
Invisibles inflows	94.1	Level of reserves	
Invisibles outflows	-96.8	end Dec.	17.7
Net transfers	-6.2	No. months of import cover	0.7
Current account balance	12.4	Aid given	3.13
– as % of GDP	3.4	– as % of GDP	0.86

Health and education

Health spending, % of GDP	8.7	Education spending, % of GDP	4.9
Doctors per 1,000 pop.	3.1	Enrolment, %: primary	108
Hospital beds per 1,000 pop.	11.3	secondary[c]	125
Improved-water source access,		tertiary	49
% of pop.	100		

Society

No. of households	6.8m	Colour TVs per 100 households	98.3
Av. no. per household	2.3	Telephone lines per 100 pop.	62.1
Marriages per 1,000 pop.	5.4	Mobile telephone subscribers	
Divorces per 1,000 pop.	2.0	per 100 pop.	73.9
Cost of living, Dec. 2001		Computers per 100 pop.	42.9
New York = 100	82	Internet hosts per 1,000 pop.	124.7

a Includes water.
b Energy trade data are distorted due to transitory and oil refining activities.
c Includes training for unemployed.

NEW ZEALAND

Area	270,534 sq km	Capital	Wellington
Arable as % of total land	6	Currency	New Zealand dollar (NZ$)

People

Population	3.8m	Life expectancy: men	75.3 yrs
Pop. per sq km	14	women	80.7 yrs
Av. ann. growth		Adult literacy	99.0%
in pop. 1995–2000	0.94%	Fertility rate (per woman)	1.97
Pop. under 15	23.0%	Urban population	87.0%
Pop. over 65	11.7%		per 1,000 pop.
No. of men per 100 women	97.2	Crude birth rate	13.7
Human Development Index	91.3	Crude death rate	7.7

The economy

GDP	NZ$110bn	GDP per head	$13,030
GDP	$49.9bn	GDP per head in purchasing	
Av. ann. growth in real		power parity (USA=100)	54.3
GDP 1990–2000	2.4%	Economic freedom index	1.70

Origins of GDP

	% of total
Agriculture	8.4
Manufacturing	16.2
Other	75.4

Components of GDP

	% of total
Private consumption	60.4
Public consumption	18.1
Investment	20.8
Exports	35.5
Imports	-34.6

Structure of employment

	% of total		% of labour force
Agriculture	9	Unemployed 2000	6.0
Industry	23	Av. ann. rate 1990–2000	7.8
Services	68		

Energy

	m TCE		
Total output	17.002	% output exported	18.2
Total consumption	22.072	% consumption imported	36.4
Consumption per head,			
kg coal equivalent	5,814		

Inflation and finance

		av. ann. increase 1995–2000	
Consumer price			
inflation 2001	2.7%	Narrow money (M1)	6.1%
Av. ann. inflation 1996–2001	1.5%	Broad money	6.0%
Money market rate, 2001	5.76%		

Exchange rates

	end 2001		December 2001
NZ$ per $	2.41	Effective rates	1995 = 100
NZ$ per SDR	3.02	– nominal	82.0
NZ$ per euro	2.17	– real	81.9

Trade

Principal exports		Principal imports	
	$bn fob		*$bn cif*
Dairy produce	2.1	Vehicles & aircraft	1.9
Meat	1.7	Machinery	1.8
Forestry products	1.5	Electrical machinery	1.5
Fruit & vegetables	0.7	Mineral fuels	1.4
Fish	0.4		
Total incl. others	**13.4**	Total incl. others	**14.1**

Main export destinations		Main origins of imports	
	% of total		*% of total*
Australia	20.4	Australia	22.5
United States	14.5	United States	17.5
Japan	13.5	Japan	11.0
United Kingdom	5.4	United Kingdom	3.8

Balance of payments, reserves and aid, $bn

Visible exports fob	13.5	Capital balance	3.2
Visible imports fob	-12.8	Overall balance	-0.1
Trade balance	0.6	Change in reserves	-1.1
Invisibles inflows	4.9	Level of reserves	
Invisibles outflows	-8.5	end Dec.	3.3
Net transfers	0.2	No. months of import cover	1.9
Current account balance	-2.7	Aid given	0.11
– as % of GDP	-5.5	– as % of GDP	0.23

Health and education

Health spending, % of GDP	8.1	Education spending, % of GDP	7.2
Doctors per 1,000 pop.	2.3	Enrolment, %: primary[a]	101
Hospital beds per 1,000 pop.	6.2	secondary[a]	113
Improved-water source access,		tertiary[a]	63
% of pop.	...		

Society

No. of households	1.3m	Colour TVs per 100 households	97.0
Av. no. per household	2.7	Telephone lines per 100 pop.	47.1
Marriages per 1,000 pop.	5.0	Mobile telephone subscribers	
Divorces per 1,000 pop.	3.2	per 100 pop.	62.1
Cost of living, Dec. 2001		Computers per 100 pop.	58.6
New York = 100	62	Internet hosts per 1,000 pop.	107.4

a 1997

NIGERIA

Area	923,768 sq km	Capital	Abuja
Arable as % of total land	31	Currency	Naira (N)

People

Population	113.9m	Life expectancy: men		52.0 yrs
Pop. per sq km	123	women		52.2 yrs
Av. ann. growth		Adult literacy		63.9%
in pop. 1995–2000	2.74%	Fertility rate (per woman)		5.42
Pop. under 15	45.1%	Urban population		43.0%
Pop. over 65	3.0%		per 1,000 pop.	
No. of men per 100 women	102	Crude birth rate		39.5
Human Development Index	45.5	Crude death rate		13.3

The economy

GDP	N4,178bn	GDP per head	$320
GDP	$41.1bn	GDP per head in purchasing	
Av. ann. growth in real		power parity (USA=100)	2.3
GDP 1990–2000	3.1%	Economic freedom index	3.60

Origins of GDP		**Components of GDP**	
	% of total		% of total
Agriculture	41.6	Private consumption	63.8
Manufacturing	6.0	Public consumption	24.9
Other	52.4	Investment	8.0
		Exports	16.7
		Imports	-13.4

Structure of employment[a]

	% of total		% of labour force
Agriculture	3	Unemployed 1997	3.2
Industry	22	Av. ann. rate 1991–97	7.1
Services	75		

Energy

	m TCE		
Total output	147.144	% output exported	87.2
Total consumption	18.941	% consumption imported	14.3
Consumption per head,			
kg coal equivalent	178		

Inflation and finance

Consumer price		av. ann. increase 1995–2000	
inflation 2000	6.9%	Narrow money (M1)	25.6%
Av. ann. inflation 1996–2000	8.0%	Broad money	26.6%
Treasury bill rate 2000	15.50%		

Exchange rates

	end 2001		December 2001
N per $	119.0	Effective rates	1995 = 100
N per SDR	149.9	– nominal	47.4
N per euro	107.1	– real	93.5

Trade

Principal exports		Principal imports	
	$bn fob		*$bn cif*
Oil	18.9	Manufactured goods	2.7
Non-oil	0.2	Machinery & transport	
		equipment	2.3
		Chemicals	2.1
		Agric products &	
		foodstuffs	1.1
Total	**19.1**	Total incl. others	**8.8**

Main export destinations		Main origins of imports	
	% of total		*% of total*
United States	46.1	United States	10.9
India	10.7	France	9.2
Spain	6.1	Germany	8.7
France	3.4	United Kingdom	7.4

Balance of payments[c], reserves and debt, $bn

Visible exports fob	12.9	Overall balance	-3.5
Visible imports fob	-8.6	Change in reserves	4.3
Trade balance	4.3	Level of reserves	
Invisibles inflows	1.2	end Dec.	9.9
Invisibles outflows	-6.3	No. months of import cover	8.6
Net transfers	1.3	Foreign debt	34.1
Current account balance	0.5	– as % of GDP	84
– as % of GDP	1.4	Debt service paid	1.0
Capital balance	-4.1	Debt service ratio	6

Health and education

Health spending, % of GDP	2.8	Education spending, % of GDP[d]	0.7
Doctors per 1,000 pop.	0.2	Enrolment, %: primary[d]	98
Hospital beds per 1,000 pop.	1.7	secondary[d]	33
Improved-water source access,		tertiary[d]	4
% of pop.	57		

Society

No. of households	22.6m	Colour TVs per 100 households	46.7
Av. no. per household	3.9	Telephone lines per 100 pop.	0.4
Marriages per 1,000 pop.	...	Mobile telephone subscribers	
Divorces per 1,000 pop.	...	per 100 pop.	0.2
Cost of living, Dec. 2001		Computers per 100 pop.	0.7
New York = 100	80	Internet hosts per 1,000 pop.	...

a 1996
b Estimate.
c 1999
d 1997

NORWAY

Area	323,878 sq km	Capital	Oslo
Arable as % of total land	3	Currency	Norwegian krone (Nkr)

People

Population	4.5m	Life expectancy: men	76.0 yrs
Pop. per sq km	14	women	81.9 yrs
Av. ann. growth		Adult literacy	99.0%
in pop. 1995–2000	0.50%	Fertility rate (per woman)	1.7
Pop. under 15	19.8%	Urban population	75.5%
Pop. over 65	15.4%		per 1,000 pop.
No. of men per 100 women	98.3	Crude birth rate	11.4
Human Development Index	93.9	Crude death rate	10.0

The economy

GDP	Nkr1,424bn	GDP per head	$36,020
GDP	$162bn	GDP per head in purchasing	
Av. ann. growth in real		power parity (USA=100)	86.9
GDP 1990–2000	3.2%	Economic freedom index	2.45

Origins of GDP		**Components of GDP**	
	% of total		% of total
Agriculture	1.9	Private consumption	42.7
Industry, of which:	30.8	Public consumption	19.0
manufacturing	...	Investment	22.1
Services	67.3	Exports	46.6
		Imports	-30.4

Structure of employment

	% of total		% of labour force
Agriculture	4	Unemployed 2000	3.4
Industry	22	Av. ann. rate 1990–2000	4.7
Services	74		

Energy

	m TCE		
Total output	239.051	% output exported	89.7
Total consumption	37.994	% consumption imported	23.4
Consumption per head,			
kg coal equivalent	8,588		

Inflation and finance

Consumer price		av. ann. increase 1995–2000	
inflation 2001	3.0%	Narrow money (M1)	9.5%
Av. ann. inflation 1996–2001	2.6%	Broad money	6.7%
Interbank rate, 2001	7.23%		

Exchange rates

	end 2001		December 2001
Nkr per $	9.01	Effective rates	1995 = 100
Nkr per SDR	11.33	– nominal	97.1
Nkr per euro	8.07	– real	127.1

Trade
Principal exports

	$bn fob
Oil, gas & products	38.1
Manufactured materials	6.7
Machinery & equipment	5.6
Food, drink & tobacco	3.8
Total incl. others	**60.0**

Principal imports

	$bn cif
Machinery & equipment	15.3
Misc. manufactures	5.1
Manufactured materials	4.9
Chemicals	3.1
Total incl. others	**34.4**

Main export destinations

	% of total
United Kingdom	20.7
Netherlands	11.4
Germany	10.3
France	10.0
Sweden	8.4
EU15	76.8

Main origins of imports

	% of total
Sweden	14.7
Germany	11.9
United States	8.2
United Kingdom	8.1
Denmark	6.4
EU15	62.5

Balance of payments, reserves and aid, $bn

Visible exports fob	60.1	Capital balance	-12.0
Visible imports fob	-34.6	Overall balance	3.7
Trade balance	25.5	Change in reserves	-0.3
Invisibles inflows	21.7	Level of reserves	
Invisibles outflows	-22.7	end Dec.	20.5
Net transfers	-1.5	No. months of import cover	4.3
Current account balance	23.0	Aid given	1.26
– as % of GDP	14.2	– as % of GDP	0.85

Health and education

Health spending, % of GDP	9.2	Education spending, % of GDP	7.7
Doctors per 1,000 pop.	2.8	Enrolment, %: primary	102
Hospital beds per 1,000 pop.	14.4	secondary	121
Improved-water source access,		tertiary	65
% of pop.	100		

Society

No. of households	2.1m	Colour TVs per 100 households	91.7
Av. no. per household	2.2	Telephone lines per 100 pop.	72.0
Marriages per 1,000 pop.	5.3	Mobile telephone subscribers	
Divorces per 1,000 pop.	2.4	per 100 pop.	82.5
Cost of living, Dec. 2001		Computers per 100 pop.	50.8
New York = 100	104	Internet hosts per 1,000 pop.	139.9

PAKISTAN

Area	803,940 sq km	Capital	Islamabad
Arable as % of total land	28	Currency	Pakistan rupee (PRs)

People

Population	141.3m	Life expectancy: men	61.2 yrs
Pop. per sq km	177	women	60.9 yrs
Av. ann. growth		Adult literacy	43.2%
in pop. 1995–2000	2.66%	Fertility rate (per woman)	5.08
Pop. under 15	41.8%	Urban population	36.0%
Pop. over 65	3.7%		per 1,000 pop.
No. of men per 100 women	106.6	Crude birth rate	36.3
Human Development Index	49.8	Crude death rate	9.7

The economy

GDP	PRs3,183bn	GDP per head	$450
GDP	$61.6bn	GDP per head in purchasing	
Av. ann. growth in real		power parity (USA=100)	5.5
GDP 1990–2000	4.0%	Economic freedom index	3.30

Origins of GDP[a]		Components of GDP[a]	
	% of total		% of total
Agriculture	24.7	Private consumption	73.0
Industry, of which:	25.1	Public consumption	9.6
manufacturing	17.4	Investment	13.4
Other	50.2	Exports	16.3
		Imports	-13.8

Structure of employment[b]

	% of total		% of labour force
Agriculture	47	Unemployed 2000	5.9
Industry	17	Av. ann. rate 1990–2000	5.4
Services	36		

Energy

	m TCE		
Total output	31.364	% output exported	1.0
Total consumption	52.316	% consumption imported	43.0
Consumption per head,			
kg coal equivalent	353		

Inflation and finance

		av. ann. increase 1995–2000	
Consumer price			
inflation 2001	3.2%	Narrow money (M1)	12.3%
Av. ann. inflation 1996–2001	5.8%	Broad money	12.7%
Money market rate, 2001	8.49%		

Exchange rates

	end 2001		December 2001
PRs per $	60.86	Effective rates	1995 = 100
PRs per SDR	76.49	– nominal	67.45
PRs per euro	54.50	– real	90.29

Trade

Principal exports[c]		Principal imports[c]	
	$bn		$bn
Textile yarn & fabrics	2.2	Machinery	2.1
Apparel & clothing accessories	1.4	Chemicals	1.9
Rice	0.6	Minerals, fuels etc	1.5
		Palm oil	0.7
Total incl. others	**8.1**	Total incl. others	**9.3**

Main export destinations		Main origins of imports	
	% of total		% of total
United States	24.8	Kuwait	11.7
United Kingdom	6.5	United Arab Emirates	10.7
United Arab Emirates	6.2	Saudi Arabia	10.5
Hong Kong	5.9	United States	6.0

Balance of payments, reserves and debt, $bn

Visible exports fob	8.7	Overall balance	-2.6
Visible imports fob	-9.9	Change in reserves	-0.0
Trade balance	-1.2	Level of reserves	
Invisibles inflows	1.5	end Dec.	2.1
Invisibles outflows	-4.6	No. months of import cover	1.7
Net transfers	4.2	Foreign debt	32.1
Current account balance	-0.1	– as % of GDP	45.0
– as % of GDP	-0.2	Debt service paid	2.9
Capital balance	-3.1	Debt service ratio	27.0

Health and education

Health spending, % of GDP	4.0	Education spending, % of GDP[d]	2.7
Doctors per 1,000 pop.	0.6	Enrolment, %: primary	86
Hospital beds per 1,000 pop.	0.7	secondary	37
Improved-water source access,		tertiary[d]	4
% of pop.	88		

Society

No. of households	20.6m	Colour TVs per 100 households	33.6
Av. no. per household	6.5	Telephone lines per 100 pop.	2.4
Marriages per 1,000 pop.	...	Mobile telephone subscribers	
Divorces per 1,000 pop.	...	per 100 pop.	0.6
Cost of living, Dec. 2001		Computers per 100 pop.	0.4
New York = 100	41	Internet hosts per 1,000 pop.	0.1

a Fiscal year ending June 30, 2001.
b 1999
c 1998
d 1997

PERU

Area	1,285,216 sq km	Capital	Lima
Arable as % of total land	3	Currency	Nuevo Sol (New Sol)

People

Population	25.7m	Life expectancy: men		67.3 yrs
Pop. per sq km	20		women	72.4 yrs
Av. ann. growth		Adult literacy[a]		90.0%
in pop. 1995–2000	1.73%	Fertility rate (per woman)		2.64
Pop. under 15	33.4%	Urban population		72.0%
Pop. over 65	4.8%			per 1,000 pop.
No. of men per 100 women	98.4	Crude birth rate		22.6
Human Development Index	74.3	Crude death rate		6.2

The economy

GDP	New Soles 187bn	GDP per head	$2,080
GDP	$53.5bn	GDP per head in purchasing	
Av. ann. growth in real		power parity (USA=100)	13.7
GDP 1990–2000	3.1%	Economic freedom index	2.75

Origins of GDP

	% of total
Agriculture	9.6
Industry, of which:	25.5
manufacturing	15.0
Services	64.9

Components of GDP

	% of total
Private consumption	71.2
Public consumption	9.7
Investment	19.5
Exports	16.5
Imports	-16.8

Structure of employment[b]

	% of total		% of labour force
Agriculture	6	Unemployed 1999	8.0
Industry	19	Av. ann. rate 1996–99	8.1
Services	75		

Energy

	m TCE		
Total output	10.737	% output exported	50.8
Total consumption	14.563	% consumption imported	63.8
Consumption per head,			
kg coal equivalent	587		

Inflation and finance

Consumer price		av. ann. increase 1995–2000	
inflation 2001	2.0%	Narrow money (M1)	23.0%
Av. ann. inflation 1996–2001	5.0%	Broad money	19.2%
Deposit rate, 2001	9.9%		

Exchange rates

	end 2001		December 2001
New Soles per $	3.44	Effective rates	1995 = 100
New Soles per SDR	4.33	– nominal	...
New Soles per Ecu	3.08	– real	...

Trade

Principal exports		Principal imports	
	$bn fob		*$bn fob*
Fish & fish products	1.1	Industrial supplies	3.7
Gold	1.1	Capital goods	2.1
Copper	0.9	Consumer goods	1.4
Textiles	0.7		
Zinc	0.5		
Total incl. others	**7.0**	Total incl. others	**7.3**

Main export destinations		Main origins of imports	
	% of total		*% of total*
United States	27.5	United States	27.0
United Kingdom	8.3	Chile	8.4
Switzerland	8.0	Spain	6.4
China	6.4	Venezuela	4.4

Balance of payments, reserves and debt, $bn

Visible exports fob	7.0	Overall balance	-0.1
Visible imports fob	-7.3	Change in reserves	-0.4
Trade balance	-0.3	Level of reserves	
Invisibles inflows	2.3	end Dec.	8.7
Invisibles outflows	-4.6	No. months of import cover	8.7
Net transfers	1.0	Foreign debt	28.6
Current account balance	-1.6	– as % of GDP	54
– as % of GDP	-3.0	Debt service paid	4.3
Capital balance	1.0	Debt service ratio	46

Health and education

Health spending, % of GDP	6.2	Education spending, % of GDP	3.2
Doctors per 1,000 pop.	0.9	Enrolment, %: primary	126
Hospital beds per 1,000 pop.	1.5	secondary	81
Improved-water source access,		tertiary	29
% of pop.	77		

Society

No. of households	5.4m	Colour TVs per 100 households	45.7
Av. no. per household	4.7	Telephone lines per 100 pop.	7.8
Marriages per 1,000 pop.	4.1	Mobile telephone subscribers	
Divorces per 1,000 pop.	...	per 100 pop.	5.9
Cost of living, Dec. 2001		Computers per 100 pop.	4.8
New York = 100	66	Internet hosts per 1,000 pop.	0.5

a Excluding indigenous jungle population.
b 1999

PHILIPPINES

Area	300,000 sq km	Capital	Manila
Arable as % of total land	19	Currency	Philippine peso (P)

People

Population	75.7m	Life expectancy: men	68.0 yrs
Pop. per sq km	252	women	72.0 yrs
Av. ann. growth		Adult literacy	95.3%
in pop. 1995–2000	2.03%	Fertility rate (per woman)	3.24
Pop. under 15	37.5%	Urban population	58.0%
Pop. over 65	3.5%		per 1,000 pop.
No. of men per 100 women	101	Crude birth rate	26.0
Human Development Index	74.9	Crude death rate	5.2

The economy

GDP	P3,303bn	GDP per head	$990
GDP	$74.7bn	GDP per head in purchasing	
Av. ann. growth in real		power parity (USA=100)	12.4
GDP 1990–2000	2.9%	Economic freedom index	2.95

Origins of GDP		Components of GDP	
	% of total		% of total
Agriculture	16.5	Private consumption	70.3
Industry, of which:	30.8	Public consumption	12.7
manufacturing	22.4	Investment	17.5
Services	52.6	Exports	55.1
		Imports	-50.7

Structure of employment[a]

	% of total		% of labour force
Agriculture	39	Unemployed 2000	10.1
Industry	16	Av. ann. rate 1990–2000	8.7
Services	45		

Energy

	m TCE		
Total output	10.108	% output exported	2.4
Total consumption	38.940	% consumption imported	84.0
Consumption per head,			
kg coal equivalent	534		

Inflation and finance

Consumer price		*av. ann. increase 1995–2000*	
inflation 2001	6.1%	Narrow money (M1)	14.9%
Av. ann. inflation 1996–2001	6.5%	Broad money	15.9%
Treasury bill rate, 2001	9.73%		

Exchange rates

	end 2001		December 2001
P per $	51.40	Effective rates	1995 = 100
P per SDR	64.60	– nominal	63.0
P per euro	46.03	– real	86.0

Trade

Principal exports		Principal imports	
	$bn fob		*$bn fob*
Electrical & electronic equipment	22.2	Semi-processed raw materials	10.7
Machinery & transport equipment	5.9	Telecom & electrical machinery	7.0
		Electrical equipment parts	4.2
Clothing	2.6	Crude petroleum	3.1
Coconut products	0.5	Chemicals	2.6
Fish	0.3	Power equipment & specialised machines	2.4
Total incl. others	**38.1**	Total incl. others	**31.4**

Main export destinations		Main origins of imports	
	% of total		*% of total*
United States	28.7	Japan	19.2
Japan	14.1	United States	15.5
Singapore	7.9	South Korea	7.5
Netherlands	7.5	Taiwan	6.2
Hong Kong	5.0	Singapore	6.1
EU15	17.9	EU15	9.2

Balance of payments, reserves and debt, $bn

Visible exports fob	37.3	Overall balance	-0.4
Visible imports fob	-30.4	Change in reserves	0.0
Trade balance	6.9	Level of reserves	
Invisibles inflows	12.0	end Dec.	15.0
Invisibles outflows	-10.2	No. months of import cover	4.4
Net transfers	0.4	Foreign debt	50.1
Current account balance	9.1	– as % of GDP	67.0
– as % of GDP	12.2	Debt service paid	6.7
Capital balance	-6.8	Debt service ratio	14

Health and education

Health spending, % of GDP	3.6	Education spending, % of GDP	3.2
Doctors per 1,000 pop.	1.2	Enrolment, %: primary[b]	117
Hospital beds per 1,000 pop.	1.1	secondary[b]	78
Improved-water source access, % of pop.	87	tertiary	28

Society

No. of households	15.3m	Colour TVs per 100 households	63.0
Av. no. per household	5.0	Telephone lines per 100 pop.	4.0
Marriages per 1,000 pop.	6.9	Mobile telephone subscribers	
Divorces per 1,000 pop.	...	per 100 pop.	13.7
Cost of living, Dec. 2001		Computers per 100 pop.	2.2
New York = 100	42	Internet hosts per 1,000 pop.	0.4

a 1999
b 1997

POLAND

Area	312,683 sq km	Capital	Warsaw
Arable as % of total land	46	Currency	Zloty (Zl)

People

Population	38.6m	Life expectancy: men	69.8 yrs
Pop. per sq km	119	women	78.0 yrs
Av. ann. growth		Adult literacy	99.7%
in pop. 1995–2000	0.01%	Fertility rate (per woman)	1.26
Pop. under 15	19.2%	Urban population	65.0%
Pop. over 65	12.1%		per 1,000 pop.
No. of men per 100 women	95	Crude birth rate	9.5
Human Development Index	82.8	Crude death rate	9.9

The economy

GDP	Zl686bn	GDP per head	$4,080
GDP	$158bn	GDP per head in purchasing	
Av. ann. growth in real		power parity (USA=100)	26.4
GDP 1991–2000	3.7%	Economic freedom index	2.70

Origins of GDP

Components of GDP

	% of total		% of total
Agriculture	3.8	Private consumption	63.3
Industry, of which:	30.5	Public consumption	20.5
manufacturing	...	Investment	28.2
Services	65.7	Exports	31.4
		Imports	-43.3

Structure of employment[a]

	% of total		% of labour force
Agriculture	19	Unemployed 2000	16.7
Industry	32	Av. ann. rate 1990–2000	12.4
Services	49		

Energy

	m TCE		
Total output	118.368	% output exported	24.8
Total consumption	131.302	% consumption imported	33.3
Consumption per head,			
kg coal equivalent	3,391		

Inflation and finance

		av. ann. increase 1995–2000	
Consumer price			
inflation 2001	5.5%	Narrow money (M1)	17.1%
Av. ann. inflation 1996–2001	10.0%	Broad money	23.1%
Money market rate, 2001	12.6%		

Exchange rates

	end 2001		December 2001
Zl per $	3.99	Effective rates	1995 = 100
Zl per SDR	5.01	– nominal	87.1
Zl per euro	3.57	– real	142.4

Trade

Principal exports		Principal imports	
	$bn fob		*$bn cif*
Machinery & transport equipment	10.8	Machinery & transport equipment	18.1
Semi-manufactured goods	7.9	Semi-manufactured goods	9.8
Other manufactured goods	6.1	Chemicals	6.9
Agric. products & foodstuffs	2.4	Mineral fuels	5.3
Chemicals	2.2	Other manufactured goods	4.2
Total incl. others	**31.7**	Total incl. others	**48.9**

Main export destinations		Main origins of imports	
	% of total		*% of total*
Germany	34.9	Germany	23.9
Italy	6.3	Russia	9.4
France	5.2	Italy	8.3
Netherlands	5.1	France	6.4
United Kingdom	4.5	United Kingdom	4.5
Czech Republic	3.8	United States	4.4

Balance of payments, reserves and debt, $bn

Visible exports fob	35.9	Overall balance	0.6
Visible imports fob	-48.2	Change in reserves	0.2
Trade balance	-12.3	Level of reserves	
Invisibles inflows	12.6	end Dec.	27.5
Invisibles outflows	-12.7	No. months of import cover	5.4
Net transfers	2.4	Foreign debt	63.6
Current account balance	-10.0	– as % of GDP	37.0
– as % of GDP	-6.3	Debt service paid	10.3
Capital balance	10.2	Debt service ratio	23.0

Health and education

Health spending, % of GDP	6.2	Education spending, % of GDP	5.4
Doctors per 1,000 pop.	2.3	Enrolment, %: primary[b]	96
Hospital beds per 1,000 pop.	5.1	secondary[b]	98
Improved-water source access, % of pop.	...	tertiary[b]	24

Society

No. of households	13.4m	Colour TVs per 100 households	82.4
Av. no. per household	2.9	Telephone lines per 100 pop.	29.5
Marriages per 1,000 pop.	3.6	Mobile telephone subscribers	
Divorces per 1,000 pop.	1.2	per 100 pop.	26.0
Cost of living, Dec. 2001		Computers per 100 pop.	8.5
New York = 100	62	Internet hosts per 1,000 pop.	16.9

a 1998
b 1997

PORTUGAL

Area	88,940 sq km	Capital	Lisbon
Arable as % of total land	22	Currency	Euro (€)

People

Population	10.0m	Life expectancy: men	72.6 yrs
Pop. per sq km	108	women	79.6 yrs
Av. ann. growth		Adult literacy	92.2%
in pop. 1995–2000	0.20%	Fertility rate (per woman)	1.45
Pop. under 15	16.7%	Urban population	63.0%
Pop. over 65	15.6%		per 1,000 pop.
No. of men per 100 women	92.7	Crude birth rate	11.0
Human Development Index	87.4	Crude death rate	10.8

The economy

GDP	Esc22,860bn	GDP per head	$10,500
GDP	$105bn	GDP per head in purchasing	
Av. ann. growth in real		power parity (USA=100)	49.8
GDP 1990–2000	2.8%	Economic freedom index	2.30

Origins of GDP		Components of GDP	
	% of total		% of total
Agriculture	3.8	Private consumption	63.3
Industry, of which:	30.5	Public consumption	20.5
manufacturing	...	Investment	28.2
Services	65.7	Exports	31.4
		Imports	-43.3

Structure of employment[a]

	% of total		% of labour force
Agriculture	13	Unemployed 2000	3.8
Industry	35	Av. ann. rate 1990–2000	5.5
Services	52		

Energy

	m TCE		
Total output	1.688	% output exported[a]	173.3
Total consumption	25.345	% consumption imported[a]	117.1
Consumption per head,			
kg coal equivalent	2,568		

Inflation and finance

Consumer price		av. ann. increase 1995–2000	
inflation 2001	4.3%	Euro area:	
Av. ann. inflation 1996–2001	2.9%	Narrow money (M1)	7.8%
Interbank rate, 2001	4.26%	Broad money	4.5%

Exchange rates

	end 2001		December 2001
Euro per $	1.13	Effective rates	1995 = 100
Euro per SDR	1.43	– nominal	93.6
		– real	99.8

Trade

Principal exports		Principal imports	
	$bn fob		*$bn cif*
Consumer goods	9.1	Capital goods	14.7
Raw materials &		Raw materials &	
semi-manufactures	7.8	semi-manufactures	12.3
Capital goods	7.0	Consumer goods	8.8
Energy products	0.6	Energy products	4.2
Total incl. others	24.4	Total incl. others	**40.0**

Main export destinations		Main origins of imports	
	% of total		*% of total*
Spain	19.2	Spain	25.3
Germany	17.6	Germany	13.7
France	12.5	France	10.6
United Kingdom	10.7	Italy	7.0
United States	6.0	United Kingdom	5.8
EU15	79.4	EU15	74.0

Balance of payments, reserves and debt, $bn

Visible exports fob	24.8	Overall balance	0.4
Visible imports fob	-38.9	Change in reserves	-0.2
Trade balance	-14.1	Level of reserves	
Invisibles inflows	13.0	end Dec.	14.3
Invisibles outflows	-13.3	No. months of import cover	3.3
Net transfers	3.4	Aid given	0.27
Current account balance	-11.0	– as % of GDP	0.26
– as % of GDP	-10.5		
Capital balance	12.6		

Health and education

Health spending, % of GDP	7.7	Education spending, % of GDP	5.7
Doctors per 1,000 pop.	3.2	Enrolment, %: primary	124
Hospital beds per 1,000 pop.	4.0	secondary[b]	113
Improved-water source access,		tertiary	45
% of pop.	...		

Society

No. of households	3.7m	Colour TVs per 100 households	98.2
Av. no. per household	2.7	Telephone lines per 100 pop.	42.9
Marriages per 1,000 pop.	6.6	Mobile telephone subscribers	
Divorces per 1,000 pop.	1.6	per 100 pop.	77.4
Cost of living, Dec. 2001		Computers per 100 pop.	11.7
New York = 100	65	Internet hosts per 1,000 pop.	26.4

a 1999
b Includes training for unemployed.

ROMANIA

Area	237,500 sq km	Capital	Bucharest
Arable as % of total land	41	Currency	Leu (L)

People

Population	22.4m	Life expectancy: men	66.5 yrs
Pop. per sq km	94	women	73.3 yrs
Av. ann. growth		Adult literacy	98.1%
in pop. 1995–2000	-0.22%	Fertility rate (per woman)	1.32
Pop. under 15	18.3%	Urban population	56.2%
Pop. over 65	13.3%		per 1,000 pop.
No. of men per 100 women	96.4	Crude birth rate	10.4
Human Development Index	77.2	Crude death rate	12.8

The economy

GDP	L797trn	GDP per head	$1,640
GDP	$36.7bn	GDP per head in purchasing	
Av. ann. growth in real		power parity (USA=100)	18.7
GDP 1990–2000	-2.2%	Economic freedom index	3.70

Origins of GDP		**Components of GDP**	
	% of total		% of total
Agriculture	11.4	Private consumption	73.9
Industry, of which:	32.4	Public consumption	12.5
manufacturing	...	Investment	19.5
Services	45.5	Exports	34.1
		Imports	-39.9

Structure of employment[a]

	% of total		% of labour force
Agriculture	42	Unemployed 2000	10.8
Industry	28	Av. ann. rate 1991–2000	7.4
Services	30		

Energy

	m TCE		
Total output	36.536	% output exported	13.0
Total consumption	50.884	% consumption imported	41.6
Consumption per head,			
kg coal equivalent	2,264		

Inflation and finance

Consumer price		*av. ann. increase 1995–2000*	
inflation 2001	34.5%	Narrow money (M1)	45.6%
Av. ann. inflation 1996–2001	63.2%	Broad money	44.7%
Treasury bill rate, 2001	42.2%		

Exchange rates

	end 2001		December 2001
L per $	31,597	Effective rates	1995 = 100
L per SDR	39,709	– nominal	0.11
L per euro	28,292	– real	114.1

SAUDI ARABIA

Area	2,200,000 sq km	Capital	Riyadh
Arable as % of total land	2	Currency	Riyal (SR)

People

Population	20.3m	Life expectancy: men	71.1 yrs
Pop. per sq km	9	women	73.7 yrs
Av. ann. growth		Adult literacy	76.3%
in pop. 1995–2000	3.49%	Fertility rate (per woman)	5.54
Pop. under 15	42.9%	Urban population	85.0%
Pop. over 65	3.0%		per 1,000 pop.
No. of men per 100 women	115	Crude birth rate	33.8
Human Development Index	75.4	Crude death rate	4.1

The economy

GDP	SR649bn	GDP per head	$8,360
GDP	$173bn	GDP per head in purchasing	
Av. ann. growth in real		power parity (USA=100)	33.4
GDP 1990–2000	2.8%	Economic freedom index	3.00

Origins of GDP
Components of GDP

	% of total		% of total
Agriculture	6.4	Private consumption	32.8
Industry, of which:	48.8	Public consumption	27.0
manufacturing	9.3	Investment	16.3
Services	44.8	Exports	49.6
		Imports	-25.7

Structure of employment[a]

	% of total		% of labour force
Agriculture	5	Unemployed 2000	
Industry	26	Av. ann. rate 1990–2000	
Services	69		

Energy

	m TCE		
Total output	714.807	% output exported	7
Total consumption	140.844	% consumption imported	
Consumption per head,			
coal equivalent	6,979		

Inflation and finance

		av. ann. increase 1995–	
Consumer price			
inflation 2001	-0.4%	Narrow money (M1)	
Av. ann. inflation 1996–2001	-0.6%	Broad money	

Exchange rates

	end 2001		December
		Effective rates	1995
SR per $	3.75	– nominal	
SR per SDR	4.71	– real	
SR per euro	3.36		

Trade

Principal exports
Principal imports

	$bn fob		$bn cif
Textiles & footwear	2.5	Machinery & equipment	3.0
Basic metals & products	1.7	Textiles & footwear	2.0
Machinery & equipment	1.5	Fuels & minerals	1.8
Minerals & fuels	0.8	Chemicals	1.0
Total incl. others	10.4	Total incl. others	12.2

Main export destinations
Main origins of imports

	% of total		% of total
Italy	22.4	Italy	18.7
Germany	15.7	Germany	14.7
France	7.0	Russia	8.6
Turkey	6.1	France	6.1
EU15	63.8	EU15	56.6

Balance of payments, reserves and debt, $bn

Visible exports fob	10.4	Overall balance	0.9
Visible imports fob	-12.1	Change in reserves	1.2
Trade balance	-1.7	Level of reserves	
Invisibles inflows	2.1	end Dec.	4.8
Invisibles outflows	-2.6	No. months of import cover	4.0
Net transfers	0.9	Foreign debt	10.2
Current account balance	-1.4	– as % of GDP	27.0
– as % of GDP	-3.7	Debt service paid	2.3
Capital balance	2.0	Debt service ratio	22

Health and education

Health spending, % of GDP	4.6	Education spending, % of GDP	4.4
Doctors per 1,000 pop.	1.8	Enrolment, %: primary	103
Hospital beds per 1,000 pop.	7.6	secondary	80
Improved-water source access,		tertiary[b]	23
% of pop.	58		

Society

No. of households	7.7m	Colour TVs per 100 households	50.1
Av. no. per household	2.9	Telephone lines per 100 pop.	18.3
Marriages per 1,000 pop.	5.9	Mobile telephone subscribers	
Divorces per 1,000 pop.	1.9	per 100 pop.	17.2
Cost of living, Dec. 2001		Computers per 100 pop.	3.6
New York = 100	43	Internet hosts per 1,000 pop.	3.1

a 1999
b 1997

RUSSIA

Area	17,075,400 sq km	Capital	Moscow
Arable as % of total land	7	Currency	Rouble (Rb)

People

Population	145.5m	Life expectancy: men	60.0 yrs
Pop. per sq km	9	women	72.5 yrs
Av. ann. growth		Adult literacy	99.6%
in pop. 1995–2000	-0.36%	Fertility rate (per woman)	1.14
Pop. under 15	18.0%	Urban population	77.7%
Pop. over 65	12.5%		per 1,000 pop.
No. of men per 100 women	87.8	Crude birth rate	8.6
Human Development Index	77.5	Crude death rate	15.3

The economy

GDP	Rb7,063bn	GDP per head	$1,730
GDP	$251bn	GDP per head in purchasing	
Av. ann. growth in real		power parity (USA=100)	23.5
GDP 1990–2000	-4.0%	Economic freedom index	3.70

Origins of GDP

	% of total
Agriculture	6.4
Industry, of which:	38.4
manufacturing	...
Services	55.2

Components of GDP

	% of total
Private consumption	49.1
Public consumption	14.6
Investment	17.6
Net exports	20.8

Structure of employment[a]

	% of total		% of labour force
Agriculture	12	Unemployed 2000	11.4
Industry	29	Av. ann. rate 1991–99	8.8
Services	59		

Energy

	m TCE		
Total output	1,377.629	% output exported	39.9
Total consumption	829.844	% consumption imported	3.9
Consumption per head,			
kg coal equivalent	5,629		

Inflation and finance

		av. ann. increase 1995–2000	
Consumer price			
inflation 2001	21.5%	Narrow money (M1)	42.2%
Av. ann. inflation 1996–2001	31.9%	Broad money	41.4%
Money market rate, 2001	10.1%		

Exchange rates

	end 2001		December 2001
Rb per $	30.14	Effective rates	1995 = 100
Rb per SDR	37.88	– nominal	36.19
Rb per euro	26.99	– real	109.61

Trade

Principal exports

	$bn fob
Fuels & energy	62.0
Metals	20.0
Machinery & equipment	7.1
Chemicals	5.9
Total incl. others	105.6

Principal imports

	$bn f
Machinery & equipment	1?
Food products	
Chemicals	
Metals	
Total incl. others	

Main export destinations

	% of total
Germany	9.0
United States	7.7
Italy	7.0
Belarus	5.4
China	5.1
Ukraine	4.9

Main origins of imports

	% o
Germany	
Belarus	
Ukraine	
United States	
Kazakhstan	
Italy	

Balance of payments, reserves and debt, $bn

Visible exports fob	105.6	Overall balance	
Visible imports fob	-44.9	Change in reserves	
Trade balance	60.7	Level of reserves	
Invisibles inflows	14.4	end Dec.	
Invisibles outflows	-28.8	No. months of import co	
Net transfers	0.1	Foreign debt	
Current account balance	46.3	– as % of GDP	
– as % of GDP	18.4	Debt service paid	
Capital balance	-23.1	Debt service ratio	

Health and education

Health spending, % of GDP	4.6	Education spending,	
Doctors per 1,000 pop.	4.2	Enrolment, %: prima	
Hospital beds per 1,000 pop.	12.1	secon	
Improved-water source access,		tertia	
% of pop.	99		

Society

No. of households	51.7m	Colour TVs per 100	
Av. no. per household	2.8	Telephone lines p	
Marriages per 1,000 pop.	5.0	Mobile telephone	
Divorces per 1,000 pop.	3.1	per 100 pop.	
Cost of living, Dec. 2001		Computers per 1	
New York = 100	84	Internet hosts p	

1999
1997

Trade

Principal exports[b]

	$bn fob
Crude oil & refined petroleum	42.6
Petrochemicals & plastics	3.4
Total incl. others	**50.8**

Principal imports[b]

	$bn cif
Machinery	6.7
Transport equipment	4.1
Chemical products	2.5
Total incl. others	**28.0**

Main export destinations

	% of total
United States	17.4
Japan	17.3
South Korea	11.7
Singapore	5.3

Main origins of imports

	% of total
United States	21.1
Japan	9.4
Germany	7.4
United Kingdom	7.3

Balance of payments, reserves and aid, $bn

Visible exports fob	77.6	Overall balance	2.7
Visible imports fob	-27.7	Change in reserves	2.5
Trade balance	49.8	Level of reserves	
Invisibles inflows	8.1	end Dec.	20.8
Invisibles outflows	-28.1	No. months of import cover	4.5
Net transfers	-15.5	Aid given	0.3
Current account balance	14.3	– as % of GDP	0.21
– as % of GDP	8.3		
Capital balance	-11.7		

Health and education

Health spending, % of GDP	8.0	Education spending, % of GDP[c]	7.5
Doctors per 1,000 pop.	1.7	Enrolment, %: primary	71
Hospital beds per 1,000 pop.	2.3	secondary	66
Improved-water source access,		tertiary	19
% of pop.	95		

Society

No. of households	2.7m	Colour TVs per 100 households	97.7
Av. no. per household	7.6	Telephone lines per 100 pop.	19.5
Marriages per 1,000 pop.	3.0	Mobile telephone subscribers	
Divorces per 1,000 pop.	...	per 100 pop.	11.3
Cost of living, Dec. 2001		Computers per 100 pop.	6.3
New York = 100	72	Internet hosts per 1,000 pop.	0.5

a % of workers, 1994.
b 1999
c 1997

SINGAPORE

Area	639 sq km	Capital	Singapore
Arable as % of total land	2	Currency	Singapore dollar (S$)

People

Population	4.0m	Life expectancy: men	75.9 yrs
Pop. per sq km	6,502	women	80.3 yrs
Av. ann. growth		Adult literacy	92.3%
in pop. 1995–2000	2.90%	Fertility rate (per woman)	1.45
Pop. under 15	21.9%	Urban population	100.0%
Pop. over 65	7.2%		per 1,000 pop.
No. of men per 100 women	101.5	Crude birth rate	10.8
Human Development Index	87.6	Crude death rate	5.3

The economy

GDP	S$159bn	GDP per head	$22,960
GDP	$92.3bn	GDP per head in purchasing	
Av. ann. growth in real		power parity (USA=100)	73.0
GDP 1990–2000	7.8%	Economic freedom index	1.55

Origins of GDP

	% of total	Components of GDP	% of total
Agriculture	0.2	Private consumption	41.7
Industry, of which:	34.2	Public consumption	10.0
manufacturing	26.4	Investment	33.9
Services	65.8	Exports less imports	15.3

Structure of employment[a]

	% of total		% of labour force
Agriculture	0	Unemployed 2000	4.4
Industry	29	Av. ann. rate 1990–2000	2.9
Services	71		

Energy

	m TCE		
Total output	...	% output exported	...
Total consumption	36.257	% consumption imported[b]	330.3
Consumption per head, kg coal equivalent	10,431		

Inflation and finance

Consumer price			av. ann. increase 1995–2000
inflation 2001	1.0%	Narrow money (M1)	5.6%
Av. ann. inflation 1996–2001	0.9%	Broad money	10.9%
Money market rate, 2001	1.99%		

Exchange rates

	end 2001		December 2001
S$ per $	1.85	Effective rates	1995 = 100
S$ per SDR	2.33	– nominal	101.1
S$ per euro	1.66	– real	93.8

Trade

Principal exports	$bn fob	Principal imports	$bn cif
Machinery & equipment	93.3	Machinery & equipment	82.0
Mineral fuels	13.4	Mineral fuels	16.3
Chemicals	9.6	Manufactured products	9.5
Manufactured products	5.2	Chemicals	7.7
Food	1.8	Food	3.0
Crude materials	1.0	Crude materials	1.0
Total incl. others	**138.3**	**Total incl. others**	**135.0**

Main export destinations	% of total	Main origins of imports	% of total
Malaysia	18.2	Japan	17.2
United States	17.3	Malaysia	17.0
Hong Kong	7.9	United States	14.8
Japan	7.6	China	5.3
Taiwan	5.7	Taiwan	4.4
Thailand	4.3	Thailand	4.3
China	3.9	Germany	3.2

Balance of payments, reserves and debt, $bn

Visible exports fob	138.9	Overall balance	6.8
Visible imports fob	-127.5	Change in reserves	3.3
Trade balance	11.4	Level of reserves	
Invisibles inflows	42.3	end Dec.	80.1
Invisibles outflows	-30.5	No. months of import cover	6.1
Net transfers	-1.4	Foreign debt	10.6
Current account balance	21.8	– as % of GDP	11.5
– as % of GDP	23.6	Debt service	3.3
Capital balance	-11.6	Debt service ratio	1.8

Health and education

Health spending, % of GDP	3.2	Education spending, % of GDP[c]	3.0
Doctors per 1,000 pop.	1.6	Enrolment, %: primary	92
Hospital beds per 1,000 pop.	3.6	secondary	67
Improved-water source access,		tertiary[c]	39
% of pop.	100		

Society

No. of households	0.9m	Colour TVs per 100 households	98.5
Av. no. per household	4.3	Telephone lines per 100 pop.	47.2
Marriages per 1,000 pop.	6.5	Mobile telephone subscribers	
Divorces per 1,000 pop.	1.8	per 100 pop.	69.2
Cost of living, Dec. 2001		Computers per 100 pop.	50.8
New York = 100	98	Internet hosts per 1,000 pop.	49.5

a 1999
b Energy trade data are distorted by transitory and oil refining activities.
c 1997

SLOVAKIA

Area	49,035 sq km	Capital	Bratislava
Arable as % of total land	31	Currency	Koruna (Kc)

People

Population	5.4m	Life expectancy: men		69.8 yrs
Pop. per sq km	110	women		77.6 yrs
Av. ann. growth		Adult literacy		99.0%
in pop. 1995–2000	0.13%	Fertility rate (per woman)		1.28
Pop. under 15	19.5%	Urban population		57.4%
Pop. over 65	11.4%			per 1,000 pop.
No. of men per 100 women	95.0	Crude birth rate		10.2
Human Development Index	83.1	Crude death rate		9.8

The economy

GDP	Kc887bn	GDP per head	$3,540
GDP	$19.1bn	GDP per head in purchasing	
Av. ann. growth in real		power parity (USA=100)	32.4
GDP 1990–2000	0.2%	Economic freedom index	2.90

Origins of GDP

	% of total
Agriculture	4.5
Industry, of which:	34.1
manufacturing	...
Services	61.4

Components of GDP

	% of total
Private consumption	53.4
Public consumption	19.0
Investment	30.0
Exports	73.5
Imports	-76.0

Structure of employment[a]

	% of total		% of labour force
Agriculture	7	Unemployed 2000	18.9
Industry	39	Av. ann. rate 1991–2000	12.8
Services	54		

Energy

	m TCE		
Total output	6.859	% output exported	50.5
Total consumption	23.400	% consumption imported	91.3
Consumption per head,			
kg coal equivalent	4,352		

Inflation and finance

Consumer price		av. ann. increase 1995–2000	
inflation 2001	7.3%	Narrow money (M1)	4.4%
Av. ann. inflation 1996–2001	8.5%	Broad money	11.2%
Money market rate, 2001	7.76%		

Exchange rates

	end 2001		December 2001
Kc per $	48.47	Effective rates	1995 = 100
Kc per SDR	60.91	– nominal	88.55
Kc per euro	43.40	– real	107.17

Trade

Principal exports

	$bn fob
Machinery & transport equipment	4.7
Intermediate manufactured goods	3.2
Other manufactured goods	1.5
Chemicals	1.0
Fuels	0.8
Total incl. others	11.9

Principal imports

	$bn fob
Machinery & transport equipment	4.6
Fuels	2.3
Intermediate manufactured goods	2.3
Chemicals	1.4
Other manufactured goods	1.1
Total incl. others	12.8

Main export destinations

	% of total
Germany	26.8
Czech Republic	17.4
Italy	9.2
Austria	8.4
EU15	59.0

Main origins of imports

	% of total
Germany	25.1
Russia	17.0
Czech Republic	14.7
Italy	6.2
EU15	48.9

Balance of payments, reserves and debt, $bn

Visible exports fob	11.9	Overall balance	0.9
Visible imports fob	-12.8	Change in reserves	0.6
Trade balance	-0.9	Level of reserves	
Invisibles inflows	2.5	end Dec.	4.4
Invisibles outflows	-4.9	No. months of import cover	3.5
Net transfers	0.1	Foreign debt	9.5
Current account balance	-0.7	– as % of GDP	46.0
– as % of GDP	-3.6	Debt service paid	2.6
Capital balance	1.6	Debt service ratio	19.0

Health and education

Health spending, % of GDP	6.5	Education spending, % of GDP	4.3
Doctors per 1,000 pop.	3.5	Enrolment, %: primary	101
Hospital beds per 1,000 pop.	7.1	secondary	86
Improved-water source access,		tertiary	27
% of pop.	100		

Society

No. of households	2.0m	Colour TVs per 100 households	87.7
Av. no. per household	2.7	Telephone lines per 100 pop.	28.8
Marriages per 1,000 pop.	5.0	Mobile telephone subscribers	
Divorces per 1,000 pop.	1.6	per 100 pop.	39.7
Cost of living, Dec. 2001		Computers per 100 pop.	14.8
New York = 100	...	Internet hosts per 1,000 pop.	12.8

a 1999

SLOVENIA

Area	20,253 sq km	Capital	Ljubljana
Arable as % of total land	9	Currency	Tolars (SIT)

People

Population	2.0m	Life expectancy: men	72.3 yrs
Pop. per sq km	98	women	79.6 yrs
Av. ann. growth		Adult literacy	99.6%
in pop. 1995–2000	-0.02%	Fertility rate (per woman)	1.14
Pop. under 15	15.9%	Urban population	50.4%
Pop. over 65	13.9%		per 1,000 pop.
No. of men per 100 women	94.5	Crude birth rate	8.2
Human Development Index	87.4	Crude death rate	9.9

The economy

GDP	SIT4,036bn	GDP per head	$9,120
GDP	$18.1bn	GDP per head in purchasing	
Av. ann. growth in real		power parity (USA=100)	50.8
GDP 1991–2000	1.8%	Economic freedom index	3.10

Origins of GDP

	% of total
Agriculture	3.3
Industry, of which:	38.3
manufacturing	27.8
Services	58.4

Components of GDP

	% of total
Private consumption	54.9
Public consumption	20.8
Investment	27.8
Exports	59.1
Imports	-62.7

Structure of employment[a]

	% of total		% of labour force
Agriculture	11	Unemployed 2000	7.5
Industry	38	Av. ann. rate 1990–2000	7.9
Services	51		

Energy

	m TCE		
Total output	3.830	% output exported	15.2
Total consumption	8.536	% consumption imported	62.0
Consumption per head,			
kg coal equivalent	4,283		

Inflation and finance

Consumer price		*av. ann. increase 1995–2000*	
inflation 2001	9.4%	Narrow money (M1)	18.7%
Av. ann. inflation 1996–2001	8.9%	Broad money	19.8%
Money market rate, 2001	6.90%		

Exchange rates

	end 2001		December 2001
SIT per $	250.9	Effective rates	1995 = 100
SIT per SDR	315.4	– nominal	...
SIT per euro	224.7	– real	...

Trade

Principal exports	$bn fob	Principal imports	$bn fob
Manufactures	4.1	Machinery & transport equipment	3.5
Machinery & transport equipment	3.1	Manufactures	3.3
Chemicals	0.9	Chemicals	1.3
Food & live animals	0.2	Mineral fuels	0.9
Total incl. others	**8.8**	Total incl. others	**9.9**

Main export destinations	% of total	Main origins of imports	% of total
Germany	27.2	Germany	19.0
Italy	13.6	Italy	17.4
Croatia	7.9	France	10.3
Austria	7.5	Austria	8.2
France	7.1	Croatia	4.4
EU15	63.9	EU15	67.8

Balance of payments, reserves and debt, $bn

Visible exports fob	8.8	Overall balance	0.2
Visible imports fob	-9.9	Change in reserves	0.0
Trade balance	-1.1	Level of reserves	
Invisibles inflows	2.3	end Dec.	3.2
Invisibles outflows	-1.9	No. months of import cover	3.2
Net transfers	0.1	Foreign debt	6.2
Current account balance	-0.6	– as % of GDP	34.3
– as % of GDP	-3.4	Debt service paid	1.0
Capital balance	0.7	Debt service ratio	9.1

Health and education

Health spending, % of GDP	7.6	Education spending, % of GDP	5.8
Doctors per 1,000 pop.	2.3	Enrolment, %: primary	98
Hospital beds per 1,000 pop.	5.7	secondary	99
Improved-water source access, % of pop.	100	tertiary	53

Society

No. of households	0.6m	Colour TVs per 100 households	89.4
Av. no. per household	3.0	Telephone lines per 100 pop.	40.1
Marriages per 1,000 pop.	3.7	Mobile telephone subscribers	
Divorces per 1,000 pop.	1.1	per 100 pop.	76.0
Cost of living, Dec. 2001		Computers per 100 pop.	27.6
New York = 100	...	Internet hosts per 1,000 pop.	13.2

a 1999

SOUTH AFRICA

Area	1,225,815 sq km	Capital	Pretoria
Arable as % of total land	12	Currency	Rand (R)

People

Population	43.3m	Life expectancy: men	46.5 yrs
Pop. per sq km	35	women	48.3 yrs
Av. ann. growth		Adult literacy	85.3%
in pop. 1995–2000	1.57%	Fertility rate (per woman)	2.85
Pop. under 15	34.0%	Urban population	55.0%
Pop. over 65	3.6%		per 1,000 pop.
No. of men per 100 women	96.5	Crude birth rate	24.6
Human Development Index	70.2	Crude death rate	17.1

The economy

GDP	R874bn	GDP per head	$2,940
GDP	$126bn	GDP per head in purchasing	
Av. ann. growth in real		power parity (USA=100)	26.9
GDP 1990–2000	1.5%	Economic freedom index	2.90

Origins of GDP

	% of total
Agriculture	4.3
Industry, of which:	32.2
manufacturing	19.8
Services	63.5

Components of GDP

	% of total
Private consumption	63.2
Public consumption	16.9
Investment	17.6
Exports	26.3
Imports	-22.5

Structure of employment[a]

	% of total		% of labour force
Agriculture	0	Unemployed 2000[b]	23.6
Industry	48	Av. ann. rate 1990–2000[b]	17.2
Services	52		

Energy

	m TCE		
Total output	188.824	% output exported	35.8
Total consumption	136.147	% consumption imported	17.4
Consumption per head,			
kg coal equivalent	2,986		

Inflation and finance

Consumer price			av. ann. increase 1995–2000
inflation 2001	3.4%	Narrow money (M1)	18.9%
Av. ann. inflation 1996–2001	5.9%	Broad money	12.7%
Money market rate, 2001	8.84%		

Exchange rates

	end 2001		December 2001
R per $	12.13	Effective rates	1995 = 100
R per SDR	15.24	– nominal	41.5
R per euro	10.86	– real	55.8

Trade

Principal exports[c]		Principal imports[c]	
	$bn fob		$bn cif
Metals & metal products	6.3	Machinery & appliances	8.9
Gold	6.0	Mineral products	3.7
Diamonds	2.9	Chemicals	3.4
Machinery & transport equipment	2.6	Transport & equipment	1.7
Total incl. others	31.0	Total incl. others	32.9

Main export destinations		Main origins of imports	
	% of total		% of total
United States	10.6	Germany	13.3
United Kingdom	7.6	United States	11.9
Japan	7.1	United Kingdom	9.4
Germany	7.0	Japan	7.3
Italy	6.4		

Balance of payments, reserves and debt, $bn

Visible exports fob	31.4	Overall balance	0.4
Visible imports fob	-27.2	Change in reserves	0.2
Trade balance	4.2	Level of reserves	
Invisibles inflows	7.3	end Dec.	7.7
Invisibles outflows	-11.0	No. months of import cover	2.4
Net transfers	-0.9	Foreign debt	24.9
Current account balance	-0.5	– as % of GDP	19
– as % of GDP	-0.4	Debt service	3.9
Capital balance	-1.6	Debt service ratio	11

Health and education

Health spending, % of GDP	7.2	Education spending, % of GDP	6.1
Doctors per 1,000 pop.	0.6	Enrolment, %: primary	127
Hospital beds per 1,000 pop.	...	secondary	104
Improved-water source access, % of pop.	86	tertiary	17

Society

No. of households	9.8m	Colour TVs per 100 households	63.4
Av. no. per household	4.3	Telephone lines per 100 pop.	11.4
Marriages per 1,000 pop.	4.1	Mobile telephone subscribers	
Divorces per 1,000 pop.	0.9	per 100 pop.	21.0
Cost of living, Dec. 2001		Computers per 100 pop.	6.7
New York = 100	44	Internet hosts per 1,000 pop.	5.5

a 1993
b Not whole country coverage.
c 1997

SOUTH KOREA

Area	99,274 sq km	Capital	Seoul
Arable as % of total land	17	Currency	Won (W)

People

Population	46.7m	Life expectancy: men	71.8 yrs
Pop. per sq km	472	women	79.1 yrs
Av. ann. growth		Adult literacy	97.8%
in pop. 1995–2000	0.78%	Fertility rate (per woman)	1.51
Pop. under 15	20.8%	Urban population	81.0%
Pop. over 65	7.1%		per 1,000 pop.
No. of men per 100 women	101	Crude birth rate	12.8
Human Development Index	87.5	Crude death rate	5.9

The economy

GDP	W517rn	GDP per head	$9,670
GDP	$457bn	GDP per head in purchasing	
Av. ann. growth in real		power parity (USA=100)	50.7
GDP 1990–2000	6.4%	Economic freedom index	2.50

Origins of GDP		Components of GDP	
	% of total		% of total
Agriculture	4.6	Private consumption	57.3
Industry, of which:	42.8	Public consumption	10.2
manufacturing	31.5	Investment	28.7
Services	52.6	Exports	45.0
		Imports	-42.2

Structure of employment

	% of total		% of labour force
Agriculture	11	Unemployed 2000	4.1
Industry	28	Av. ann. rate 1990–2000	3.3
Services	61		

Energy

	m TCE		
Total output	36.917	% output exported	131.0
Total consumption	187.542	% consumption imported	127.5
Consumption per head,			
kg coal equivalent	4,067		

Inflation and finance

Consumer price		av. ann. increase 1995–2000	
inflation 2001	4.3%	Narrow money (M1)	3.9%
Av. ann. inflation 1996–2001	3.8%	Broad money	21.8%
Money market rate, 2001	4.7%		

Exchange rates

	end 2001		December 2001
W per $	1,314	Effective rates	1995 = 100
W per SDR	1,651	– nominal	...
W per euro	1,177	– real	...

Trade

Principal exports	$bn fob	Principal imports	$bn cif
Electronic products	62.0	Electrical machinery	43.3
Machinery	12.1	Crude petroleum	25.2
Metal goods	11.4	Machinery & equipment	18.4
Chemicals	11.1	Chemicals	11.8
Motor vehicles	11.1	Iron & steel products	6.0
Total incl. others	**174.0**	Total incl. others	**163.2**

Main export destinations	% of total	Main origins of imports	% of total
United States	21.8	Japan	19.8
Japan	11.9	United States	18.2
China	10.7	China	8.0
Hong Kong	6.2	Saudi Arabia	6.0
Taiwan	4.7	Australia	3.7

Balance of payments, reserves and debt, $bn

Visible exports fob	175.9	Overall balance	23.8
Visible imports fob	-159.1	Change in reserves	22.1
Trade balance	16.9	Level of reserves	
Invisibles inflows	36.1	end Dec.	96.3
Invisibles outflows	-42.2	No. months of import cover	5.7
Net transfers	0.7	Foreign debt	134.4
Current account balance	11.4	– as % of GDP	33
– as % of GDP	2.5	Debt service paid	23.2
Capital balance	12.1	Debt service ratio	13

Health and education

Health spending, % of GDP	5.4	Education spending, % of GDP	4.1
Doctors per 1,000 pop.	1.3	Enrolment, %: primary[a]	94
Hospital beds per 1,000 pop.	5.5	secondary[a]	102
Improved-water source access,		tertiary[a]	68
% of pop.	92		

Society

No. of households	14.1m	Colour TVs per 100 households	92.5
Av. no. per household	3.3	Telephone lines per 100 pop.	47.6
Marriages per 1,000 pop.	6.7	Mobile telephone subscribers	
Divorces per 1,000 pop.	1.5	per 100 pop.	60.8
Cost of living, Dec. 2001		Computers per 100 pop.	25.1
New York = 100	90	Internet hosts per 1,000 pop.	9.4

a 1997

SPAIN

Area	504,782 sq km	Capital	Madrid
Arable as % of total land	27	Currency	Euro (€)

People

Population	39.9m	Life expectancy: men	75.4 yrs
Pop. per sq km	79	women	82.3 yrs
Av. ann. growth		Adult literacy	97.6%
in pop. 1995–2000	0.09%	Fertility rate (per woman)	1.13
Pop. under 15	14.7%	Urban population	77.6%
Pop. over 65	17.0%		per 1,000 pop.
No. of men per 100 women	95.7	Crude birth rate	8.9
Human Development Index	90.8	Crude death rate	9.8

The economy

GDP	Pta100,873bn	GDP per head	$14,150
GDP	$559bn	GDP per head in purchasing	
Av. ann. growth in real		power parity (USA=100)	56.5
GDP 1990–2000	2.6%	Economic freedom index	2.30

Origins of GDP

Components of GDP

	% of total		% of total
Agriculture	3.6	Private consumption	59.4
Industry, of which:	30.5	Public consumption	17.1
manufacturing	...	Investment	25.8
Services	65.9	Exports	29.9
		Imports	-32.2

Structure of employment[a]

	% of total		% of labour force
Agriculture	7	Unemployed 2000	14.1
Industry	31	Av. ann. rate 1990–2000	19.2
Services	62		

Energy

	m TCE		
Total output	40.407	% output exported[b]	24.0
Total consumption	140.356	% consumption imported[b]	95.5
Consumption per head,			
kg coal equivalent	3,542		

Inflation and finance

Consumer price			av. ann. increase 1995–2000
inflation 2001	3.6%	Euro area:	
Av. ann. inflation 1996–2001	2.6%	Narrow money (M1)	7.8%
Money market rate, 2001	4.36%	Broad money	4.5%

Exchange rates

	end 2001		December 2001
Euro per $	1.13	Effective rates	1995 = 100
Euro per SDR	1.43	– nominal	92.3
		– real	104.2

Trade

Principal exports		Principal imports	
	$bn fob		$bn cif
Raw materials &		Raw materials & intermediate	
intermediate products	49.5	products (excl. fuels)	69.4
Consumer goods	44.7	Consumer goods	37.6
Capital goods	15.1	Capital goods	27.6
Energy products	4.1	Energy products	18.5
Total incl. others	**113.4**	Total incl. others	**153.1**

Main export destinations		Main origins of imports	
	% of total		% of total
France	19.4	France	17.1
Germany	12.4	Germany	14.9
Portugal	9.4	Italy	8.8
Italy	8.8	Benelux	7.1
United Kingdom	8.3	United Kingdom	7.0
EU15	70.6	EU15	63.1

Balance of payments, reserves and aid, $bn

Visible exports fob	115.1	Capital balance	21.9
Visible imports fob	-147.8	Overall balance	-2.9
Trade balance	-32.8	Change in reserves	-2.4
Invisibles inflows	68.3	Level of reserves	
Invisibles outflows	-54.4	end Dec.	35.6
Net transfers	1.6	No. months of import cover	2.1
Current account balance	-17.3	Aid given	1.19
– as % of GDP	-3.1	– as % of GDP	0.22

Health and education

Health spending, % of GDP	7.0	Education spending, % of GDP	4.5
Doctors per 1,000 pop.	3.1	Enrolment, %: primary	108
Hospital beds per 1,000 pop.	3.9	secondary	113
Improved-water source access,		tertiary	56
% of pop.	...		

Society

No. of households	12.5m	Colour TVs per 100 households	98.2
Av. no. per household	3.2	Telephone lines per 100 pop.	43.1
Marriages per 1,000 pop.	5.2	Mobile telephone subscribers	
Divorces per 1,000 pop.	0.8	per 100 pop.	65.5
Cost of living, Dec. 2001		Computers per 100 pop.	16.8
New York = 100	69	Internet hosts per 1,000 pop.	37.5

a 1999
b Energy trade data are distorted by transitory and oil refining activities.

SWEDEN

Area	449,964 sq km	Capital	Stockholm
Arable as % of total land	7	Currency	Swedish krona (Skr)

People

Population	8.8m	Life expectancy: men		77.6 yrs
Pop. per sq km	20		women	82.8 yrs
Av. ann. growth		Adult literacy		99.0%
in pop. 1995–2000	0.03%	Fertility rate (per woman)		1.29
Pop. under 15	18.2%	Urban population		83.3%
Pop. over 65	17.4%			per 1,000 pop.
No. of men per 100 women	98.4	Crude birth rate		8.2
Human Development Index	93.6	Crude death rate		10.6

The economy

GDP	Skr2,083bn	GDP per head	$25,630
GDP	$227bn	GDP per head in purchasing	
Av. ann. growth in real		power parity (USA=100)	70.3
GDP 1990–2000	1.7%	Economic freedom index	2.05

Origins of GDP

	% of total
Agriculture	2.0
Industry, of which:	28.7
manufacturing	...
Services	69.3

Components of GDP

	% of total
Private consumption	50.4
Public consumption	26.3
Investment	17.9
Exports	47.4
Imports	-42.1

Structure of employment[a]

	% of total		% of labour force
Agriculture	3	Unemployed 2000	5.1
Industry	25	Av. ann. rate 1990–2000	7.2
Services	72		

Energy

	m TCE		
Total output	37.021	% output exported	39.1
Total consumption	58.786	% consumption imported	72.0
Consumption per head,			
kg coal equivalent	6,624		

Inflation and finance

Consumer price			av. ann. increase 1995–2000
inflation 2001	2.9%	Narrow money (M1)	...
Av. ann. inflation 1996–2001	1.0%	Broad money	3.9%
Money market rate, 2001	4.08%		

Exchange rates

	end 2001		December 2001
			1995 = 100
Skr per $	10.67	Effective rates	
Skr per SDR	13.41	– nominal	91.8
Skr per euro	9.55	– real	92.9

Trade

Principal exports		Principal imports	
	$bn fob		*$bn cif*
Electrical machinery & transport equipment	30.6	Electrical machinery & transport equipment	23.2
Non-electrical machinery	12.4	Non-electrical machinery	7.8
Wood & paper products	10.7	Chemicals	6.7
Chemicals	8.0	Food, beverages & tobacco	4.2
Total incl. others	**86.9**	Total incl. others	**72.8**

Main export destinations		Main origins of imports	
	% of total		*% of total*
Germany	10.6	Germany	16.3
United States	9.5	United Kingdom	8.8
United Kingdom	9.1	Norway	8.2
Norway	7.5	Denmark	6.7
Denmark	5.3	United States	6.7
EU15	53.6	EU15	60.3

Balance of payments, reserves and aid, $bn

Visible exports fob	87.4	Capital balance	-2.9
Visible imports fob	-72.2	Overall balance	0.2
Trade balance	15.2	Change in reserves	-0.3
Invisibles inflows	40.3	Level of reserves	
Invisibles outflows	-45.6	end Dec.	16.5
Net transfers	-3.3	No. months of import cover	1.7
Current account balance	6.6	Aid given	1.80
– as % of GDP	2.9	– as % of GDP	0.79

Health and education

Health spending, % of GDP	7.9	Education spending, % of GDP	8.0
Doctors per 1,000 pop.	3.1	Enrolment, %: primary	111
Hospital beds per 1,000 pop.	3.7	secondary[b]	161
Improved-water source access,		tertiary	63
% of pop.	100		

Society

No. of households	4.4m	Colour TVs per 100 households	97.3
Av. no. per household	2.0	Telephone lines per 100 pop.	73.9
Marriages per 1,000 pop.	4.6	Mobile telephone subscribers	
Divorces per 1,000 pop.	2.3	per 100 pop.	77.1
Cost of living, Dec. 2001		Computers per 100 pop.	56.1
New York = 100	78	Internet hosts per 1,000 pop.	129.7

a 1999
b Includes training for unemployed.

SWITZERLAND

Area	41,293 sq km	Capital	Berne
Arable as % of total land	10	Currency	Swiss franc (SFr)

People

Population	7.2m	Life expectancy: men		75.9 yrs
Pop. per sq km	174		women	82.3 yrs
Av. ann. growth		Adult literacy		99.0%
in pop. 1995–2000	0.15%	Fertility rate (per woman)		1.38
Pop. under 15	16.7%	Urban population		67.7%
Pop. over 65	16.0%			per 1,000 pop.
No. of men per 100 women	97.8	Crude birth rate		8.6
Human Development Index	92.4	Crude death rate		9.8

The economy

GDP	SFr405bn	GDP per head	$33,390
GDP	$240bn	GDP per head in purchasing	
Av. ann. growth in real		power parity (USA=100)	89.3
GDP 1990–2000	1.1%	Economic freedom index	1.90

Origins of GDP[a]		Components of GDP	
	% of total		% of total
Agriculture	1.6	Private consumption	59.8
Industry, of which:	33.8	Public consumption	14.3
manufacturing	...	Investment	21.2
Services	64.6	Exports	46.3
		Imports	-41.6

Structure of employment

	% of total		% of labour force
Agriculture	5	Unemployed 2000	2.7
Industry	26	Av. ann. rate 1990–2000	3.0
Services	69		

Energy

	m TCE		
Total output	13.871	% output exported	31.1
Total consumption	33.496	% consumption imported	77.6
Consumption per head,			
kg coal equivalent	4,569		

Inflation and finance

Consumer price		av. ann. increase 1996–2000	
inflation 2001	1.0%	Narrow money (M1)	4.5%
Av. ann. inflation 1996–2001	0.8%	Broad money	1.1%
Money market rate, 2001	1.65%		

Exchange rates

	end 2001		December 2001
SFr per $	1.67	Effective rates	1995 = 100
SFr per SDR	2.11	– nominal	98.9
SFr per euro	1.50	– real	108.5

Trade

Principal exports	$bn	Principal imports	$bn
Machinery	22.0	Machinery	18.7
Chemicals	21.2	Chemicals	13.0
Precision instruments,		Motor vehicles	8.8
watches & jewellery	12.1	Metals & metals manufactures	6.4
Metals & metal manufactures	6.4	Agricultural products	5.9
Textiles & clothing	1.6		
Total incl. others	**74.9**	Total incl. others	**76.1**

Main export destinations	% of total	Main origins of imports	% of total
Germany	22.2	Germany	31.2
United States	11.6	France	10.8
France	9.0	Italy	10.0
Italy	7.6	United States	6.8
United Kingdom	5.4	Netherlands	6.1
Japan	3.8	United Kingdom	4.5
EU15	60.4	EU15	77.7

Balance of payments, reserves and aid, $bn

Visible exports fob	93.3	Capital balance	-31.8
Visible imports fob	-92.9	Overall balance	-4.0
Trade balance	0.4	Change in reserves	-6.9
Invisibles inflows	89.1	Level of reserves	
Invisibles outflows	-53.2	end Dec.	53.6
Net transfers	-3.8	No. months of import cover	4.4
Current account balance	32.5	Aid given	0.89
– as % of GDP	13.6	– as % of GDP	0.37

Health and education

Health spending, % of GDP	10.4	Education spending, % of GDP	5.5
Doctors per 1,000 pop.	3.4	Enrolment, %: primary	102
Hospital beds per 1,000 pop.	18.1	secondary	94
Improved-water source access,		tertiary	36
% of pop.	100		

Society

No. of households	3.1m	Colour TVs per 100 households	97.2
Av. no. per household	2.3	Telephone lines per 100 pop.	71.8
Marriages per 1,000 pop.	5.0	Mobile telephone subscribers	
Divorces per 1,000 pop.	2.6	per 100 pop.	72.4
Cost of living, Dec. 2001		Computers per 100 pop.	50.0
New York = 100	100	Internet hosts per 1,000 pop.	85.3

a 1998

TAIWAN

Area	36,179 sq km	Capital	Taipei
Arable as % of total land	25	Currency	Taiwan dollar (T$)

People

Population	22.2m	Life expectancy: men	72.6
Pop. per sq km	617	women	78.4
Av. ann. growth		Adult literacy	...
in pop. 1995–98	0.87%	Fertility rate (per woman)	1.8
Pop. under 15	22.0%	Urban population	...
Pop. over 65	8.6%		per 1,000 pop.
No. of men per 100 women	105.2	Crude birth rate	12.9
Human Development Index	...	Crude death rate[a]	6.0

The economy

GDP	T$9,686bn	GDP per head	$13,950
GDP	$310bn	GDP per head in purchasing	
Av. ann. growth in real		power parity (USA=100)	66.7
GDP 1990–2000	6.1%	Economic freedom index	2.35

Origins of GDP

	% of total
Agriculture	2.1
Industry, of which:	31.9
manufacturing	26.3
Services	66.0

Components of GDP

	% of total
Private consumption	62.2
Public consumption	13.0
Investment	22.8
Exports	54.2
Imports	-52.2

Structure of employment

	% of total		% of labour force
Agriculture	8	Unemployed 2000	2.9
Industry	37	Av. ann. rate 1990–2000	2.3
Services	55		

Energy

	m TCE		
Total output	...	% output exported	...
Total consumption	...	% consumption imported	...
Consumption per head, kg coal equivalent	...		

Inflation and finance

Consumer price			av. ann. increase 1995–2000
inflation 2001	0.0%	Narrow money (M1)	7.3%
Av. ann. inflation 1996–2001	0.8%	Broad money	8.1%

Exchange rates

	end 2001		December 2001
			1995 = 100
T$ per $	35.1	Effective rates	
T$ per SDR	44.2	– nominal	...
T$ per euro	31.6	– real	...

Trade

Principal exports		Principal imports	
	$bn fob		*$bn cif*
Machinery & electrical		Machinery & electrical	
equipment	82.6	equipment	66.0
Textiles & clothing	15.2	Minerals	14.1
Base metals & manufactures	13.5	Chemicals	13.1
Plastics and rubber products	9.1	Metals	11.0
Vehicles, aircraft & ships	5.8	Precision instruments, clocks	
		& watches	9.1
Total incl. others	**148.3**	Total incl. others	**140.0**

Main export destinations		Main origins of imports	
	% of total		*% of total*
United States	23.5	Japan	27.5
Hong Kong	21.1	United States	17.9
Japan	11.2	South Korea	6.4
Singapore	3.7	Germany	4.0
Germany	3.3	Malaysia	3.8
Netherlands	3.3	Australia	2.5
United Kingdom	3.0	Indonesia	2.2

Balance of payments, reserves and debt, $bn

Visible exports fob	147.6	Overall balance	2.5
Visible imports fob	-133.6	Change in reserves	0.5
Trade balance	14.0	Level of reserves	
Invisibles inflows	29.5	end Dec.	106.7
Invisibles outflows	-31.6	No. months of import cover	7.9
Net transfers	-2.6	Foreign debt	21.8
Current account balance	9.3	– as % of GDP	7.0
– as % of GDP	3.0	Debt service paid	3.7
Capital balance	-8.3	Debt service ratio	2.1

Health and education

Health spending, % of GDP	6.2	Education spending, % of GDP	...
Doctors per 1,000 pop.	0.4	Enrolment, %: primary[b]	89
Hospital beds per 1,000 pop.	2.0	secondary[b]	59
Improved-water source access,		tertiary[b]	21
% of pop.	...		

Society

No. of households	6.6m	Colour TVs per 100 households	99.4
Av. no. per household	3.3	Telephone lines per 100 pop.	57.3
Marriages per 1,000 pop.	7.9	Mobile telephone subscribers	
Divorces per 1,000 pop.	1.8	per 100 pop.	96.6
Cost of living, Dec. 2001		Computers per 100 pop.	22.3
New York = 100	91	Internet hosts per 1,000 pop.	75.8

a 2001 estimate.
b 1997

THAILAND

Area	513,115 sq km	Capital	Bangkok
Arable as % of total land	29	Currency	Baht (Bt)

People

Population	62.8m	Life expectancy:	men	67.9 yrs
Pop. per sq km	122		women	73.8 yrs
Av. ann. growth		Adult literacy		95.5%
in pop. 1995–2000	1.34%	Fertility rate (per woman)		2.0
Pop. under 15	26.7%	Urban population		21.6%
Pop. over 65	5.2%			per 1,000 pop.
No. of men per 100 women	98	Crude birth rate		17.8
Human Development Index	75.7	Crude death rate		6.2

The economy

GDP	Bt4,900bn	GDP per head	$2,010
GDP	$122bn	GDP per head in purchasing	
Av. ann. growth in real		power parity (USA=100)	18.5
GDP 1990–2000	5.0%	Economic freedom index	2.40

Origins of GDP		**Components of GDP**	
	% of total		% of total
Agriculture	10.0	Private consumption	53.8
Industry, of which:	44.3	Public consumption	9.5
manufacturing	36.4	Investment	20.6
Services	45.7	Exports	65.1
		Imports	-48.1

Structure of employment[a]

	% of total		% of labour force
Agriculture	49	Unemployed 2000	2.4
Industry	18	Av. ann. rate 1990–2000	1.9
Services	33		

Energy

	m TCE		
Total output	40.671	% output exported	17.7
Total consumption	79.593	% consumption imported	65.3
Consumption per head,			
kg coal equivalent	1,320		

Inflation and finance

Consumer price			av. ann. increase 1995–2000
inflation 2001	1.7%	Narrow money (M1)	12.0%
Av. ann. inflation 1996–2001	3.4%	Broad money	9.4%
Money market rate, 2001	2.00%		

Exchange rates

	end 2001		December 2001
Bt per $	44.22	Effective rates	1995 = 100
Bt per SDR	55.58	– nominal	...
Bt per euro	39.60	– real	...

Trade

Principal exports		Principal imports	
	$bn fob		*$bn cif*
Computers & parts	8.5	Capital goods	29.0
Textiles & clothing	4.7	Raw materials & intermediates	16.8
Integrated circuits	4.5	Petroleum & products	6.9
Rice	1.6	Consumer goods	6.6
Total incl. others	**69.3**	Total incl. others	**62.2**

Main export destinations		Main origins of imports	
	% of total		*% of total*
United States	21.2	Japan	23.7
Japan	14.8	United States	10.7
Singapore	8.7	Singapore	9.7
Hong Kong	5.0	Malaysia	5.4
Malaysia	4.1	Hong Kong	4.5

Balance of payments, reserves and debt, $bn

Visible exports fob	67.9	Overall balance	-1.8
Visible imports fob	-56.2	Change in reserves	-2.1
Trade balance	11.8	Level of reserves	
Invisibles inflows	18.1	end Dec.	32.7
Invisibles outflows	-21.1	No. months of import cover	5.1
Net transfers	0.6	Foreign debt	79.7
Current account balance	9.4	– as % of GDP	66
– as % of GDP	7.7	Debt service paid	14.0
Capital balance	-10.2	Debt service ratio	18

Health and education

Health spending, % of GDP	6.0	Education spending, % of GDP	4.7
Doctors per 1,000 pop.	0.4	Enrolment, %: primary	94
Hospital beds per 1,000 pop.	2.0	secondary	88
Improved-water source access,		tertiary	30
% of pop.	80		

Society

No. of households	15.7m	Colour TVs per 100 households	80.2
Av. no. per household	3.9	Telephone lines per 100 pop.	9.4
Marriages per 1,000 pop.	6.9	Mobile telephone subscribers	
Divorces per 1,000 pop.	1.1	per 100 pop.	11.9
Cost of living, Dec. 2001		Computers per 100 pop.	2.7
New York = 100	54	Internet hosts per 1,000 pop.	1.3

a 1999

TURKEY

Area	779,452 sq km	Capital	Ankara
Arable as % of total land	31	Currency	Turkish Lira (L)

People

Population	66.7m	Life expectancy:	men	68.0 yrs
Pop. per sq km	86		women	73.2 yrs
Av. ann. growth		Adult literacy		85.1%
in pop. 1995–2000	1.62%	Fertility rate (per woman)		2.3
Pop. under 15	30.0%	Urban population		74.0%
Pop. over 65	5.8%			per 1,000 pop.
No. of men per 100 women	102.0	Crude birth rate		20.1
Human Development Index	73.5	Crude death rate		6.2

The economy

GDP	L124,982trn	GDP per head	$3,060
GDP	$200bn	GDP per head in purchasing	
Av. ann. growth in real		power parity (USA=100)	20.6
GDP 1990–2000	4.0%	Economic freedom index	3.35

Origins of GDP		Components of GDP	
	% of total		% of total
Agriculture	14.5	Private consumption	71.5
Industry, of which:	28.3	Public consumption	14.1
manufacturing	...	Investment	24.6
Services	57.2	Exports	24.0
		Imports	-31.5

Structure of employment[a]

	% of total		% of labour force
Agriculture	46	Unemployed 2000	8.3
Industry	20	Av. ann. rate 1990–2000	7.4
Services	34		

Energy

	m TCE		
Total output	31.343	% output exported	7.7
Total consumption	87.298	% consumption imported	74.9
Consumption per head,			
kg coal equivalent	1,354		

Inflation and finance

Consumer price		av. ann. increase 1995–2000	
inflation 2001	54.5%	Narrow money (M1)	76.6%
Av. ann. inflation 1996–2001	68.4%	Broad money	86.6%
Money market rate, 2001	92.00%		

Exchange rates

	end 2001		December 2001
L per $	1,450,127	Effective rates	1995 = 100
L per SDR	1,822,418	– nominal	...
L per euro	1,298,589	– real	...

Trade

Principal exports		Principal imports	
	$bn fob		*$bn cif*
Clothing & textiles	7.5	Machinery	13.8
Machinery	3.3	Petroleum & products	9.5
Iron & steel	1.5	Vehicles	5.4
Vehicles	1.5	Iron & steel	2.7
Total incl. others	**27.8**	Total incl. others	**54.5**

Main export destinations		Main origins of imports	
	% of total		*% of total*
Germany	18.8	Germany	13.2
United States	11.2	Italy	8.0
United Kingdom	7.4	Russia	7.2
Italy	6.4	United States	7.2
France	6.0	France	6.5
EU15	52.5	EU15	48.9

Balance of payments, reserves and debt, $bn

Visible exports fob	31.7	Overall balance	-2.9
Visible imports fob	-54.0	Change in reserves	-0.9
Trade balance	-22.4	Level of reserves	
Invisibles inflows	22.3	end Dec.	23.5
Invisibles outflows	-15.0	No. months of import cover	4.1
Net transfers	5.2	Foreign debt	116.2
Current account balance	-9.8	– as % of GDP	58
– as % of GDP	-4.9	Debt service paid	21.1
Capital balance	9.4	Debt service ratio	37

Health and education

Health spending, % of GDP	4.8	Education spending, % of GDP[b]	2.2
Doctors per 1,000 pop.	1.2	Enrolment, %: primary[b]	107
Hospital beds per 1,000 pop.	2.6	secondary	70
Improved-water source access,		tertiary	14
% of pop.	83		

Society

No. of households	15.8m	Colour TVs per 100 households	67.0
Av. no. per household	4.0	Telephone lines per 100 pop.	28.5
Marriages per 1,000 pop.	8.1	Mobile telephone subscribers	
Divorces per 1,000 pop.	0.6	per 100 pop.	30.2
Cost of living, Dec. 2001		Computers per 100 pop.	4.1
New York = 100	47	Internet hosts per 1,000 pop.	2.1

a 1999
b 1997

UKRAINE

Area	603,700 sq km	Capital	Kiev
Arable as % of total land	56	Currency	Hryvnya (UAH)

People

Population	49.6m	Life expectancy:	men	62.7 yrs
Pop. per sq km	82		women	73.5 yrs
Av. ann. growth		Adult literacy		99.6%
in pop. 1995–2000	-0.78%	Fertility rate (per woman)		1.1
Pop. under 15	17.8%	Urban population		68.0%
Pop. over 65	13.8%			per 1,000 pop.
No. of men per 100 women	87.2	Crude birth rate		8.1
Human Development Index	74.2	Crude death rate		15.4

The economy

GDP	UAH173bn	GDP per head	$640
GDP	$31.8bn	GDP per head in purchasing	
Av. ann. growth in real		power parity (USA=100)	10.9
GDP 1990–2000	-7.9%	Economic freedom index	3.85

Origins of GDP[a]		Components of GDP[a]	
	% of total		% of total
Agriculture	13	Private consumption	60.2
Industry, of which:	38	Public consumption	19.0
manufacturing	33	Investment	19.8
Services	49	Exports	52.6
		Imports	-51.5

Structure of employment[a]

	% of total		% of labour force
Agriculture	26	Unemployed 1999	11.9
Industry	26	Av. ann. rate 1995–99	9.1
Services	48		

Energy

	m TCE		
Total output	116.177	% output exported	5.5
Total consumption	209.679	% consumption imported	48.8
Consumption per head,			
kg coal equivalent	4,123		

Inflation and finance

Consumer price		av. ann. increase 1995–2000	
inflation 2001	12.0%	Narrow money (M1)	34.6%
Av. ann. inflation 1996–2001	17.7%	Broad money	35.2%
Money market rate, 2001	16.57%		

Exchange rates

	end 2001		December 2001
UAH per $	5.30	Effective rates	1995 = 100
UAH per SDR	6.66	– nominal	127.3
UAH per euro	4.75	– real	121.7

Trade

Principal exports	$bn fob	Principal imports	$bn cif
Metals	6.0	Fuels, mineral products	6.0
Chemicals	1.8	Machinery & transport	
Machinery & transport		equipment	2.4
equipment	1.7	Chemicals	1.5
Food & agricultural produce	1.3	Food & agricultural produce	0.8
Total incl. others	**14.6**	Total incl. others	**13.9**

Main export destinations	% of total	Main origins of imports	% of total
Russia	24.1	Russia	41.7
Turkey	6.0	Germany	8.1
Germany	5.1	Turkmenistan	6.8
Italy	4.4	United States	2.6

Balance of payments, reserves and debt, $bn

Visible exports fob	15.7	Overall balance	0.9
Visible imports fob	-14.9	Change in reserves	0.4
Trade balance	0.8	Level of reserves	
Invisibles inflows	3.9	end Dec.	1.5
Invisibles outflows	-4.3	No. months of import cover	0.9
Net transfers	1.0	Foreign debt	12.2
Current account balance	1.5	– as % of GDP	34
– as % of GDP	4.7	Debt service paid	3.4
Capital balance	-0.4	Debt service ratio	20

Health and education

Health spending, % of GDP	4.4	Education spending, % of GDP	4.5
Doctors per 1,000 pop.	3.0	Enrolment, %: primary	...
Hospital beds per 1,000 pop.	11.8	secondary	...
Improved-water source access,		tertiary[b]	42
% of pop.	...		

Society

No. of households	18.7m	Colour TVs per 100 households	73.7
Av. no. per household	2.6	Telephone lines per 100 pop.	21.2
Marriages per 1,000 pop.	6.0	Mobile telephone subscribers	
Divorces per 1,000 pop.	3.5	per 100 pop.	4.4
Cost of living, Dec. 2001		Computers per 100 pop.	1.8
New York = 100	63	Internet hosts per 1,000 pop.	1.1

a 1999
b 1997

UNITED KINGDOM

Area	242,534 sq km	Capital	London
Arable as % of total land	25	Currency	Pound (£)

People

Population	59.4m	Life expectancy: men	75.7 yrs
Pop. per sq km	243	women	80.7 yrs
Av. ann. growth		Adult literacy	99.0%
in pop. 1995–2000	0.27%	Fertility rate (per woman)	1.61
Pop. under 15	19.0%	Urban population	89.5%
Pop. over 65	15.8%		per 1,000 pop.
No. of men per 100 women	97	Crude birth rate	10.6
Human Development Index	92.3	Crude death rate	10.5

The economy

GDP	£935bn	GDP per head	$23,680
GDP	$1,415bn	GDP per head in purchasing	
Av. ann. growth in real		power parity (USA=100)	69.1
GDP 1990–2000	2.1%	Economic freedom index	1.85

Origins of GDP

Components of GDP

	% of total		% of total
Agriculture	1.4	Private consumption	65.5
Industry, of which:	24.9	Public consumption	18.5
manufacturing	19.9	Investment	17.7
Services	73.7	Exports	28.1
		Imports	-29.8

Structure of employment

	% of total		% of labour force
Agriculture	2	Unemployed 2000	5.3
Industry	25	Av. ann. rate 1990–2000	7.8
Services	73		

Energy

	m TCE		
Total output	400.381	% output exported	38.3
Total consumption	332.209	% consumption imported	32.2
Consumption per head,			
kg coal equivalent	5,664		

Inflation and finance

Consumer price		av. ann. increase 1995–2000	
inflation 2001	1.8%	Narrow money (M0)	7.1%
Av. ann. inflation 1996–2001	2.6%	Broad money	7.2%
Money market rate, 2001	4.90%		

Exchange rates

	end 2001		December 2001
£ per $	0.69	Effective rates	1995 = 100
£ per SDR	0.87	– nominal	125.3
£ per euro	0.62	– real	144.3

Trade

Principal exports		Principal imports	
	$bn fob		*$bn fob*
Finished manufactured products	164.4	Finished manufactured products	199.3
Semi-manufactured products	72.0	Semi-manufactured products	75.4
Fuels	25.2	Food, beverages & tobacco	24.5
Food, beverages & tobacco	15.0	Fuels	15.1
Basic materials	3.9	Basic materials	9.6
Total incl. others	**283.7**	Total incl. others	**326.8**

Main export destinations		Main origins of imports	
	% of total		*% of total*
United States	15.7	United States	13.2
Germany	12.1	Germany	12.8
France	9.9	France	8.2
Netherlands	8.0	Netherlands	6.9
Ireland	6.5	Japan	4.7
EU15	57.2	EU15	50.5

Balance of payments, reserves and aid, $bn

Visible exports fob	284.6	Capital balance	32.9
Visible imports fob	-330.0	Overall balance	5.3
Trade balance	-45.4	Change in reserves	6.4
Invisibles inflows	320.8	Level of reserves	
Invisibles outflows	-286.9	end Dec.	48.2
Net transfers	-14.0	No. months of import cover	0.9
Current account balance	-25.6	Aid given	4.50
– as % of GDP	-1.8	– as % of GDP	0.32

Health and education

Health spending, % of GDP	6.9	Education spending, % of GDP	4.7
Doctors per 1,000 pop.	1.8	Enrolment, %: primary	102
Hospital beds per 1,000 pop.	4.1	secondary[a]	156
Improved-water source access,		tertiary	58
% of pop.	100		

Society

No. of households	24.3m	Colour TVs per 100 households	98.2
Av. no. per household	2.4	Telephone lines per 100 pop.	57.8
Marriages per 1,000 pop.	10.6	Mobile telephone subscribers	
Divorces per 1,000 pop.	3.2	per 100 pop.	78.3
Cost of living, Dec. 2001		Computers per 100 pop.	36.6
New York = 100	102	Internet hosts per 1,000 pop.	41.5

a Includes training for unemployed.

UNITED STATES

Area	9,372,610 sq km	Capital	Washington DC
Arable as % of total land	19	Currency	US dollar ($)

People

Population	283.2m	Life expectancy: men	74.6 yrs
Pop. per sq km	30	women	80.4 yrs
Av. ann. growth		Adult literacy	99.0%
in pop. 1995–2000	1.05%	Fertility rate (per woman)	1.93
Pop. under 15	21.7%	Urban population	77.2%
Pop. over 65	12.3%		per 1,000 pop.
No. of men per 100 women	97.2	Crude birth rate	13.1
Human Development Index	93.4	Crude death rate	8.4

The economy

GDP	$9,837bn	GDP per head	$34,940
Av. ann. growth in real		GDP per head in purchasing	
GDP 1990–2000	3.1%	power parity (USA=100)	100
		Economic freedom index	1.80

Origins of GDP		Components of GDP	
	% of total		% of total
Agriculture	1.4	Private consumption	68.2
Industry, of which:	21.9	Public consumption	17.7
manufacturing	15.9	Investment	17.9
Services[a]	76.7	Exports	11.2
		Imports	-14.9

Structure of employment

	% of total		% of labour force
Agriculture	3	Unemployed 2000	4.1
Industry	23	Av. ann. rate 1990–2000	5.6
Services	74		

Energy

	m TCE		
Total output	2,377.484	% output exported	4.6
Total consumption	2,986.958	% consumption imported	29.7
Consumption per head,			
kg coal equivalent	10,900		

Inflation and finance

Consumer price		av. ann. increase 1995–2000	
inflation 2001	2.8%	Narrow money (M1)	-0.7%
Av. ann. inflation 1996–2001	2.5%	Broad money	9.0%
Treasury bill rate, 2001	3.45%		

Exchange rates

	end 2001		December 2001
$ per SDR	1.26	Effective rates	1995 = 100
$ per euro	0.90	– nominal	131.6
		– real	138.9

Trade

Principal exports		Principal imports	
	$bn fob		*$bn fob*
Capital goods, excl. vehicles	357.0	Capital goods, excl. vehicles	346.7
Industrial supplies	171.9	Industrial supplies	299.8
Consumer goods, excl. vehicles	90.6	Consumer goods, excl. vehicles	281.4
Vehicles & products	80.2	Vehicles & products	195.9
Food & beverages	47.5	Food & beverages	46.0
Total incl. others	**781.9**	Total incl. others	**1,218.0**

Main export destinations		Main origins of imports	
	% of total		*% of total*
Canada	22.9	Canada	19.0
Mexico	14.2	Japan	12.0
Japan	8.3	Mexico	11.2
United Kingdom	5.3	China	8.2
Germany	3.8	Germany	4.8
EU15	21.1	EU15	18.1

Balance of payments, reserves and aid, $bn

Visible exports fob	774.9	Capital balance	444.3
Visible imports fob	-1,224.4	Overall balance	0.3
Trade balance	-449.6	Change in reserves	-8.1
Invisibles inflows	643.8	Level of reserves	
Invisibles outflows	-584.8	end Dec.	128.4
Net transfers	-54.2	No. months of import cover	0.9
Current account balance	-444.7	Aid given	9.95
– as % of GDP	-4.5	– as % of GDP	0.10

Health and education

Health spending, % of GDP	12.9	Education spending, % of GDP	5.0
Doctors per 1,000 pop.	2.7	Enrolment, %: primary	102
Hospital beds per 1,000 pop.	3.6	secondary	97
Improved-water source access,		tertiary	77
% of pop.	100		

Society

No. of households	103.8m	Colour TVs per 100 households	99.3
Av. no. per household	2.5	Telephone lines per 100 pop.	66.5
Marriages per 1,000 pop.	8.5	Mobile telephone subscribers	
Divorces per 1,000 pop.	4.6	per 100 pop.	44.4
Cost of living, Dec. 2001		Computers per 100 pop.	62.3
New York = 100	100	Internet hosts per 1,000 pop.[b]	344.1

a Including utilities.
b Includes all hosts ending ".com", ".net" and ".org" which exaggerates the numbers.

VENEZUELA

Area	912,050 sq km	Capital	Caracas
Arable as % of total land	3	Currency	Bolivar (Bs)

People

Population	24.2m	Life expectancy:	men	70.9 yrs
Pop. per sq km	27		women	76.7 yrs
Av. ann. growth		Adult literacy		92.6%
in pop. 1995–2000	2.02%	Fertility rate (per woman)		2.72
Pop. under 15	34.0%	Urban population		86.9%
Pop. over 65	4.4%			per 1,000 pop.
No. of men per 100 women	101.3	Crude birth rate		22.8
Human Development Index	76.5	Crude death rate		4.7

The economy

GDP	Bs81,924bn	GDP per head	$4,980
GDP	$121bn	GDP per head in purchasing	
Av. ann. growth in real		power parity (USA=100)	16.8
GDP 1990–2000	2.4%	Economic freedom index	3.65

Origins of GDP		**Components of GDP**	
	% of total		% of total
Agriculture	4.7	Private consumption	63.1
Industry, of which:	46.6	Public consumption	7.0
manufacturing	14.1	Investment	17.5
Services	46.0	Exports	29.4
		Imports	-17.0

Structure of employment[a]

	% of total		% of labour force
Agriculture	11	Unemployed 1999	14.9
Industry	24	Av. ann. rate 1990–99	10.3
Services	65		

Energy

	m TCE		
Total output	324.780	% output exported	70.5
Total consumption	93.129	% consumption imported	1.8
Consumption per head,			
kg coal equivalent	4,007		

Inflation and finance

Consumer price		av. ann. increase 1995–2000	
inflation 2001	6.5%	Narrow money (M1)	43.0%
Av. ann. inflation 1996–2001	23.2%	Broad money	33.1%
Money market rate, 2001	13.33%		

Exchange rates

	end 2001		December 2001
Bs per $	763	Effective rates	1995 = 100
Bs per SDR	959	– nominal	29.6
Bs per euro	683	– real	175.2

Trade

Principal exports		Principal imports	
	$bn fob		$bn fob
Oil	27.5	Intermediate goods	11.2
Chemicals	1.1	Capital goods	2.5
Steel	1.0	Consumer goods	2.4
Plastics	0.2		
Total incl. others	**31.8**	Total incl. others	**16.1**

Main export destinations		Main origins of imports	
	% of total		% of total
United States	60.0	United States	35.8
Brazil	5.5	Colombia	6.8
Colombia	3.5	Brazil	4.5
Italy	3.5	Italy	3.9

Balance of payments, reserves and debt, $bn

Visible exports fob	33.0	Overall balance	5.8
Visible imports fob	-15.5	Change in reserves	0.8
Trade balance	17.5	Level of reserves	
Invisibles inflows	4.2	end Dec.	15.9
Invisibles outflows	-8.4	No. months of import cover	8.0
Net transfers	-0.2	Foreign debt	38.2
Current account balance	13.1	– as % of GDP	37
– as % of GDP	10.9	Debt service paid	5.8
Capital balance	-2.8	Debt service ratio	21

Health and education

Health spending, % of GDP	4.2	Education spending, % of GDP[a]	5.2
Doctors per 1,000 pop.	2.4	Enrolment, %: primary[a]	91
Hospital beds per 1,000 pop.	1.5	secondary[a]	40
Improved-water source access,		tertiary[a]	25
% of pop.	84		

Society

No. of households	5.1m	Colour TVs per 100 households	90.4
Av. no. per household	4.7	Telephone lines per 100 pop.	11.2
Marriages per 1,000 pop.	3.8	Mobile telephone subscribers	
Divorces per 1,000 pop.	1.0	per 100 pop.	26.4
Cost of living, Dec. 2001		Computers per 100 pop.	5.3
New York = 100	77	Internet hosts per 1,000 pop.	0.9

a 1997

VIETNAM

Area	331,114 sq km	Capital	Hanoi
Arable as % of total land	18	Currency	Dong (D)

People

Population	78.1m	Life expectancy: men	66.9 yrs
Pop. per sq km	236	women	71.6 yrs
Av. ann. growth		Adult literacy	93.4%
in pop. 1995–2000	1.4%	Fertility rate (per woman)	2.25
Pop. under 15	33.4%	Urban population	19.7%
Pop. over 65	5.3%		per 1,000 pop.
No. of men per 100 women	99	Crude birth rate	19.7
Human Development Index	68.2	Crude death rate	6.4

The economy

GDP	D444trn	GDP per head	$400
GDP	$31.3bn	GDP per head in purchasing	
Av. ann. growth in real		power parity (USA=100)	5.9
GDP 1990–2000	7.2%	Economic freedom index	3.85

Origins of GDP

	% of total
Agriculture	23.2
Industry, of which:	35.4
manufacturing	...
Services	41.4

Components of GDP

	% of total
Private consumption	66.4
Public consumption	6.3
Investment	29.5
Exports	54.7
Imports	-56.8

Structure of employment[a]

	% of total		% of labour force
Agriculture	70	Unemployed 2000	...
Industry	13	Av. ann. rate 1990–2000	...
Services	17		

Energy

	m TCE		
Total output	31.702	% output exported	64.7
Total consumption	18.281	% consumption imported	54.6
Consumption per head,			
kg coal equivalent	236		

Inflation and finance

		av. ann. increase 1995–2000	
Consumer price			
inflation 2001	-0.4%	Narrow money (M1)	27.8
Av. ann. inflation 1996–2001	2.6%	Broad money	34.2
Treasury bill rate, 2001	5.25%		

Exchange rates

	end 2001		December 2001
D per $	15,084	Effective rates	1995 = 100
D per SDR	18,957	– nominal	...
D per euro	13,508	– real	...

Trade

Principal exports		Principal imports	
	$bn fob		*$bn cif*
Crude oil	3.5	Petroleum products	2.1
Textiles & garments	1.9	Motorcycles	0.8
Fisheries products	1.5	Steel	0.8
Footwear	1.5	Fertiliser	0.5
Rice	0.7		
Total incl. others	**14.4**	Total incl. others	**15.6**

Main export destinations		Main origins of imports	
	% of total		*% of total*
Japan	18.1	Singapore	17.7
China	10.6	Japan	14.4
Australia	8.8	Taiwan	12.1
Singapore	6.1	South Korea	11.1
Taiwan	5.2	Sweden	9.1
Germany	5.1	Thailand	5.2

Balance of payments, reserves and debt, $bn

Visible exports fob	14.4	Overall balance	0.1
Visible imports fob	-14.1	Change in reserves	0.1
Trade balance	0.4	Level of reserves	
Invisibles inflows	2.9	end Dec.	3.4
Invisibles outflows	-4.0	No. months of import cover	2.3
Net transfers	1.7	Foreign debt	12.8
Current account balance	1.0	– as % of GDP	38
– as % of GDP	3.1	Debt service paid	1.3
Capital balance	-0.3	Debt service ratio	9

Health and education

Health spending, % of GDP	4.8	Education spending, % of GDP[b]	3.0
Doctors per 1,000 pop.	0.5	Enrolment, %: primary	110
Hospital beds per 1,000 pop.	1.7	secondary	61
Improved-water source access,		tertiary	11
% of pop.	56		

Society

No. of households	15.5m	Colour TVs per 100 households	36.5
Av. no. per household	4.8	Telephone lines per 100 pop.	3.8
Marriages per 1,000 pop.	...	Mobile telephone subscribers	
Divorces per 1,000 pop.	...	per 100 pop.	1.5
Cost of living, Dec. 2001		Computers per 100 pop.	1.0
New York = 100	69	Internet hosts per 1,000 pop.	...

a 1995
b 1997

ZIMBABWE

Area	390,759 sq km	Capital	Harare
Arable as % of total land	8	Currency	Zimbabwe dollar (Z$)

People

Population	12.6m	Life expectancy: men		43.3 yrs
Pop. per sq km	32		women	42.4 yrs
Av. ann. growth		Adult literacy		88.7%
in pop. 1995–2000	1.91%	Fertility rate (per woman)		4.5
Pop. under 15	45.2%	Urban population		35.3%
Pop. over 65	3.2%			per 1,000 pop.
No. of men per 100 women	100	Crude birth rate		35.1
Human Development Index	55.4	Crude death rate		17.8

The economy

GDP	Z$320bn	GDP per head	$590
GDP	$7.4bn	GDP per head in purchasing	
Av. ann. growth in real		power parity (USA=100)	7.5
GDP 1990–2000	2.1%	Economic freedom index	4.30

Origins of GDP[a]		Components of GDP[a]	
	% of total		% of total
Agriculture	20	Private consumption	74.0
Industry, of which:	25	Public consumption	14.9
manufacturing	17	Investment	11.4
Services	55	Net exports	-0.4

Structure of employment[b]

	% of total		% of labour force
Agriculture	26	Unemployed 1999	6
Industry	28	Av. ann. rate 1990–99	...
Services	46		

Energy

	m TCE		
Total output	5.284	% output exported	4.1
Total consumption	5.854	% consumption imported	18.4
Consumption per head,			
kg coal equivalent	515		

Inflation and finance

Consumer price		av. ann. increase 1995–2000	
inflation 2001	74.5%	Narrow money (M1)	37.0%
Av. ann. inflation 1996–2001	46.5%	Broad money	36.9%
Money market rate, 2001	21.52%		

Exchange rates

	end 2001		December 2001
Z$ per $	54.95	Effective rates	1995 = 100
Z$ per SDR	68.97	– nominal	...
Z$ per euro	49.21	– real	...

Trade

Principal exports		Principal imports	
	$m fob		$m cif
Tobacco	547	Machinery & transport	
Gold	284	equipment	439
Ferro-alloys	124	Manufactured products	252
Textiles & clothing	79	Chemicals	250
		Petroleum products &	
		electricity	167
Total incl. others	**2,138**	Total incl. others	**1,507**

Main export destinations[c]		Main origins of imports	
	% of total		% of total
South Africa	13.1	South Africa	41.8
United Kingdom	9.3	United Kingdom	7.1
Japan	8.4	Mozambique	3.9
Germany	6.5	United States	3.2
China	5.9	Germany	2.6

Balance of payments[ad], reserves and debt, $bn

Visible exports fob	1.9	Overall balance	-0.05
Visible imports fob	-1.7	Change in reserves	-0.2
Trade balance	0.2	Level of reserves	
Invisibles inflows	0.7	end Dec.	0.3
Invisibles outflows	-0.8	No. months of import cover	2.3
Net transfers	0.2	Foreign debt	4.0
Current account balance	0.05	– as % of GDP	59
– as % of GDP	0.6	Debt service paid	0.2
Capital balance	-0.02	Debt service ratio	20

Health and education

Health spending, % of GDP	8.1	Education spending, % of GDP	10.8
Doctors per 1,000 pop.	0.1	Enrolment, %: primary[e]	112
Hospital beds per 1,000 pop.	0.5	secondary[e]	50
Improved-water source access,		tertiary[e]	7
% of pop.	85		

Society

No. of households	3.2m	Colour TVs per 100 households	3.0
Av. no. per household	3.6	Telephone lines per 100 pop.[a]	1.9
Marriages per 1,000 pop.	...	Mobile telephone subscribers	
Divorces per 1,000 pop.	...	per 100 pop.	2.4
Cost of living, Dec. 2001		Computers per 100 pop.	1.2
New York = 100	71	Internet hosts per 1,000 pop.	0.3

a 1999
b 1994
c Excluding gold.
d Provisional, does not sum to total.
e 1997

Glossary

Balance of payments The record of a country's transactions with the rest of the world. The **current account** of the balance of payments consists of: visible trade (goods); "invisible" trade (services and income); private transfer payments (eg, remittances from those working abroad); official transfers (eg, payments to international organisations, famine relief). Visible imports and exports are normally compiled on rather different definitions to those used in the trade statistics (shown in principal imports and exports) and therefore the statistics do not match. The **capital account** consists of long- and short-term transactions relating to a country's assets and liabilities (eg, loans and borrowings). Adding the current to the capital account gives the **overall balance**. This is compensated by net monetary movements and changes in reserves. In practice methods of statistical recording are neither complete nor accurate and an errors and omissions item, sometimes quite large, will appear. In the country pages of this book this item is included in the overall balance. **Changes in reserves** exclude revaluation effects and are shown without the practice often followed in balance of payments presentations of reversing the sign.

CFA Communauté Financière Africaine. Its members, most of the francophone African nations, share a common currency, the CFA franc, which used to be pegged to the French franc but is now pegged to the euro.

Cif/fob Measures of the value of merchandise trade. Imports include the cost of "carriage, insurance and freight" (cif) from the exporting country to the importing. The value of exports des not include these elements and is recorded 'free on board" (fob). Balance of payments statistics are generally adjusted so that both exports and imports are shown fob; the cif elements are included in invisibles.

Commonwealth of Independent States All former Soviet Union Republics, excluding Estonia, Latvia and Lithuania. It was established January 1 1992; Azerbaijan joined in September 1993 and Georgia in December 1993.

Crude birth rate The number of live births in a year per 1,000 population. The crude birth rate will automatically be relatively high if a large proportion of the population is of childbearing age.

Crude death rate The number of deaths in a year per 1,000 population. Also affected by the population's age structure.

Debt, foreign Financial obligations owed by a country to the rest of the world and repayable in foreign currency. **Debt service paid** is the sum of principal repayments and interest payments actually made. **The debt service ratio** is debt service expressed as a percentage of the country's earnings from exports of goods and services.

EU European Union. Members are: Austria, Belgium, Denmark, Finland, France, Germany, Greece, Ireland, Italy, Luxembourg, Netherlands, Portugal, Spain, Sweden and the United Kingdom.

Effective exchange rate The nominal index measures a currency's depreciation (figures below 100) or appreciation (figures over 100) from a base date against a trade weighted basket of the currencies of the country's main trading partners. The real effective exchange rate reflects adjustments for relative movements in prices or costs.

Euro Replaced the ecu (European currency unit), on a one-to-one basis on January 1 1999. The currencies of the 11 euro area members have irrevocably fixed conversion rates for the euro. Notes and coins went into circulation on January 1 2002.

Euro area Members are those of the EU except Denmark, Sweden and the United Kingdom. Greece joined on January 1 2001 so is not included in the euro area figures in this book, unless otherwise stated.

Fertility rate The average number of children born to a woman who completes her childbearing years.

GDP Gross domestic product. The sum of all output produced by economic activity within a country. GNP (gross national product) and GNI (gross national income) include net income from abroad eg, rent, profits.

Import cover The number of months of imports covered by reserves, ie reserves ÷ ½₂ annual imports (visibles and invisibles).

Inflation The annual rate at which prices are increasing. The most common measure and the one shown here is the increase in the consumer price index.

Internet hosts Websites and other computers that sit permanently on the Internet.

Life expectancy The average length of time a baby born today can expect to live.

Literacy is defined by UNESCO as the ability to read and write a simple sentence, but definitions can vary from country to country.

Median age Divides the age distribution into two halves. Half of the population is above and half below the median age.

Money supply A measure of the "money" available to buy goods and services. Various definitions exist. The measures shown here are based on definitions used by the IMF and may differ from measures used nationally. Narrow money (M1) consists of cash in circulation and demand deposits (bank deposits that can be withdrawn on demand). "Quasi-money" (time, savings and foreign currency deposits) is added to this to create broad money.

OECD Organisation for Economic Co-operation and Development. The "rich countries" club was established in 1961 to promote economic growth and the expansion of world trade. It is based in Paris and now has 29 members.

Opec Organisation of Petroleum Exporting Countries. Set up in 1960 and based in Vienna, Opec is mainly concerned with oil pricing and production issues. Members are; Algeria, Indonesia, Iran, Iraq, Kuwait, Libya, Nigeria, Qatar, Saudi Arabia, United Arab Emirates and Venezuela.

PPP Purchasing power parity. PPP statistics adjust for cost of living differences by replacing normal exchange rates with rates designed to equalise the prices of a standard "basket"of goods and services. These are used to obtain PPP estimates of GDP per head. PPP estimates are normally shown on a scale of 1 to 100, taking the United States as 100.

Real terms Figures adjusted to exclude the effect of inflation.

Reserves The stock of gold and foreign currency held by a country to finance any calls that may be made for the settlement of foreign debt.

SDR Special drawing right. The reserve currency, introduced by the IMF in 1970, was intended to replace gold and national currencies in settling international transactions. The IMF uses SDRs for book-keeping purposes and issues them to member countries. Their value is based on a basket of the US dollar (with a weight of 45%), the euro (29%), the Japanese yen (15%) and the pound sterling (11%).

List of countries

Whenever data is available, the world rankings consider 174 countries: all those which had (in 2000) or have recently had a population of at least 1m or a GDP of at least $1bn. Here is a list of them.

	Population	GDP	GDP per head	Area	Median age
	m	$bn	$PPP	'000 sq km	years
Afghanistan	21.8	21.0[a]	960[a]	652	18.1
Albania	3.1	3.8	3,600	29	26.5
Algeria	30.3	53.3	5,040	2,382	21.8
Angola	13.1	8.8	1,180	1,247	15.9
Argentina	37.0	285.5	12,050	2,767	27.8
Armenia	3.8	1.9	2,580	30	30.4
Aruba	0.1	2.0	28,000[a]	0.2	35.0[a]
Australia	19.1	390.1	24,970	7,682	35.2
Austria	8.1	189.0	26,330	84	38.4
Azerbaijan	8.0	5.3	2,740	87	26.7
Bahamas	0.3	4.8	16,400	14	26.2
Bahrain	0.6	8.0	17,400[a]	1	29.6
Bangladesh	137.4	47.1	1,590	144	20.2
Barbados	0.3	2.6	15,020	0.4	32.6
Belarus	10.2	30.0	7,550	208	36.3
Belgium	10.2	226.6	27,470	31	39.1
Benin	6.3	2.2	980	113	16.6
Bermuda	0.1	2.7[a]	33,000[a]	1	...
Bhutan	2.1	0.5	1,440	47	18.4
Bolivia	8.3	8.3	2,360	1,099	20.0
Bosnia	4.0	4.4	1,700[a]	51	35.1
Botswana	1.5	5.3	7,170	581	18.2
Brazil	170.4	595.5	7,300	8,512	25.8
Brunei	0.3	4.8[a]	17,600[a]	6	25.7
Bulgaria	7.9	12.0	5,560	111	39.1
Burkina Faso	11.5	2.2	970	274	15.6
Burundi	6.4	0.7	580	28	16.0
Cambodia	13.1	3.2	1,440	181	17.4
Cameroon	14.9	8.9	1,590	475	18.1
Canada	30.8	687.9	27,170	9,971	36.9
Central African Rep	3.7	1.0	1,160	622	18.3
Chad	7.9	1.4	870	1,284	16.7
Chile	15.2	70.5	9,100	757	28.3
China	1,275.1	1,079.9	3,920	9,561	30.0
Colombia	42.1	81.3	6,060	1,142	24.0
Congo	50.9	31.0[a]	600[a]	342	15.6
Congo-Brazzaville	3.0	3.2	570	2,345	16.8
Costa Rica	4.0	15.9	7,980	51	24.2
Côte d'Ivoire	16.0	9.4	1,500	322	18.3
Croatia	4.7	19.0	7,960	57	37.9
Cuba	11.2	19.2[a]	1,700[a]	111	23.9
Cyprus	0.8	8.7	20,780	9	33.4
Czech Republic	10.3	50.8	13,780	79	37.6
Denmark	5.3	162.3	27,250	43	38.7

	Population	GDP	GDP per head	Area	Median age
	m	$bn	$PPP	'000 sq km	years
Dominican Republic	8.4	19.7	5,710	48	23.1
Ecuador	12.6	13.6	2,910	272	22.9
Egypt	67.9	98.7	3,670	1,000	21.9
El Salvador	6.3	13.2	4,410	21	21.8
Eritrea	3.7	0.6	960	117	17.9
Estonia	1.4	5.0	9,340	45	37.3
Ethiopia	62.9	6.4	660	1,134	17.3
Fiji	0.8	1.5	4,480	18	23.1
Finland	5.2	121.5	24,570	338	39.4
France	59.2	1,294.2[b]	24,420	544	37.6
French Polynesia	0.2	3.9	23,340	3	25.1
Gabon	1.2	4.9	5,360	268	20.4
Gambia, The	1.3	0.4	1,620	11	20.2
Georgia	5.3	3.0	2,680	70	34.8
Germany	82.0	1,873.0	24,920	358	40.1
Ghana	19.3	5.2	1,910	239	18.9
Greece	10.6	112.6	16,860	132	39.1
Guadeloupe	0.4	5.7[c]	12,650[c]	2	30.5
Guatemala	11.4	19.0	3,770	109	17.8
Guinea	8.2	3.0	1,930	246	17.7
Guinea-Bissau	1.2	0.2	710	36	18.2
Haiti	8.1	4.1	1,470	28	18.9
Honduras	6.4	5.9	2,400	112	18.7
Hong Kong	6.9	162.6	25,990	1	36.0
Hungary	10.0	45.6	11,990	93	38.1
Iceland	0.3	8.5	28,710	103	32.9
India	1,008.9	457.0	2,340	3,287	23.7
Indonesia	212.1	153.3	2,830	1,904	24.6
Iran	70.3	104.9	5,910	1,648	19.9
Iraq	22.9	23.7[a]	3,540[a]	438	18.8
Ireland	3.8	93.9	25,520	70	31.9
Israel	6.0	110.4	19,330	21	27.9
Italy	57.5	1,074.0	23,470	301	40.2
Jamaica	2.6	7.4	3,440	11	24.2
Japan	127.1	4,841.6	27,080	378	41.2
Jordan	4.9	8.3	3,950	89	19.5
Kazakhstan	16.2	18.2	5,490	2,717	28.0
Kenya	30.7	10.4	1,010	583	17.6
Kirgizstan	4.9	1.3	2,540	583	23.2
Kuwait	1.9	37.8	18,690	18	22.7
Laos	5.3	1.7	1,540	237	18.5
Latvia	2.4	7.2	7,070	64	37.8
Lebanon	3.5	16.5	4,550	10	25.1
Lesotho	2.0	0.9	2,590	30	20.1
Liberia	2.9	0.5[a]	1,100[a]	111	17.8
Libya	5.3	40.4[a]	10,500[a]	1,760	21.4
Lithuania	3.7	11.3	6,980	65	35.7

	Population	GDP	GDP per head	Area	Median age
	m	$bn	$PPP	'000 sq km	years
Luxembourg	0.4	18.9	45,470	3	37.7
Macau	0.4	6.2	18,190	0.02	34.2
Macedonia	2.0	3.6	5,020	26	32.3
Madagascar	16.0	3.9	820	587	17.5
Malawi	11.3	1.7	600	118	16.7
Malaysia	22.2	89.7	8,330	333	23.3
Mali	11.4	2.3	780	1,240	16.8
Malta	0.4	3.6	16,530	0.3	36.5
Martinique	0.4	6.0c	14,420c	1	32.3
Mauritania	2.7	0.9	1,630	1,031	17.7
Mauritius	1.2	4.4	9,940	2	28.9
Mexico	98.9	574.5	8,790	1,973	23.3
Moldova	4.3	1.3	2,230	34	31.5
Mongolia	2.5	1.0	1,760	1,565	21.8
Morocco	29.9	33.3	3,450	447	22.3
Mozambique	18.3	3.8	800	799	17.9
Myanmar	47.7	6.6a	780a	677	23.4
Namibia	1.2	3.5	6,410	824	18.0
Nepal	23.0	5.5	1,370	147	19.4
Netherlands	15.9	364.8	25,850	42	37.7
Netherlands Antilles	0.2	2.4a	11,400a	1	32.0
New Caledonia	0.2	3.1	21,820	19	26.9
New Zealand	3.8	49.9	18,530	271	34.4
Nicaragua	5.1	2.4	2,080	130	18.1
Niger	10.8	1.8	740	1,267	15.1
Nigeria	113.9	41.1	800	924	17.2
North Korea	22.3	22.0a	1,000a	121	29.4
Norway	4.5	161.8	29,630	324	37.2
Oman	2.5	20.0	11,100a	310	17.7
Pakistan	141.3	61.6	1,860	804	18.9
Panama	2.9	9.9	5,680	77	25.2
Papua New Guinea	4.8	3.8	2,180	463	19.4
Paraguay	5.5	7.5	4,450	407	19.8
Peru	25.7	53.5	4,660	1,285	23.1
Philippines	75.7	74.7	4,220	300	20.9
Poland	38.6	157.7	9,000	313	35.2
Portugal	10.0	105.1	16,990	89	37.0
Puerto Rico	3.9	41.4	10,000a	9	30.6
Qatar	0.6	14.5	29,600a	11	32.1
Réunion	0.7	8.2c	11,570c	3	27.6
Romania	22.4	36.7	6,360	238	34.6
Russia	145.5	251.1	8,010	17,075	36.8
Rwanda	7.6	1.8	930	26	17.3
Saudi Arabia	20.3	173.3	11,390	2,200	18.4
Senegal	9.4	4.4	1,480	197	17.6
Serbia & Montenegro	10.6	8.4	2,840a	102	35.4
Sierra Leone	4.4	0.6	480	72	17.8

	Population	GDP	GDP per head	Area	Median age
	m	*$bn*	*$PPP*	*'000 sq km*	*years*
Singapore	4.0	92.3	24,910	1	34.5
Slovakia	5.4	19.1	11,040	49	34.0
Slovenia	2.0	18.1	17,310	20	38.1
Somalia	8.8	4.3[a]	600[a]	638	16.0
South Africa	43.3	125.9	9,160	1,226	22.6
South Korea	46.7	457.2	17,300	99	31.8
Spain	39.9	558.6	19,260	505	37.7
Sri Lanka	18.9	16.3	3,460	66	27.8
Sudan	31.1	11.5	1,520	2,506	19.7
Suriname	0.4	0.8	3,480	164	24.0
Swaziland	0.9	1.5	4,600	17	18.9
Sweden	8.8	227.3	23,970	450	39.7
Switzerland	7.2	239.8	30,450	41	40.2
Syria	16.2	17.0	3,340	185	18.7
Taiwan	22.2	310.0	22,700[a]	36	32.1[a]
Tajikistan	6.1	1.0	1,090	143	19.9
Tanzania	35.1	9.0	520	945	17.2
Thailand	62.8	122.2	6,320	513	27.5
Togo	4.5	1.2	1,410	57	17.6
Trinidad & Tobago	1.3	7.3	8,220	5	27.7
Tunisia	9.5	19.5	6,070	164	24.6
Turkey	66.7	199.9	7,030	779	24.9
Turkmenistan	4.7	4.4	3,800	488	21.1
Uganda	23.3	6.2	1,210	241	15.4
Ukraine	49.6	31.8	3,700	604	37.3
United Arab Emirates	2.6	65.9[a]	16,300[ac]	84	31.3
United Kingdom	59.4	1,414.6	23,550	243	37.7
United States	283.2	9,837.4	34,100	9,373	35.5
Uruguay	3.3	19.7	8,880	176	31.4
Uzbekistan	24.9	7.7	2,360	447	21.6
Venezuela	24.2	120.5	5,740	912	23.1
Vietnam	78.1	31.3	2,000	331	23.1
West Bank and Gaza	3.2	4.4	1,320[a]	6	16.8
Yemen	18.3	8.5	770	528	15.0
Zambia	10.4	2.9	750	753	16.5
Zimbabwe	12.6	7.4	2,550	391	17.0
Euro area (11)	292.2	5,919.6	23,340	2,365	38.8
Euro area (12)	302.8	6,032.2	23,120	2,497	38.9

a Estimate.
b Including French Guiana, Guadeloupe, Martinique and Réunion.
c 1999
d At market exchange rates.

Sources

Airports Council International, *Worldwide Airport Traffic Report*

BP, *Statistical Review of World Energy*

British Mountaineering Council

Centre for International Earth Science Information Network, Columbia University

Corporate Resources Group, *Quality of Living Report*

Council of Europe

Demographia

The Economist Intelligence Unit, *Business Operating Costs; Cost of Living Survey; Country Forecasts; Country Reports; Country Risk Service; Global Outlook – Business Environment Rankings*

ERC Statistics International, *World Cigarette Report*

Euromonitor, *International Marketing Data and Statistics; European Marketing Data and Statistics*

Europa Publications, *The Europa World Yearbook*

European Bank for Reconstruction and Development, *Transition Report*

Eurostat, *Statistics in Focus*

FAO, *FAOSTAT database*

Financial Times Business Information, *The Banker*

The Heritage Foundation, *The 2001 Index of Economic Freedom*

IMD, *World Competitiveness Yearbook*

IMF, *Direction of Trade; International Financial Statistics; World Economic Outlook*

International Cocoa Organisation, *Quarterly Bulletin of Cocoa Statistics*

International Civil Aviation Organisation, *Civil Aviation Statistics of the World*

International Coffee Organisation

International Cotton Advisory Committee, *Bulletin*

International Criminal Police Organisation (Interpol), *International Crime Statistics*

International Road Federation, *World Road Statistics*

International Rubber Study Group, *Rubber Statistical Bulletin*

International Federation of the Phonographic Industry

International Grains Council, *The Grain Market Report*

International Sugar Organisation, *Sugar Yearbook*

International Tea Committee, *Annual Bulletin of Statistics*

International Telecommunication Union, *ITU Indicators*

International Wool Textile Organisation

ISTA Mielke, *Oil World*

Lloyd's Register, *Statistical Tables*

William M. Mercer Limited

National statistics offices

Network Wizards

Nobel Foundation

OECD, *Development Assistance Committee Report; Environmental Data*

Standard & Poor's *Emerging Stock Markets Factbook*

Swiss Re, *sigma*

Taiwan Statistical Data Book

The Times, *Atlas of the World*

Time Inc Magazines, *Fortune International*

Transparency International

UN, *Energy Statistics Yearbook; Global Refugee Trends; Global Urban Indicators Database; State of World Population Report; Statistical Chart on World Families; Urban Agglomerations; World Population; World Population Prospects*

UN Development Programme, *Human Development Report*

Unicef *Global Database of Fertility and Contraceptive Use*

UNESCO, website: unescostat. unesco.org

Union Internationale des Chemins de Fer, *Statistiques Internationales des Chemins de Fer*

US Department of Agriculture, *Rice Report*

University of Michigan, Windows to the Universe website

WHO, *Weekly Epidemiological Record; World Health Statistics Annual*

World Bank, *Global Development Finance; World Development Indicators; World Development Report*

World Bureau of Metal Statistics, *World Metal Statistics*

World Economic Forum/Harvard University, *Global Competitiveness Yearbook*

World Economic Forum/Yale University/Columbia University, *Environmental Sustainability Index*

World Resources Institute, *World Resources*

World Tourist Organisation, *Yearbook of Tourism Statistics*

World Trade Organisation, *Annual Report*